Economic Thought and Political Theory

RECENT ECONOMIC THOUGHT SERIES

Editors:

Warren J. Samuels
Michigan State University
East Lansing, Michigan, USA

William Darity, Jr.
University of North Carolina
Chapel Hill, North Carolina, USA

Other books in the series:

DeGregori, T.:
DEVELOPMENT ECONOMICS
Nowotny, K.:
PUBLIC UTILITY REGULATION
Horowitz, I.:
ORGANIZATION AND DECISION THEORY
Mercuro, N.:
LAW AND ECONOMICS
Hennings, K. and Samuels, W.:
NEOCLASSICAL ECONOMIC THEORY, 1870 to 1930
Samuels, W.:
ECONOMICS AS DISCOURSE
Lutz, M.:
SOCIAL ECONOMICS
Weimer, D.:
POLICY ANALYSIS AND ECONOMICS
Bromley, D. and Segerson, K.:
THE SOCIAL RESPONSE TO ENVIRONMENTAL RISK
Roberts, B. and Feiner, S.:
RADICAL ECONOMICS
Mercuro, N.:
TAKING PROPERTY AND JUST COMPENSATION
de Marchi, N.:
POST-POPPERIAN METHODOLOGY OF ECONOMICS
Capinski, J.:
THE ECONOMICS OF SAVING
Darity, W.:
LABOR ECONOMICS: PROBLEMS IN ANALYZING LABOR MARKETS
Caldwell, B. and Boehm, S.:
AUSTRIAN ECONOMICS: TENSIONS AND DIRECTIONS
Tool, Marc R.:
INSTITUTIONAL ECONOMICS: THEORY, METHOD, POLICY

Economic Thought and Political Theory

Edited by
David Reisman
University of Surrey

Kluwer Academic Publishers
Boston/Dordrecht/London

Distributors for North America:
Kluwer Academic Publishers
101 Philip Drive
Assinippi Park
Norwell, Massachusetts 02061 USA

Distributors for all other countries:
Kluwer Academic Publishers Group
Distribution Centre
Post Office Box 322
3300 AH Dordrecht, THE NETHERLANDS

Library of Congress Cataloging-in-Publication Data

Economic thought and political theory / edited by David Reisman.
p. cm.—(Recent economic thought series)
Includes index.
ISBN 0-7923-9433-X (HB)
1. Economic policy. 2. Economics—History. 3. Economic history.
I. Reisman, David A. II. Series.
HD87.E264 1994
330'.01—dc20

93-42898
CIP

Printed on acid-free paper.

Printed in the United States of America

Contents

Contributing Authors

Samuel Bostaph is an Associate Professor and Chairman of the Department of Economics, University of Dallas, where he has taught since 1981. He earned his PhD from Southern Illinois University at Carbondale.

Samuel Hollander is University Professor of Economics in the University of Toronto. He is the author of *The Sources of Increased Efficiency: A Case-Study of Dupont Rayon Plants*, *The Economics of Adam Smith*, *The Economics of David Ricardo, The Economics of John Stuart Mill*, and *Classical Economics.*

Anastassios Karayiannis is Assistant Professor in the Department of Economics at the University of Piraeus. He received his MPhil from the University of Dundee in 1988 and his PhD from the University of Piraeus in 1987. He has published several articles on the history of economic thought and the book *General Economic Equilibrium: A Critical Analysis of the Modern Model* (in Greek). His research interests focus on the history of economic thought, economic methodology, and entrepreneurship.

Thomas Nitsch is Professor of Economics in the College of Business Administration at Creighton University. He has authored numerous articles and essays in social economics and the history of economic thought, including 'Social Economics: The First 200 Years', in *Social Economics: Retrospect and Prospect.*

David Reisman is Senior Lecturer in Economics, University of Surrey. His books include *Adam Smith's Sociological Economics*, *Alfred Marshall's Mission, The Political Economy of James Buchanan*, and *Market and Health.*

A. Allan Schmid is Professor of Agricultural Economics, Michigan State University. His teaching and research interests relate to law and economics, public choice, and public investment analysis. He is the author of *Property, Power and Public Choice* and *Benefit-Cost Analysis: A Political Economy Approach.* Recently he has served as consultant on Eastern Europe to the World Bank and the United Nations.

David Simpson is Economist at the Standard Life Assurance Company. He was formerly Professor of Economics at the University of Strathclyde and Director of the Fraser of Allander Institute; Associate Statistician at the United Nations; and Instructor in Economics at Harvard University. He has published a number of books and articles on a range of economic topics, in particular input-output analysis, political economy, and economic growth.

Viktor Vanberg is Professor of Economics and Editorial Director at the Center for Study of Public Choice, George Mason University. He is co-editor of *Constitutional Political Economy*. His recent publications include a number of papers on rational choice and institutional arrangements, together with a book, *The Economics of Rules: Essays in Constitutional Political Economy*.

INTRODUCTION

David Reisman

For many, the distinction is clear. Economics is about the market, about individuals maximizing utility and firms maximizing profit. Politics is about the state, about constitutional rules and piecemeal interventions. The two realms are separate and distinct. They are studied by different disciplines, taught in different departments, analyzed in different journals.

Reality, however, is less tidy. Economy trespasses on polity where elected officials are conceived as policy-merchants paid in votes, where civil servants are believed to be self-interested and not self-sacrificing. Polity trespasses on economy where law and order makes possible negotiated contracts, where markets fail and citizens demand public services instead. Analytically as separate as allocation and leadership, the simple fact is that all known economies are mixed economies and that the real-world frontiers have always been impossible to police.

This book is concerned with important thinkers of the past and present who have this in common, that they make no effort to put up barriers where nature intended no dam or obstruction. In that sense this book is concerned with synthesis and bringing together, not with reduction or pulling apart. Yet this book is more than a demonstration that interdisciplinarity matters. It also shows that ideas matter and that economic systems are often best understood when interpreted with the aid of an intellectual template that guides the investigation. In an era of systemic upheaval such as our own, few things can be more important than for perceptions to move in step with events—and for political economists to learn to trade in the scarce commodity of abstract thought.

This book is made up of eight chapters. The starting point is Plato who, in Samuel Bostaph's essay, is seen to have tried to explain how ancient Sparta sought to reconcile the communism of property rights with a high degree of authoritarianism in the state. Bostaph's comparisons with Marx and Engels look forward from ancient Athens to a different tradition that nonetheless shares with Plato an interest in justice and belonging, the individual and the community, the propertied and the disaffected, elitism and dictatorship. They also look forward to the Scottish Enlightenment when, as Anastassios Karayiannis shows in his chapter, Sir James Steuart wrote of the managed market and the beneficient statesman at the very time when Adam Smith was defending the invisible hand and the automatic process. Steuart was impressed by the Mercantilists' propensity to make the nation and not the individual the centerpiece of economic theory. He was also concerned about the failure of the market to restore full employment in the long run. His views on the money supply and the public debt recall those of Keynes on the role of discretionary intervention in a drifting economy that has lost its way.

John Stuart Mill is often cited as a theorist who, unlike Plato or Steuart, tended to conceive of economics as virtually synonymous with competitive markets and maximizing behavior. Samuel Hollander's essay clarifies the matter by showing that Mill was attracted by abstraction while fully appreciating just how much of institutional reality was deliberately being left for separate study. Mill compared economic orders in his account of socialism; he discussed state education and other forms of intervention; he explored the economic origins of social stratification; and he showed a sociologist's awareness of customs and norms. Hollander reaches the conclusion that "Mill would have looked aghast at much of what today passes for Economics." In reading Hollander's essay, one is strongly tempted to imitate Mill and to look aghast as well.

Thomas Nitsch continues the theme of motivation and integration. Writing of Christian (and particularly of Catholic) economics, Nitsch argues that voluntary and self-help organizations may be seen as providing a stimulus to intelligence and freedom that it is at least the equal of the textbook's possessive individualism. Of particular interest is his contention that the Catholic doctrine is committed to the middle way, neither laissez-faire capitalism nor central planning and command. Now that the monolithic structures of Eastern Europe are thawing into decentralization and hopefully also into democracy, Nitsch's chapter on the state as a part of the society rather than as a night watchman or a dictator apart would seem to be very much in sympathy with the search for a compromise that is being undertaken by so many intellectuals in the vacuum of the transition that is the subject of A. Allan Schmid's contribution to this book. Schmid's theme is property rights and transfer of title, but it must not be inferred that he expects the state in the East to wither away. Rather, his position is scrupulously agnostic. Before we can predict how the state will react to joblessness, welfare, or agricultural support, Schmid says, we need to discover who in the East will acquire a property in the opportunity to influence the state. Schmid also makes the important observation about rights and their transfer that "commercial law is more adapted to preventing breach of contract than failure to contract." Where something could happen and does not happen, the inference might be that there is an opportunity for a pragmatic state Nitsch-like to get involved.

Yet the case for the market is strong, and not least because of ignorance: since no leader can be certain of the future, there must be a temptation, eschewing paternalism and guidance, to tell history-to-come to mind its own business without relying on Sir for a compass that he does not and cannot be expected to possess. The concluding three chapters of the book are concerned with Sir and with spontaneity.

Thus David Simpson, writing about Schumpeter's pessimistic predictions, argues that capitalism need not be destroyed by its success. Privatization, de-regulation, and lower tax rates all suggest to him that the controlling state need not be just around the corner even if the entrepreneur is indeed giving way to the bureaucrat in the large-firm sector. His theme of dynamism is continued by Viktor Vanberg in his chapter on historical evolution as a discovery process. Building on the insights of Hayek, Vanberg argues that functionality is more likely than not to be the unintended outcome of conjectures and refutations, survivals and failures, in a competitive environment that winnows and sifts.

Vanberg's discussion of the constitutional framework that would circumscribe individual experimentation with the reason of rules provides the link to my own chapter, the last in the volume. Taking the example of health and health care, I examine the economic thought of James Buchanan in order to establish the direction in which the precommitment of consent and the in-period calculus are likely to point when the pulse is racing and the joints creak. Buchanan once said that "if socialism fails in the large it also fails in the small." My chapter, concerned not with the national economy but with a single sector, considers the extent to which the contractarian analysis may be employed to establish the proper balance between market and state.

My discussion does not conclude that there is a single "right" answer that makes all other answers useless and out of date. What it does suggest is that the discussion of ideas is a civilized activity—a process and not an endstate—that is more likely to be of cultural benefit than is a dogmatic intolerance that shouts down all opposition. It is likely that Vanberg and Simpson, Hayek and Schumpeter, would be broadly in sympathy with the notion that human experience is a search for explanations. So almost certainly would the other authors, the other subjects, of the chapters in this book.

1 COMMUNISM, SPARTA, AND PLATO

Samuel Bostaph

The organization of our forces is a thing calling in its nature for much advice and the framing of many rules, but the principal [first] is this—that no man, and no woman, be ever suffered to live without an officer set over them, and no soul of man to learn the trick of doing one single thing of its own sole motion, in play or in earnest, but, in peace as in war, ever to live with the commander in sight, to follow his leading and take its motions from him to the last detail . . . in a word, to teach one's soul the habit of never so much as thinking to do one single act apart from one's fellows, of making life, to the very uttermost, an unbroken consort, society, and community of all with all.

—Plato, *Laws*, 942a–c

Introduction

Was Plato a socialist or communist theorist? Was he the author of a socialist or communist utopian ideal? Was ancient Sparta a socialist or communist society? What is or was the relationship between the actual regime of ancient Sparta and the attempts by Plato to envision an ideal polis? These questions are the focus of this chapter.

The belief that Sparta was in some sense a communist society and Plato an ancient source of argument for communism is widespread, especially among journalists and the general public. Because a substantial number of scholars and other students of history share that belief, this chapter is primarily addressed to them. Of course, the terms *socialist* and *communist* must first be given some meaning—or at least the meaning they have for those who have used such terms to describe ancient Sparta and to refer to Plato must be indicated. This is done in the next section.

Because ancient Sparta came before Plato, and many of its core institutions and practices are acknowledged, discussed, and used by Plato in his attempts to envision an ideal regime, Sparta is discussed in the third section. It is then possible in the fourth section to examine Plato's vision in the context of what is known of Sparta, and to reach some conclusions concerning their historical and theoretical relationship. Given those, the relationship of the political economies of socialism and communism to both the Spartan actual regime and the Platonic ideal regime is briefly explored.

The general conclusion of the chapter is that historical Sparta was no socialist or communist society and Plato can be identified as an author of theoretical communism or socialism only in some trivial sense. Communal elements did exist in historical Sparta, just as they did in Plato's visions of the ideal regime; however, those aspects were incidental to the form and substance of Sparta, and they are neither central to Plato's purpose nor crucial to the structure of his ideal. If to be an author of theoretical communism or socialism is to present a vision of a society in which communist elements are a central and unifying theme, Plato is no such author. By the same token, the relative unimportance of communal elements to the basic nature and purpose of Spartan society means that Sparta was no socialist or communist society.

What Is a Communist?

In Marx's inaugural article (October 16, 1842) as the editor of the *Rheinische Zeitung* (1972, pp. 47–48), he identifies Plato as a communist theorist. At the same time Marx rejects "communist ideas in their present form" and pronounces "their practical realization" to be both undesirable and impossible. Of course, this is no rejection of theoretical communism per se. In fact, Marx goes on to claim that in the theory of communism, rather than its practice, "the reality of communist ideas" and thus their "true danger" to existing regimes is found. For the theoretical development of communist ideas might engender conviction, making them "ideas to which reason has riveted our conscience, and chains from which one cannot break loose without breaking one's heart." This is in contrast to the practical efforts of any actual communist revolutionaries, which "can be answered with a cannon."

Unfortunately, neither in that article nor in any subsequent publication does Marx indicate why he includes Plato among past theorists of communism, or what Platonic arguments are the rivets that might bind the consciences of some men to that ideal. Even further, what indeed does Marx mean by "communists" and "communism"? As is well known, nowhere in Marx's writings is any serious attempt made at a theory of any communistic economic system or of a society of communism, in contrast to his extensive treatment of capitalism.

Certainly, in the third of Marx's *Economic and Philosophic Manuscripts of 1844* are fragmentary comments that attempt to differentiate "crude" or historical communism from the system as an intellectually and historically evolving social "solution to the riddle of history" (p. 155) and ultimate "objectification of human essence" (p. 162). As far as its historical or crude forms are concerned (pp. 152–153), he indicates that they follow the abolition of privately held property, but always fail to abolish the property relation itself. Crude communism retains community or "general private property," such as communal capital or communal property in women, as well as that "alienating" manifestation of private property—the division of labor (p. 187). As Marx asserts that "real" communism is a system that abolishes (p. 155) or annuls (p. 213) the institution of private property itself; it is a final system that history will produce (p. 176). Given these two alternatives, and certain well-known "general private property" elements in Plato's *Republic* and *Laws*, perhaps Marx intended to include Plato among the theorists of crude communism. If so, he does not say it.

The German Ideology (1845–1846) slightly extends Marx's critique of crude as contrasted with real communism in the context of the development of his historical materialism argument. Among other things he asserts that in the communism of the future, to be established by means of revolution, there will be no exclusivistic or excludivist division of labor and no class structure. Thirty years later, in his May 1875 *Critique of the Gotha Program*, Marx stigmatizes as "vulgar socialism" any practical focus by members of the communist movement on questions of distribution. In response to such a focus in the draft program of the German Social Democratic Party, he divides into two phases the communism that is to follow the demise of the capitalist mode of production after the proletarian revolution. The first will have common ownership of "the means of production," which will be "cooperatively regulated" under the "revolutionary dictatorship of the proletariat," and individual labor will be rewarded according to its productivity. This "defective" phase or "political transition period" is to be the forerunner of the eventual "higher phase of communist society," where there will be no state, no classes, no division of labor and the individual will produce according to ability and consume according to need. Thus, for Marx, the practice of the higher phase of communism cannot be introduced into any existing regime; it will be found in the future after the end of regimes.

After Marx, Lenin later (1965, pp. 88–93) argues that the exact way in which the dictatorship of the proletariat will be transformed into the higher phase of communism cannot be known "for there is *no* material for answering these questions" (p. 88). Perhaps as a result of the influence of Stalin (von Mises, 1951, pp. 552–553), it has become conventional for modern Marxists to refer to the first phase as either "socialism" or "state socialism," that phase to be followed at some point by a stateless, higher, and true or pure "communism."

While Marx's reasons for terming Plato a communist theorist are not clear, Emile Durkheim, in his classic study of Saint-Simonian socialism, not only refers to Plato as a "disciple" of communism (1962, p. 50), but alleges that it was Plato who "first gave in antiquity a systematic formula" (p. 64) to the theory of communism, of which all later theories are "hardly more than variations" (p. 68). He further characterizes Plato's system as one that looks to the past, "openly reproduc[ing] the ancient organization of Sparta" (p. 79), thus implying that Spartan society was a communist one.

Just as Marx had drawn a difference between phases of communism, Durkheim distinguishes carefully between theories or systems of socialism and those of communism. He uses the term *socialism* to describe systems of state-managed industrial activities, whether consumption is state-managed or not. Durkheim's socialism seems to correspond to Marx's final conception of the first or "lower" phase of communism. Durkheim reserves the term *communism* for social orders in which there is no private property permitted for its members, and the political and economic orders (the latter of which he appears to confine to production activities) are entirely separated.

Durkheim's use of the term *communism* thus refers to a theory or system of state-managed consumption, with the consumption goods provided somehow outside political control, rather than to the state-less Marxian "higher phase" of communism that incorporates both production and consumption. Durkheim identifies Sparta as an example of the former social order and Plato as a theorist of it. Although agreeing with Marx that Plato was a progenitor of communist theory, Durkheim means something different by that theory than Marx does.[1]

Identifying communism as "the socialism of consumption" (p. 496), the historian of socialism Alexander Gray identifies Plato as the originator of "the theory and the vision" (1968, p. 11) of it and the inspiration of later utopians. He presents Sparta as an example of "Greek communism in practice"; although he emphasizes the military nature of Spartan society which, with its subordination of the individual to social ends, "is, of course, of the very essence of socialism in its general sense, as distinguished from that species of socialism generally referred to as communism" (p. 12*ff*.). Plato's own vision is argued to be one restricted to the ruling classes within the greater society and dependent on the material support provided by that society. The result is a restricted "communism of poverty and of asceticism, of abnegation and renunciation" (p. 12) in contrast to the wealth- and income-equalizing theories of later ages. Gray's typology of Plato is closer to Durkheim's than to Marx's.

Alban Winspear (1940, p. 262) credits Plato with the crucial insight that it is economics, and primarily the institution of private property, that creates social division. Plato's purported reaction was to envision an "upper-class communism" (p. 249) based on Spartan and Cretan practice. Winspear chides Plato for not having gone far enough in his search for "a unified state" by including the lower classes in his communist scheme.

Among other historians of socialism, Max Beer asserts that Plato produced "a theory of Communism" (1957, p. 14), to be applied to all Greeks (p. 97). He further describes the Spartans as having "accomplished a communist revolution" (pp. 60*ff*.) under the leadership of Lykourgos, "a communist revolutionary" who constitutionally established a communism of consumption in Sparta. Harry Laidler describes Plato's ideal as a state that unites "the moral individual with the socialized state" (1968, p. 10) in a "dictatorship of philosophic communists" (p. 12); while Igor Shafarevich describes the *Republic* and the *Laws* as an ideal "chiliastic socialism" (p. 7), that is, as a socialist analogue to the religious ideal of the "thousand-year Kingdom of God upon earth."

Only a few general historians of economic thought include some mention of communistic aspects of Plato's ideal polis. Lewis Haney refers to Plato's "communistic beliefs" (1949, p. 59) and his desire for a "complete communism" (p. 61) among the upper classes in his ideal state; Eric Roll characterizes the life of the "elite" in the *Republic* as "a communistic life of Spartan rigour" (1974, p. 29); Gide and Rist label Plato an "utopian communist" (n.d., p. 213); while Ekelund and Hebert point out that Plato "proposed that communism be imposed on the rulers" (1990, p. 18) of his ideal state so that they would be incorruptible.

In contrast, and with his characteristic independence, Schumpeter declines to identify Plato as either a communist or a socialist, preferring to label him as merely influential on later communist "schemes" while his own is closer to "fascistic" in nature (1954, p. 55). Most recently, Spiegel rejects both the communist and fascist labels, if they would imply any of what is meant by such labels today, and remarks on the contrast between the ascetic purpose of the communal elements in Plato's politically "authoritarian" republic and the "utilitarian lineage of communism" (1991, p. 22).

Obviously opinions are mixed regarding the question of Plato's status in the intellectual lineage of the theory of communism, if there is such a theory distinct from that of socialism. In addition, some believe that historical Sparta has a place in the history of actual communist social orders. But should it? One suspects a linkage between the two questions. Plato's reliance on aspects of historical Sparta in constructing his poleis of the imagination is apparent in his many references to Spartan institutions and Spartan society, as will be shown below. Especially for those who believe that Plato is a theoretician of communism (of some sort) does this encourage a view of Sparta as an historical communist social order. And that is one possible truth of the relationship between historical Sparta and Plato's ideal.

Of course, Plato could have misunderstood Sparta or misused what he knew of it in his own communist enterprise. Therefore, Plato could be the father of communist theory, but Sparta no example of historical communism. Alternatively, Sparta may have been a communist society, but Plato no communist theorist; however, by introducing aspects of Spartan society into his own social ideal, he colored his own ideal with communism and, for many, became its seminal theorist. Finally, Plato may have been no theorist of communism; he may have understood Sparta and represented what he knew accurately. However, by having been later mistakenly characterized as a "communist theorist," he inadvertently contributed to a mistaken appraisal of Sparta as itself a communist society. Guilt by association, as it were.

I will show that the last of these alternatives is most likely the correct one. To do so, it is first necessary to examine historical Sparta. Because knowledge of many aspects of ancient Spartan society is both fragmentary and controversial, the reconstruction presented here may be too simplified and is certainly speculative; however, it does have the virtue of bringing coherence to the historical sources. And isn't coherence a presupposition of those who label Sparta as communist? It will prove useful at first to review the political aspects of Spartan society separately from the economic aspects. This is not to suggest, however, that the Spartan economy was either separable from, or independent of, the political, cultural, and institutional framework of Spartan society (Austin and Vidal-Naquet, 1977, p. 8).

Sparta

The Political Order

The political foundations of the Spartan polis were laid during the Archaic Age in Greek history (800–500 B.C.) by descendants of the Dorian tribes that swept into the Peloponnese and Crete after the mysterious destruction of the Bronze Age Mycenaean civilization. This migration probably occurred during the eleventh century (Finley, 1970, p. 72). The political order of the Mycenaeans had resembled the monarchical system of the Near East coupled with a palace bureaucracy, while the Dorian "semi-nomadic warriors . . . governed themselves in tribal assemblies," the king ruling only with the consent of his soldiers (Huxley, 1962, p. 15). This political structure was by no means unusual (Starr, 1977, p. 30; Prentice, 1940, p. 138) since virtually all the various peoples on the Greek continent and in Ionia were organized tribally at that time.

The following centuries saw a continuing struggle for political power between the Dorian kings and the aristocracy. By the end of the Archaic Age, the unique political organization of the Greek polis existed throughout the Hellenic world, with each community having attained that organization in its own way. The arbitrary will of particular men as the principle of political rulership had been discarded, and the members of the community that constituted each polis had become subject to the rule of law, as interpreted and applied by their various councils, officers, and assemblies.[2]

Lykourgos of Sparta was one of the earliest reputed codifiers of the laws and (perhaps) mythic founder of the Spartan constitution (*c.* 825–800 B.C., according to Hammond, 1986, p. 103, who depends on Thucydides; *c.* 700–670 B.C., according to Huxley, 1962, p. 49, and Forrest, 1968, p. 58, who argue the logic of the historical evidence). In doing this, he may (Aristotle, *Politics*, 1271b20*ff.*) have adopted some of the main elements of the constitutions of Dorian poleis on Crete, which in turn were supposedly adopted from the constitution introduced by the (perhaps) mythic Minos. In any event, Sparta became famous as the first of the classic Greek poleis considered to be a community of free citizens possessing equal, given and publicly known political rights (Finley, 1973, pp. 154–155) that granted them "a defined and substantial say in running their city" (Forrest, 1968, p. 152). The reforms attributed to Lykourgos occurred at a crucial point in the early history of the Spartan state.

Sparta was originally formed by the union of the three Dorian tribes, Pamphyloi, Hylleis, and Dymanes, under the two royal houses, the Agiad and Eurypontid, named for the kings Agis I and Eurypon of the latter two tribes.[3] These warrior tribesmen conquered Laconia and settled in four villages *c.* 800 B.C. (Huxley, 1962, pp. 16*ff.*). About 750 B.C. the village of Amyclae was captured and added to the others. Although the number of tribes did not increase, the number of tribesmen did through natural increase as well as the adoption into the existing tribes of kinship groups or clans (*obai*) having hereditary chiefs and common lands (Huxley, 1962, p. 24). Tribal membership therefore was based on heredity, and obal membership combined heredity and geographic location.

Throughout the eighth century, the united tribes expanded their conquest of Laconia to the mountain barriers east and west of the Eurotas valley, and the sea to the south. Inhabitants of conquered cities became the *perioikoi*, a class of subjects with no political rights in the Spartan state but nevertheless responsible for paying tribute and supplying troops. In the late eighth century, Helos on the southern coast of the Peloponnese was captured. It was apparently at that point that the Spartan system of land division among citizens began (Huxley, 1962, p. 31).

In this first or "old allotment," the land of Laconia was divided into allotments (*kleroi*), each of which was assigned to a Spartan citizen or "equal" (*homoios*) to be worked by people tied to the land (the "helots"), with one-half the produce to go to the absentee landholder. Thus, each citizen now had a landed estate on the income of which he was to subsist and make his contributions to the community. In addition, the helots were also liable for military service.

Then followed the First Messenian War, the results of which were the additions of the fertile lands and inhabitants of Messenia to the Spartan domain, Division of this additional land and its new helots among the *homoioi* would enable virtual self-sufficiency for them; however, it also engendered political discord because the Spartan aristocrats got the lion's share of the spoils as compared to that given to the ordinary *homoios* (Jones, 1967, p. 43). This may have reflected the power of the royal families and their entourage, which had increased since the time when warrior assemblies ruled the tribe (Michell, 1964, p. 23). The degree of social strife (*stasis*) after the war is underscored by the fact that it was at this time (708 B.C.) that one of the only Spartan colonies (Taras or Tarentum) was founded, but not for the reasons of overpopulation or trading purposes that motivated the founding of colonies by other Greek poleis (Jones, 1967, pp. 11–12). Sparta had no population problem and had a subsistence agricultural economy, which was only enriched by the conquest of Messenia. It is most likely that Taras was founded by political refugees forced out of Sparta (Forrest, 1968, p. 61).

Whatever the source of the existing strife between the ordinary citizen and the aristocracy, the Spartan constitution strove to eliminate it. It did so by restoring the ancient power of the tribal assembly, while providing a more formal political structure for governing the polis. Introducing the constitution was the service reputedly performed by Lykourgos, who, after visiting Crete, went to the Cretan priests of Apollo at Delphi and secured the "Great Rhetra" or oracle on which to found the new political order (Huxley, 1962, p. 43, n. 283).

The Rhetra instructed the Spartan *homoioi* to build a shrine to Zeus and Athena and celebrate the feast of Apollo; to establish a *gerousia*, or council of 30 elders, that included the two kings; and to legislate by initiatives from either the council or the whole citizenry, with the latter having the final word in regular public assemblies. This gave the predominance of political power to the citizenry; however, the Rhetra was later amended during the Second Messenian War to grant veto power over citizen initiatives to the council of elders, thus effectively balancing the political power of the general citizenry against that of the *gerousia* (Plutarch, *Lycurgus*, n.d., p. 54; Huxley, 1962, p. 54).

The *gerousia* itself likely consisted of 27 elected members, each of whom represented one of the tribal warrior brotherhoods into which the *homoioi* were subdivided (Huxley, 1962, pp. 47–49; Forrest, 1968, pp. 45–46). This unit was the *phratry* (from which the military company or *lochos* was taken, three of which formed a *mora*, a regiment of the army). Three *phratries* formed an *obe*—each of the three coming from a different tribe. There were thus nine *obes* in existence at the time of the Rhetra. If there were about 330 men in a *phratry*, then each *obe* was about 1,000 men and each tribe about 3,000, for a total Spartan citizenry of about 9,000 men when the constitution was established. (Forrest, 1968, p. 45).

The remaining three members of the council were the two kings and a third leader, perhaps a leader representing the Pamphyloi tribe because they supplied no king.[4] If so, this would have provided a council that combined representation of the individual tribal brotherhoods within each tribe, with overall representation for each of the three. It is not known whether the five *Ephors*, or city magistrates, of Sparta existed prior to this constitution. Huxley (1962, p. 38) believes so; Plutarch (*Lycurgus*, n.d., p. 54), Jones (1967, pp. 30–31), and others believe the Ephorate was created later. In any event, the result of the Lykourgan reforms was to make the Spartan political order both reflective of its military organization and of its tribal past (Michell, 1964, pp. 93–94). Sparta thus became a warrior tribesmen state, a polis (Plato, *Laws*, 666e) organized more like an ancient army than a true community, and dedicated (Aristotle, *Politics*, 1984, 1324b7) to preparation for war. Later (506 B.C.), the conflicts between the two kings during military campaigns would result in one being designated to lead the army in each campaign while the other remained at home.

Also attributed to Lykourgos and his reforms are the distinctive educational system and domestic customs that together formed the Spartan system of military training or *agoge*. The *agoge* included elements similar to those found in other ancient warrior societies (Jones, 1967, p. 34; Michell, 1964, pp. 176, 281–286), as well as in some existing today (Forrest, 1968, p. 53).[5] It even extended to a preference for choral music and to dancing that mimicked warfare (Michell, 1964, pp. 185*ff*.; Barnstone, 1988, p. 8), much as the *kata* (forms) of the Asian martial arts are sham *kumite* (fights). The *agoge* can only be understood if it is recognized that its purpose was to create and maintain an army of professional soldiers in a high state of discipline and readiness, both to retain control of Spartan lands and to provide defense from all outside threats (Michell, 1964, p. 165).

The inside threat of a revolt of the helots was very real. This is shown by the size of the subject population relative to that of the Spartan rulers (perhaps as much as 20 or 30 to 1) and the ethnic and tribal homogeneity, and thus common interests, in each of the several subject peoples as opposed to that of the Spartans (Forrest, 1968, p. 39). In fact, several revolts did occur, and Sparta insisted, in making alliances with other poleis, that they agree to render assistance in the event of such revolts (Jones, 1967, p. 9).

The element of the *agoge* that was most immediately relevant to the needs of a warrior state was the system of public education of the youth. From the ages of 7 to 30 Spartan males lived apart from their families and underwent intense military training. It was supervised by the Ephors and designed to instill a level of obedience, courage, physical fitness, and endurance superior to that of any other army (Michell, 1964, p. 128). The training included physical exercise and intentional deprivation, trials of courage and initiative, and instruction in skills and obedience by peers as well as elders. Indeed, Plutarch (*Lycurgus*, p. 67) remarks of their training that it was intended to rival the conditions of the battlefield so that war demanded less of them than their education. At the age of 19, the young *homoioi* became part of the Spartan army; full citizenship and the right to live with wives and family were only obtained after completion of training at age 30. Military service continued until age 60 or death, whichever came first.

In addition, the period of childhood before the formal period of training was regulated by eugenic laws and customs to encourage the bearing and rearing of healthy children of "good stock." Wives were not held in common, but occasionally were "shared" (Xenophon, "Constitution," 1942, p. 659); some husbands lending their wives to conceive the children of other men with desired qualities. This also may have represented an attempt to compensate for childless marriages in the face of decline of the *homoioi* population (Michell, 1964, pp. 56, 230–231), as well as the general fear of childlessness itself (Zimmern, 1961, p. 74). Nevertheless, male children who were presumed weak or apparently malformed were killed.

The one communal institution to which the young warrior was introduced during his military training and that continued even after he married and established a family was the *syssition*, or compulsory communal evening meal—the earlier of the two daily meals being taken (Zimmern, 1961, p. 50) in the middle of the workday. The *syssition* was, in origin at least, the military mess of the *phratry* to which he belonged and to which, after he became a full citizen, he was required to make a fixed monthly contribution from the produce of his *kleros* (Michell, 1964, pp. 281–282; Forrest, 1968, pp. 45–46).[6] In fact, failure to maintain that contribution led to the loss of full citizenship rights, expulsion from the *syssition* and demotion from the status of *homoios* to that of *hypomeion*, an impoverished member of the Spartan community (Forrest, 1968, p. 124). It is not known whether a *hypomeion* retained his membership and voting rights in the assembly.

Participation in the nightly *syssition* no doubt aided the continuance of the traditions and camaraderie necessary to the preservation of a warrior state (Powell, 1988, p. 222). Perhaps that was its main purpose. Complementing this was its use as a forum for educating the young in politics, manners, and temperance (Plutarch, *Lycurgus*, n.d., p. 58). Regarding instruction in the latter virtue, if Plutarch (p. 71) is correct in relating the Spartans' use of drunken helots as objects of ridicule during the *syssitia*, then Sparta also retained another characteristic of primitive societies (David, 1989, pp. 7–17). This was the use of the degradation and humiliation of those low in the social hierarchy to enhance its rigidity as well as the sense of superiority enjoyed by those at the top, the *homoioi*.

Whatever its social purposes, the *syssition* was by no means a communal meal to which each contributed an equal share and that was the same in all *phratries*. Much as dining varies from one college to another at Oxford, dependent on the wealth of each college, so dining varied from one *phratry* to another in ancient Sparta, dependent on the wealth and good fortune in the hunt of its members (Fisher, 1989, pp. 31–32). Each was responsible for a basic contribution, but some gave more than others for reasons of prestige and patronage, so that "hierarchy in the *syssition* was extremely important" (*ibid.*, p. 37). On the other hand, the sharing of income and wealth in this way would likely alleviate some of the resentment engendered by wealth and income inequalities (*ibid.*, p. 39), perhaps in the same way that patronage of the arts and other civic activities by the wealthy often accomplish the same end today.

It should be clear from this brief review of the political order of Sparta, and its main supporting institutions, that the political and social hierarchy were exceedingly rigid—and intentionally so.[7] According to political distinction, and in descending order of political importance, there were *homoioi*, *perioikoi*, helots, and slaves. Helots given freedom in return for military service became the *neodamodeis*, virtual mercenaries in the Spartan army (Forrest, 1968, p. 128; Oliva, 1971, p. 107). Those who elected to serve in the Spartan navy became the *desposionautai* (Huxley, 1962, p. 73). Furthermore, (Michell, 1964, p. 230) entry into full citizenship by means other than being born the son of a *homoios* was seldom granted after the introduction of the constitution.

Significant distinctions based on heredity, age, and the fulfilment of obligations even existed among the *homoioi* themselves. Obviously, the aristocratic *homoios* was privileged in comparison to *homoioi* who were not members of the royal families. Additional distinctions were made according to parentage, the *mothakes* being sons of *hypomeiones* and who served as companions of sons of *homoioi* (Jones, 1967, p. 37). Also, *homoioi* who failed to marry, or were convicted of cowardice, were subject to social discrimination, and only those who died on the battlefield were given state burials and marked graves. Some of the "equals" were obviously and perpetually more equal than others.

The Economic Order

The economic aspects of the history of Sparta prior to the conquest of Helos in the late eighth century are obscure. All that is known is that after the settlement of the original four villages that would become Sparta, the indigenous Achaean population of most of the cities conquered in Laconia in the wars of the eighth century became the *perioikoi* (Huxley, 1962, p. 16*ff.*).

As previously mentioned, once Helos and all Laconia were secure, the Spartans divided the land outside the perioikic cities into separate agricultural estates (*kleroi*) which, with their inhabitants, were then assigned to individual Spartan homoioi to provide them regular incomes. This assignment was originally not a transfer of ownership, but rather made each *homoios* a conservator of state property who retained the *kleros* and its associated inhabitants and income by right of his citizenship, with that retention dependent on good conduct (Michell, 1964, p. 205). The former nomadic warrior tribesmen thus became surrogate rentiers of estates worked by the helots, who were tied to the land. From the rents each *homoios* received, he provided for his family, made his compulsory contribution to his *syssition* and to occasional civic needs and religious festivals, and outfitted himself for war. Transfer of the *kleros* and its helots remained a state decision until the fourth-century Law of Epitadeus gave the right of disposition of the *kleros* to the incumbent *homoios* (Oliva, 1971, pp. 188–190).[8]

Following the conquest of Messenia and the second allotment of estates, the total agricultural wealth under Spartan dominance assured its citizens virtual self-sufficiency in necessities, as long as they retained political control (Huxley, 1962, p. 41). The tasks of retaining that control by suppressing a rebellion of the helots in the Second Messenian War and pursuing wars against hostile cities outside Sparta's borders occupied the army for the rest of the seventh century. By the end of the sixth, Sparta ruled Laconia, Messenia, and much of Arcadia; had conquered its main enemy Argos; and was powerful enough to intervene in Athenian politics. It had, however, irrevocably committed itself to an agrarian economic base (Forrest, 1968, p. 38).

This was a result of the central economic role of the land-tenure system. It supported both the rigid political hierarchy and the standing army necessary to retain political control of the occupied lands, as well as to repel potential invaders. It also reflected (Austin and Vidal-Naquet, 1977, pp. 14–15) the commitment to the basically aristocratic value system of ancient Greece, which enobled war and leisure—and, to a lesser extent, agriculture—while denigrating trade or production activities, where one man might be subject to the will of another. What commercial activity existed in Sparta was the province of the subjugated *perioikoi* (Hamilton, 1979, p. 61).[9]

Despite the periodic wars, the latter part of the seventh century and the whole of the sixth were characterized by relative peace and prosperity in comparison with earlier conditions (Huxley, 1962, pp. 61–65; Michell, 1964, pp. 11–12).[10] There were even significant increases in trade between Sparta and other poleis.[11] Although there was allegedly an internal ban on the use of coined precious metal for money, it was used in external trade after its introduction in the Peloponnese in the sixth century.[12]

For Huxley (1962, p. 73), it was the rise of Athens and Persia that brought an end to this prosperity and initiated the isolation and increased bellicosity for which Sparta was known in the fifth century. This interpretation reinforces the conclusion of Thucydides (I, 1951, 88) and Hasebroek (1965, p. 144) that the Peloponnesian War was the result of Spartan fear of Athenian imperial power, although it does not necessarily mean that the war was commercially motivated (Finley, 1973, p. 158).[13] Although successful in that war, the defeat of Sparta by Thebes at Leuktra in 371 B.C. and the other military failures of the fourth century, culminating in the loss of Messenia, crippled the agricultural base of classic Sparta, consigned Spartan armies to the status of mercenaries, and reduced the Spartan economy to the level prevailing prior to the First Messenian War 400 years earlier.

During the long period of relative Spartan prosperity, the political equality of the *homoioi* was not at all matched by economic equality, as one reference by Plato (*Laws*, 683d–685a) might imply, and some later commentators (Jones, 1967, p. 41) have suggested. There were great disparities in wealth and income among the *homoioi* (Jones, 1967, p. 36; Michell, 1964, pp. 35, 207*ff.*) as there were also class (Ridley, 1974, p. 291) and wealth (Forrest, 1968, p. 30) differences among the *perioikoi* and even among the helots (Michell, 1964, p. 78)—who, if they satisfied the 50 percent tithe and survived their military service, were otherwise free to manage their own economic affairs. The percentage tithe could even be seen as an incentive to production in that both the helot and his rentier stood to benefit from increases.

Several factors contributed through time to an increasing inequality of wealth and income among the *homoioi*. Unequal estates were alloted among the nobility and the ordinary *homoioi* at the beginning of the land-tenure system, and this situation persisted. Managerial abilities and luck were not equally distributed among the *homoioi*, and this led to differences in their incomes while in possession of their *kleroi*. As a result of an understandable desire to prevent the reduction—or even to encourage an increase—of wealth and income, there was an incentive for marital arrangements aimed at preserving or concentrating landholdings.[14] Also, inheritance customs that dispersed holdings among male descendants created an incentive to restrict the size of families; and this, given the higher mortality rates of Spartan males, increased the probability of having a surviving daughter for whom to find a suitable marriage, rather than a son to inherit.[15] There were also the key demographic factors of the continuing absolute attrition of the *homoioi* through wars and the unwillingness to extend citizenship beyond tribal membership.[16]

Over the centuries between the capture of Helos and the defeat of the Spartan army at Leuktra in 371 B.C., the number of *homoioi* shrank steadily—possibly being fewer than a thousand by the latter date (Austin and Vidal-Naquet, 1977, p. 82)—while the disparities of wealth between the richer and poorer citizens grew greater and the land became increasingly concentrated in the hands of the female population. Michell (1964, p. 334) even goes so far as to characterize the economic inequality among the *homoioi* that resulted from the land tenure system as exceeding that found in any other polis. These inequalities, and the associated debt of the poorer members of the community, were to culminate in the third century in social stasis, a situation resolved by debt cancellation, land redistribution, and reinstitution of the *agoge* by Agis IV, Kleomenes III, and Nabis.

Spartan state finances, like those of Athens and the other Greek poleis, were handled on a cash-flow basis. When there was cash, it flowed. Otherwise, there is little evidence of any attempt at systematic public finance and none of state economic planning. Despite the fact that the Spartan economy was virtually a permanent war economy—the income from the *kleroi* being primarily devoted to support of the standing army—there was no attempt to anticipate and prepare for war expenditures. For the expenditures that did become necessary, perioikic tribute was used, resources were seized, or citizens were compelled to make contributions to meet specific needs. No direct taxes (Michell, 1964, p. 308) were levied, save the obligatory monthly contribution to the *syssitia.* It was only after the defeat of Athens in 404 B.C. that Sparta attempted to adopt the Athenian system of extracting tribute from its allies (*ibid.*, p. 312). For the brief period before defeat at Leuktra it flowed into Sparta, but left no lasting imprint such as that left by the tribute that had built Periklean Athens.

Summary

How should post-Lykourgan Sparta be characterized? It is tempting to regard the political order established by Lykourgos as (Aristotle, *Politics*, 1984, 1265b34–42) a mixture of monarchy, oligarchy, and democracy; however, such an approach is not really very informative. It uses terms intended to reveal the locus of legitimized physical coercion (political power) in an entire social order to characterize contending power centers within such an order. Without knowing the exact governmental structure and the rules according to which political power is exercised, one could not anticipate how that order might have functioned. On the other hand, if one knew that structure and rules, the particular terms used to denote its parts would be irrelevant to its understanding.

It is also tempting to characterize the political order of Sparta as a balance of powers between the executive, the legislative, and the judicial branches of the government (Forrest, 1968, pp. 17–18). Unfortunately, any attempt to do so founders on the difficulty of identifying which were which within the Spartan structure. Each major element—the kings, the *gerousia*, the assembly, the *ephors*—combined the duties of originating law, executing law and judging transgressions of the law (Jones, 1967, pp. 15*ff.*). Again, if characterizing a political order is to convey understanding of how it functions, inappropriate or anachronous analogs cannot be used.

The position taken here is that the Spartan polis is best understood as what it was in itself, rather than what it was or is called. There were two kings, a *gerousia*, an assembly, and *ephors*. Each part obtained particular constitutional responsibilities as a result of historical compromises in the struggle for political power. The political order among the *homoioi* combined the representation of their tribal past, their geographical present, and the military foundation blocks within Spartan society. It was not, at least in structure, dominated by the *demos*, the kings, the aristocracy, or the army; instead, it balanced those (potentially) contending factions (Plato, *Laws*, 691e–692a, and *Letters*, VIII, 354b–c).[17]

Sparta was, like the other Greek poleis, exclusivistic in that only a minority of the population had full political rights. In that sense, it was an authoritarian regime. The rest of the population—women, *perioikoi*, helots, slaves, et alia—were ruled by, and had their rights defined by, the *homoioi* minority. In classic Greek fashion, the political distance from citizenship was measured by the degree to which one's will was subject to that of those at the top, the *homoioi*. There were thus no classes in the Marxian sense of peasants, proletariat, and bourgeoisie; status was politically rather than economically defined.

Even further, culture and economic structure were strongly influenced, if not solely determined, by the political necessities created by the seizure and determination to retain control of Laconia and Messenia. The eugenic practices, the educational system, and other elements of the *agoge* united to provide the needed standing professional army, while freezing the social structure and introducing that relative stability (*eunomia*) so admired by outsiders. The kleroikic system, intended to provide self-sufficiency for the army, in like manner froze the economic structure into a subsistence agrarian mold that retarded the economic development of Sparta. When the army was defeated and the land was lost, the gains of several centuries evaporated.

Plato's *Republic* and *Laws*

The purpose of this section is to explore the influence of Sparta on Plato's vision of the ideal political and economic regime; however, historical Sparta was only one of the influences on Plato. He taught and wrote in a cultural context that also must be appreciated if his work is to be understood. It will help to review that context briefly before narrowing the focus to the specific influence of Sparta. Then it will be possible to ask in what sense, if any, either historical Sparta or Plato's ideal regime might be termed communist or socialist, given what has been learned.

The Cultural Context

Above the social frame of any particular polis arched the metaphysical epistemological, religious, and ethical context within which Hellenes existed. Their belief in the unity of nature and the existence of order in the universe, concomitant with the belief in the efficacy of reason to reveal that order, grew with the rise of philosophy to make Hellenic civilization the seedbed of both scientific and moral thinking in the West. As early as Homer's *Iliad* and *Odyssey* (*c.* 750 according to Forrest, 1966) the concept of universal moral law and the necessity of obedience to it had been expressed, as well as its central role in human affairs. In this earliest conception (Bowra, 1959, p. 79), the natural melded with the moral in the divine law as "the will of the gods" and myth provided a basis for order in society; but even the gods were believed to be subject to Necessity (*ananke*) and Fate (*moira*).

Human nature, being part of Nature, was taken to mean that moral and natural law must have the same foundation; social law was to express the realization of natural law in society. The highest function of social law would be that of "a creative, formative agent" for both securing and inculcating justice (*dike*) (Kitto, 1951, p. 94). The basic laws (*nomoi*) of the polis thus aimed at creating the ideal citizen. The relation between religion and man-made law became that of the former providing the confirmation, rather than the basis, for the latter.

There exists no better summary of the primary values intended to motivate "the best men" (*aristoi*) of ancient Greece than the two inscribed aphorisms of the Delphic Oracle, "Nothing in Excess" and "Know Thyself." The search for "the good life" and the attempt to achieve the ideal of "the good man" as exemplar of that life through the practice of moderation or temperance (*sophrosune*) embodied the spirit of these aphorisms. This meant "accepting the bounds excellence laid down for human nature, restraining impulses to unrestricted freedom . . . [and] obeying the inner laws of harmony and proportion" (Hamilton, 1964, p. 21).

Kitto (1951, p. 252) emphasizes the consequent importance to the Greeks of the doctrine of the Mean, whereby the will was to master the extremes of the passions to produce a man who was like a tuned string, which "did not imply the absence of tension and lack of passion, but the correct tension which gives out the true and clear note." *Eros* was believed to be the force that animated the highest blend of the intellectual and spiritual to achieve the greatest ends, one that produced "a properly balanced personality," and a life devoted to achieving and exhibiting the four cardinal virtues of courage, wisdom, temperance, and justice (Bowra, 1959, p. 209).

The ancient Greeks were certainly not ascetics; however, there was an element of asceticism in this emphasis on the virtue of temperance and the exertion of the will, inspired by eros, to achieve harmony of soul, body, and polis.[18] There was also an element of individualism in their emphasis (Finley, 1970, pp. 130–131) on self-reliance and the value of innovation, although they were not truly individualistic (Starr, 1977, p. 137). The family (*oikos*) and polis remained the fundamental social units. Aristotle's argument in the *Politics* that concludes with the famous words "man is by nature a political animal" (1253a3) (*zoon politikon*) is better understood by the modern reader in its more literal translation of "man is an animal whose characteristic it is to live in a polis" (Kitto, 1951, p. 11).

It was further believed that for *aristoi* to achieve excellence of character (*arete*),[19] they required a setting of leisure, health, beauty, wealth, and community that was not possible to everyone and in which only certain men would be ultimately successful.[20] The specific aristocratic ethos within which *arete* was to be sought was a constellation of values maintained by education, the arts, and religious and social institutions that first appeared in the eighth century (Starr, 1977, pp. 120*ff.*). By the fifth century, it was believed that "*arete* was found in the full development of the individual inside the social frame" (Bowra, 1959, p. 211). This evolved into the fourth-century ideal of *paideia*, or civic cultural education, as the supreme means to *arete* (Jaeger, vol. I, 1945, p. 204). Significantly, only Sparta (Aristotle, *Nicomachean Ethics*, 1947, 1180a25) had such a public education.

Plato's concept of the *paideia* that would produce *arete*, and achieve the just man and the just polis, is presented in arguments for its ideal form as well as for its practical realization.[21] *Republic* argues the ideal; *Laws* is concerned with practice in the face of "frail human nature" (875b). Only *Laws* concerns a truly constitutional polis—a polis under the rule of law. It is thus appropriate that Sparta, the first constitutional Greek polis, provides only a springboard for Plato's ideal, while presenting (in conjunction with those of Crete) key institutional patterns for his practical regime. The narrative structures of *Republic* and *Laws* are well known and will not be summarized here; it is only necessary to review the elements relevant to the question of the degree to which Spartan influence is apparent.

Republic

In *Gorgias*, Plato argues (506e) that it is the presence of the order appropriate to a thing that makes it good. Thus, *paideia* is the perfection of man's character in accordance with nature to make him good (Jaeger, vol. II, 1945, pp. 133, 146). Plato's purpose in *Republic* is to present a *paideia* for self-realization, as well as a vision of the ideal polis (Brann, 1979, p. xxxvi). The order of the ideal polis is used (592b) as an exemplar for achieving an inner *eunomia*, or harmony, for the parts of the soul (410c). As each class of the just city (rulers, auxiliaries, and nonguardians) is associated with a particular virtue, and maintaining the natural order of the whole is what makes it just (433e), so each of the parts of the whole person (the intellect, the spirit, and the desires) is to be dedicated to the achievement of its proper virtue (wisdom, courage, and temperance) while the whole is to be so ordered as to achieve a person's greatest good (justice), and thus happiness (443d).

Plato's "city of words" thus anticipates what he argues is needed to be a just man (435b); it does so as "a projection of justice on the largest possible screen . . . so that its nature may be easier to discern" (Brann, 1979, p. xliv). The aristocratic city is ruled by the philosopher king to achieve the good through his wise policies and their implementation by the guardians. Analogously, the *aristos* is ruled by his reason to achieve the good through wisdom in his thought and courageous action. This is the guardian city and the best man idealized in *Republic*. Replace the dominance of wisdom with that of courage and one has timocratic man, whose parallel city is timocracy (545a).

Of all existing regimes it was Sparta that Plato most admired. This is apparent in his use of Sparta as representative of timocracy—the first degenerate or unjust real regime (*Republic*, 544c–551b). The most admirable elements of Sparta are given as those that make it most resemble the just but nonexistent regime, aristocracy, namely: "honoring its rulers and in the abstention of its warrior class from farming and handicraft and money-making in general, and in the provision of common public tables and the devotion to physical training and expertness in the game and contest of war . . ." (547d). But most admirable of all was the thoroughgoing *paideia* of Sparta, devoted as it was to imposing order on the entire community (Jaeger, vol. III, 1945, p. 168)—albeit wrongly, as it was not the order of aristocracy dominated by wisdom, but that of timocracy dominated by courage and "with a view to war" (*Laws*, 626b).

Plato's admiration for Sparta is also revealed in his argument for the inevitable degeneration of aristocracy into timocracy. Decay begins with an innocent failure in the eugenic calculations by the rulers of the aristocratic regime. This produces future members of the ruling class lacking in attention to *paideia*. The result is dissension among the guardians to the point that houses and land are privatized, members of the nonguardian class are brought into subjection as *perioikoi* and serfs, and the guardian class occupies itself with repression of its subjects and war against its neighbors. The similarities to Sparta and her political history, related in an earlier section, should be apparent.

The degenerate Spartan regime of timocracy arises from innocent error, and it does preserve much of aristocracy; however, its failure to be just lies in the emphasis on the virtue of courage and the dominance of the warriors within the guardian class, to the exclusion of wisdom and wise men. The lack of the class order intended by nature, where each person does that for which he is uniquely suited, and the emphasis on gymnastics to the detriment of poetry (422a) is what makes timocracy and timocratic man unjust and, in consequence, unstable and ripe for degeneration into oligarchy—an even more unjust regime.

Given Plato's admiration for Sparta, how did it affect his vision of the ideal or just polis? First, the aspects of Sparta praised explicitly by Plato (547d) are constituent elements of his ideal and require little comment. The Spartan class structure and predominance of the *homoioi* finds its reflection in the predominance of the guardians, and especially in those who are the warriors. The warrior guardians obviously mirror the character of the *homoioi* as a standing army, uninvolved in farming or commerce, and their public messes bear some resemblance to the Spartan *syssitia*, although there is insufficient detail in *Republic* to say how close it is.[22] Also, the emphasis on gymnastics and preparation for war in Sparta is part of the *paideia* of Plato's warriors.

Other elements of the Spartan *agoge* seem more like springboards to the *paideia* of Plato's just polis. Among these are included the partial application of the *agoge* to Spartan girls, the administration of the *agoge* to all male children of *homoioi* until the age of 30 by members (the *ephors*) of the ruling class, the emphasis by the *homoioi* on the virtue of courage and the honours paid to heroism in battle, the marital and eugenic practices of the *homoioi*, and, last, the hereditary aristocracy. In Plato's vision, the guardians are both male and female, they receive the same education until the age of 50, they have all their major possessions, their children, and each other in common; they are subject to exact eugenic planning; and, most important, the wisest become the rulers. This was not Sparta; however, for Plato, it might have been Sparta purified to achieve *eunomia* through a universal *paideia*, the elimination of any potential sources of dissension, and the establishment of the rule of natural aristocrats.

As far as the economic order of *Republic* is concerned, it should first be noted that Plato attributes the origin of the polis (369b) to the individual's lack of self-sufficiency in the face of scarcity. Further, he describes the growth of the polis as contingent on extending the division of labor according to comparative advantage, with the subsequent development of an exchange economy. The introduction of a marketplace and a token currency to support the division of labor, of a merchant class acting to reduce transactions costs, and of an unskilled laboring class completes the founding of Plato's "city of words."

The guardian class arises after the city has expanded to include industrial and service sectors producing luxury goods, and the unbridled requirements of the increasing population requires an army for territorial expansion. This hypothetical or "conjectural" history of the polis thus depends strongly on the economic principle of the division of labor, driven by the attempt to satisfy more completely the needs of the citizenry. In a sense, the consequent class division into rulers, guardians, farmers and craftsmen, merchants, traders, and laborers is a result of stopping that division of labor at the level of whole professions. Further, it is only when "each perform(s) his one task as one man and (i)s not a versatile busybody" (433d) that justice exists in the polis. Thus, economics has partially founded the polis, as well as provided the basis for a just order, given the proper *paideia*.

The other founding principle is that of the different qualities of men that suit them for their respective professions and classes, and of which it is the purpose of eugenics and education to determine. The politically just order is thus a mirror that reflects both economic and natural necessity. Beyond maintaining the division of professions and classes according to natural aptitudes, the guardians also strive to preserve *eunomia* among members of the nonguardian class by preventing extremes of wealth or income (421e). *Eunomia* among the guardians themselves is to be preserved by their communal institutions (464), which focus their thoughts and actions on the collective good rather than on their individual satisfactions (462).

Entirely missing is any concern with extensive political control of economic activity. The guardians receive their minimal required sustenance from the output of the nonguardian class, much as the *homoioi* received their incomes from their helot-worked *kleroi.* Beyond that, there is only minimal interpenetration of political and economic activity in Plato's ideal regime, as there was in historical Sparta. Apart from sequestration of the share of output devoted to provisioning the guardians, the existence of relatively free production and trade sectors is entirely compatible with both *Republic* and what is known of the Spartan economy.[23]

The "Second-Best" Regime

Plato's concern with the form of the good polis led in *Statesman* to the attempt to define the true statesman—for a just polis would only be possible if it were ruled in justice. To Plato this meant the determination of the justice appropriate to the circumstances of each person. If the exercise of authority requires the same qualitative knowledge at the level of the household as it does at the level of the polis (259b), then the true statesman is he who has that knowledge and is thus able to rule every man justly and at all levels of social aggregation (294a). The just polis is the one in which he rules.

This precludes the rule of law as the highest political principle, and the constitutional polis as the just polis. In the absence of such a statesman, Plato argues, the constitutional polis is the second-best. This leads to the attempt in *Laws* to define that second-best regime, the one in which "frail human nature" requires the rule of law for approximate justice. While doing so, Plato cannot resist occasional references to the ideal or "best" regime, which is an autocracy (710e) ruled by a wise, temperate autocrat (712a), and which resembles (739c–e) the circumstances under which only the guardians were to live in *Republic* (543a).

As he does in *Republic*, in *Laws* Plato presents an argument for the origin of the polis, or state; however, this time his emphases are on actual history and on authority. The regimes within which actual men have lived and may live determine his focus.[24] In particular, he traces the evolution of the historical states of Sparta and Crete from beginnings in the mythical Age of Cronus to the contemporary blend of authority and liberty that marks their superiority as regimes (701e) compared with both the Persian monarchy (698a) and the Athenian democracy (699e). Especially is Sparta praised for the stability and longevity engendered by the balance of power (691e) maintained by the political order of the double kingship, the ephorate, and the *gerousia*.[25]

On the other hand, Plato also presents its history to illustrate the weakness of Sparta in that it became a regime organized like an army and perpetually at war (685). This he attributes to its laws, or constitution, the main purpose of which is to instill the virtue of courage rather than that of wisdom (688). Underlying this critique is Plato's basic view that the purpose of law is to instill virtue (630c), while the purpose of education is to instill the law (690d). So, while he clearly admires Sparta above all existing regimes, Plato sees a fatal flaw that prevents attaining the peace and order of the best regime possible to "frail human nature."

It is the main purpose of the rest of *Laws* to outline that second-best regime in a hypothetical argument for how the new city of Magnesia might be established in Crete. The influence of Sparta is even more evident here than it is in *Republic*.[26] Again, the aspects of Sparta that Plato explicitly praised in *Republic* (547d) are constituent elements of his real, or second-best, regime, and Sparta is explicitly praised for its resemblance to the regime envisioned (*Laws*, 836b)—especially in those (controversial) respects in which Sparta differs from other poleis.

Magnesia is to be an autarchic inland polis, with no city walls, no gold or silver money, and a population fixed at 5,040 male citizen landholders divided into four classes according to their property holdings. The wealthiest will possess no more than four times the property of the poorest, since excess wealth breeds discord (729a) and no really wealthy man can be either good or happy (743). Citizens and their servants or slaves practice no trades and receive their incomes from the serfs who work their *kleroi*. All tradesmen and craftsmen are resident foreigners who each practice only one trade and are subject to a fixed term of residence and no possibility of attaining citizenship. The produce of the agricultural sector is divided into three portions: one going to the citizens, a second administered by them for their households and servants, and the third going to the foreigners. Only the last portion may be the object of trade on the market.

The political order is maintained by the code of laws, which is administered by officials, magistrates, and commissioners, who are both elected and chosen by lot. There is a ruling council of 360, one-fourth of which is elected from each of the four property classes. Thirty of the council members form a monthly governing board and may convene general meetings of the citizenry. Although all citizens are trained as soldiers and are part of the standing army, only those between the ages of 25 and 30 serve full-time as police or rural guards. Nevertheless, all citizens mess together and there are also common messes for the women.

There is no state eugenic control because of the potential for resentment (773c), but like are encouraged to marry like, and all men are encouraged to marry and procreate. Should they not do so, they are penalized by law and lack of deference. Because "the child is even more the property of the state than of his parents," the children are educated by the state from the age of six, the sexes being segregated, but receiving a comparable education in music, gymnastics, and military training (804e). Most significantly, the office of supervisor of public education is by "far the most important of the highest offices in the state" (765e) given the purpose of education to instill the code of law that, in turn, will instill virtue.

Other than the proscription of pederasty and the more ambitious scope of education (837*ff.*), the institutions of Magnesia that differ significantly from those of Sparta are mainly economic.[27] They are better understood if it is borne in mind that Plato's ideal human community, or touchpoint to which the regimes possible to actual man are to be compared, is that of the mythical age of Cronus when there was no scarcity and men were ruled in complete justice by gods (713b–e). In recounting the Cronus legend in *Statesman* (271c*ff.*), Plato emphasizes the age of scarcity and human weakness that follows the rewinding of the universe and the end of godly rule. Although the gifts of the gods enable man to alleviate this scarcity, man needs the rule of a statesman in place of the lost rule of the gods to establish order and eliminate dissension. In the absence of either such a statesman or godly rule, man needs laws patterned after "the immortal element within us" for "we should do our utmost . . . to reproduce the life of the age of Cronus" (*Laws*, 713e).

In its material abundance, the Age of Cronus resembled the earliest point of another of Plato's conjectural histories, when the simple survivors of some massive calamity are supposedly bereft of both tools and guile, but live peaceably in conditions of plenty amid neither riches nor poverty (677*ff.*). Again, in *Critias* Plato describes the Athens of the age of the mythical island of Atlantis as one in which there was great abundance and a class structure similar to that of his ideal regime in *Republic*, including the communal institutions of the guardians (110c–e). Thus, the keys to understanding the economic side of the regime in *Laws* would seem to be Plato's desire to encourage abundance and order, and the consequent desire to eliminate possible sources of dissension.

There are regulations to increase agricultural yields (842c–e), to redistribute wealth to prevent extremes (744d–e), to provide public works and social services (761), to protect property (843c) and enforce contracts (920d), and to punish violence and property crimes. In light of the flaw of self-love (731e) and its tendency to stimulate greed and corruption in commerce (918d), only a small number of the lowest of foreigners are to be allowed to engage in it (919c), and it is to be regulated to increase available supplies (913*ff.*), and to prevent fraud and excessive profits. Of course, no citizen is permitted to engage in commerce. Again, it is clear that this regulation is intended to promote abundance and *eunomia*, since "public well-being should be considered before private" (875b).

All in all, when the regime in *Laws* is compared to Sparta, it is Sparta adjusted to instill wisdom, temperance, and justice, as well as courage, to promote abundance and to eliminate sources of dissension. The ideal remains that of the unity of thought and action of a society of gods, or sons of gods, or of the guardians of *Republic*, promoted by their communal institutions, the key to which is the lack of property in things or themselves (739c). The reality is that there are no such men and so the second-best regime is one regulated by ordinance and law to prevent extremes in property ownership and promote virtuous behavior (875c).

Summary

Teaching and writing in the midst of Athenian political decline, Plato attempted to develop political theory in the light of what he believed were the successes and mistakes of the political past, while retaining his commitment to basic Hellenic values. His main purpose was to define the ideal of justice and the *paideia*, life and political regime appropriate to its achievement. He found that ideal in a concept of the natural social order, ruled and guided by a knowledgeable elite to achieve *eunomia* and stability. In the existent world of imperfect man, the rule of law would provide a second-best solution.

Plato drew on many sources, including his culture and his own life experience during the disorders of the Peloponnesian War, the democracy, the tyranny of "The Thirty," the execution of his beloved teacher, and the continued strife of the fourth century. Historical Sparta was a useful source of material, both for outlining his ideal and for contrast with it; it showed the weaknesses that he thought would bring down any regime and life short of that ideal. In the light of the historical accounts summarized earlier, it is plain that Plato knew much about Sparta.

What Plato admired most in Sparta was the stability of the social structure—a division of labor that led to what seemed an harmonious social whole—with clearly defined political classes functioning to provide social cohesion. He made those the central institutional elements of his ideal. What Plato disliked was the *purpose* of Spartan society—war—and the primary virtue—courage—that impelled (he believed) its downfall. In their respective places he substituted the achievement of the good and the wisdom to do so. Both of these required the central intellectual element absent from Spartan society—philosophy.

The communal elements in the Spartan polis, vestiges of its tribal past, had been adapted to serve as training and unifying elements for a citizenry that lived as an occupying army. Eschewing the general purpose of Sparta, but admiring its unity and stability, Plato adapted the *syssitia*, the pedagogy, and a much-extended ideal of common property to his own uses. These were: (1) the promotion of unity; (2) the public education of the rulers; and (3) the elimination of anything that might stimulate the desiring part of man (*Republic*, 442b, and *Laws*, 731e) to create dissension and disharmony among the guardians in his ideal polis (*Republic*, 462a–c), or among the "gods, or sons of gods" (*Laws*, 739c–e) in a paradigmatic polis. For the second-best regime of flawed human beings, he thought it enough to publicly educate all citizens, to eliminate extremes of wealth and poverty, to promote material abundance, and to restrict and regulate commerce.

Evaluations and Conclusions

Was Sparta a Socialist or Communist Society?

In turning to the specific questions that were raised at the beginning of this chapter, it should be clear from what is known of historical Sparta that it cannot be described meaningfully as having been either a socialist or a communist society according to any of the senses given to those terms by those who have so used them. Rather than being keys to its understanding, the social and economic structure of classical Sparta were derivative of its political purpose—collectivistic tools of its collective end. That purpose, in turn, was the outcome of the warrior tribal nature of ancient Sparta, carried over into the classical era as the *homoioi* became a permanent occupying army, intent on retaining political control of the occupied lands and their peoples.

There were great disparities in incomes and wealth throughout Spartan society, and these grew over the centuries. There was no "communal capital" in the *kleroi*: they were individually assigned; their incomes were individually received and disbursed; and they were eventually individually owned. It may be that in the sense that the Spartan *homoioi* can be said to have produced, they produced according to their respective abilities; however, this is also the rule by which they received—in both the economic and military dimensions of their lives. In the use of their incomes there is little evidence, beyond the *syssitia* contribution, of any "communism of consumption."

The *syssitia*, or communal meals, are best understood as a remnant of warrior tribalism and a reinforcing element of what was, in essence, a society as a permanent military camp. Syssitia even differed in quality and abundance from one *phratry* to another. Military units, like families, mess together; however, we do not, for that reason alone, refer to either as "communistic."

The family was, in fact, an important element of Spartan society, and there was no community of women, only an occasional sharing of a wife under particular and culturally compelling circumstances.[28] There were no common homes, except the military barracks of *homoioi* youths, and no common personal possessions, although Aristotle (*Politics*, 1263a35–7) notes a practice of sharing personal possessions according to the (Pythagorean) proverb, "The things of friends are common," a practice which Plato longed to see (*Laws*, 739c) generalized in the "first-best" society. Nevertheless, in the face of everything else known about Sparta, there is far from any indication of the classless society of pure communism—even among the *homoioi*.

The division of labor certainly existed among the *homoioi* in their military and political structures, as well as in economic activity existing throughout Sparta. And the self-interested actions of the *homoioi* were manifest not only in the growing inequality of incomes and wealth but also in their reputation for corruption and susceptibility to bribery (Michell, 1964, p. 303). There is also no evidence of any attempt at the state planning of production, or of specific interventions to increase production, even in the restricted sense that Xenophon ("Ways and Means") proposed as means to enhance the revenues of Athens. There was not even simple state financial planning in Sparta. In summary, there is no historical support for Sparta's having been a communist society or having had a "dictatorship of the proletariat" or other state socialist regime. Even the description of the sway of the *homoioi* over the rest of the population as "authoritarian" relates Sparta only distantly to socialist aspirations.

Was Plato a Socialist or Communist Theorist?

If socialism or communism are to be more than labels for a subset of institutions or practices existent within a greater society, the terms must refer to something that differentiates that society from others in an essential way. That is, each term must be used to include that society in its extension because, in essentials, it fits the intension or definition of the term. Only in this way does meaningfulness replace ambiguity, as Plato is at pains to demonstrate in *Euthyphro*. A thing is not what it is because we think it so; we think it so because of what it is. For this reason, Sparta should not be termed a communist or socialist society because what is known of its essentials does not fit the intension given those terms by those who have used them to refer to Sparta.

The same argument applies to the characterization of theories. For a theory to be socialist or communist, its essential elements must be those included in the intension of the terms. This is why the answer to the question at the head of this section must be "no," if socialism or communism is what Marx or Durkheim, or those who agree with them, say it is.

Of the early attempts made by Marx to visualize communism, his characterization of "crude" communism might be thought applicable to Plato's guardians in the ideal regime of *Republic*, or to his regime of "gods, or sons of gods" in *Laws* (739c–3). There are "general private property" communal elements present in each; however, they are not central elements of either the political or economic structure of Plato's ideal in *Republic*, and both political and economic structures are undefined in what little Plato says of a first-best regime in *Laws*. The division of labor is a residue of capitalism that continues in crude communism, and it is crucial to both *Republic* and *Laws*; however, like the property relation itself, the division of labor could hardly be part of the definiens of both capitalism and "crude" communism. Surely, it is the communal elements that set communism—crude or real—apart from capitalism and, as has been shown, they were peripheral to both Plato's purpose and the structure of his ideal.

As far as the two phases of communism sketched in Marx's later work, neither seems in any way evocative of Plato's theoretical constructs. Perhaps the real regime in *Laws* might be impugned as "vulgar socialism"; but Marx obviously meant that as an epithet, not a theory.

What else might be said to indicate the gulf that lies between what Plato sought and what Marx's (alleged) theory of communism seeks to depict? Plato's concept of a fixed human nature surely conflicts with Marx's view that the "higher phase" of communism will change man's nature. To Plato the attainment of *arete* is the supreme personal goal; Marx's historical materialism obviates personal virtues as well as vices. Further, the abstemiousness of the guardians of *Republic* is to remove any tendency to feed their self-love, whereas the end of scarcity under Marx's communism would seem to enable its total fulfilment. Also, the division of labor is crucial to Plato's ideal regime, whereas at the end of history in Marx's communist paradise, there is to be no division of labor. Further, Plato ranks material goods lowest of all, where to Marx the principle of their production and consumption defines the perfect political economy. Finally, for Plato the end of history is one enshrining the perfect state, and the rulers in Plato's vision are the elite, the *aristoi*; Marx foretells the dictatorship of the proletariat, and then no state or rule at all.

Durkheim's depiction of socialism as, essentially, state-managed industrial activities is obviously inapplicable to *Republic*, where industrial activity is unregulated. In *Laws*, the state regulates agriculture to increase yields, and commerce to minimize dissension; it does not manage industry beyond the provision of infrastructure and certain minimal social services. This is hardly a warrant to describe the real regime in *Laws* as Durkheimian socialism.

At first glance, Durkheim's communism, and his identification of Plato as a theorist of it, seems almost a fit because of the ideal regime of *Republic*, with its absence of private property among the guardians and the separation of the political and economic orders. However, Durkheim's communism is for all members of that society, while the communal elements are confined to the guardians in Plato's ideal. The nonguardian members of the polis are the property owners and producers whom the guardians rule and guard and on whose production they subsist. Plato's ideal and his theoretical context included that whole polis, conceived in both its political and economic dimensions. His social theory could never be characterized as one of guardian consumption. Again, the secondary importance of the communal institutions in *Republic* speaks against an aggrandizement such as Durkheim attempts.

Others who have used the term *communism* to refer to the practices of the guardians or some alleged theory of those practices fail less grandly than Durkheim in realizing what Plato attempted to achieve. Plato's regimes of the imagination are politically authoritarian and, in light of the quotation that opens this chapter, he may even have aspired to totalitarianism; however, it is difficult to avoid the general judgment that to refer to Plato as either a socialist or communist theorist is to focus on a few peripheral practices included in his attempts to envision a just society and thus to trivialize what he sought to do. It also restricts the meaning of socialism or communism for those who are directed to the less significant aspects of Plato's work to find a "theory."

Acknowledgments

I am especially grateful to Eva T.H. Brann, Francis Swietek, and Wayne Ambler for valuable comments and suggestions. Nonetheless, any remaining errors are solely my responsibility.

Notes

1. In the process of arguing that Plato's conception of the best state changed from the *Republic* to the *Laws* as a result of the influence of contemporary history, Welles refers to "the communism of Plato's political writings" (1948, p. 101). The commonality of property among the guardians in the *Republic* is referred to as "real communism" (p. 109), while the city described in the *Laws*, "whether we choose to call this state socialism, or communism, or something else" (p. 114), presents "the pattern of the modern authoritarian state" (p. 101). The differences in Plato's conception between *Republic* and *Laws* will be discussed later. It is understandable, though regrettable, that in accomplishing his main purpose Welles presents little to justify these appellations, despite a stated intention "to suggest how fundamentally Plato grasped the principles of a communist state, practically and theoretically." There is also a curious omission of the influence of historical Sparta on both of Plato's fictive cities in favor of that of Athens, and this despite Plato's own references to Spartan institutions, customs, and practices throughout both works. On this point see also Powell (1988, p. 156).

2. The distinctive Greek political institution of tyranny can be viewed as an interruption of the development that culminated in the classic polis, tyranny being mainly important from the mid-seventh to the end of the sixth century. Its beneficial aspects in aiding the transition from oligarchical to democratic government in some poleis are argued in Prentice (1940, pp. 85*ff.*) and Kitto (1951, pp. 102*ff.*). Also see Finley (1970, pp. 103*ff.*) and Forrest (1966, pp. 104*ff.*). Compare this with Plato's view (*Republic*, 565–568) that tyranny is the last degenerate regime. Popper (1966, vol. 1, p. 198 and p. 315, n. 63) argues that Plato so identifies tyranny and hated it *because* it destroyed oligarchy. Sparta, which Plato admired, never experienced tyranny and never made the transition to democracy.

3. Theoretically, a tribe was a kinship unit formed like a pyramid (Forrest, 1966, pp. 50–55), at the base of which was the family (*oikos*) of an historical male aristocrat. Several families having a common male ancestor formed a clan (*genos*), several of which in turn formed a phratry (from *phratores*—"brothers"). A tribe was a combination of phratries, headed by a *basileus* or king. Its status depended on the status of its supposed male progenitor. The importance of this to the Greeks is shown in that Herakles was claimed as an ancestor of both Spartan ruling royal houses (Herodotus, 1972, 7.204 and 8.133), and Herakles was believed to be the son of Zeus and Alcmene (Hesiod, *Theogony*, 1977, 525). At some point before the Lykourgan reforms, and for unknown reasons, the three kings of the tribes that formed the Spartan state became the two that traced their lineage through the Agiadai and Eurypontidai. Oliva (1971, p. 26) speculates that, as it later was for the federation of the Iroquois in North America, this may have been an expedient to prevent one tribe from dominating the others in military as well as civil matters.

4. Huxley (1962, p. 49) speculates that the third leader was an Aigiad, arguing that the two kings and an Aigiad commanded the army in the First Messenian War; however, he also says that the three would thus provide a representative from each tribe. Because one of the

two kings was an Agiad (*ibid.*, p. 17), the two statements are inconsistent. To represent each tribe with a tribal leader would require the third leader on the council to be a Pamphyloid.

5. For a comparison of the Spartan *agoge* and the military training and regimen of the nineteenth-century Zulus, see Ferguson (1918). As "both alike made war, and preparation for war, the primary aims of their association" (p. 197), the educational and military organizational similarities are striking despite the great differences in the political orders and cultures.

6. Plutarch (*Lycurgus*, n.d., p. 57) and, after him, Michell (1964, p. 282) include only 15 men in each mess group; however, these common messes were found in other and earlier Dorian communities, such as those in Crete. Because the Cretan *syssitia* were one to each *phratry*, and the Spartan polis had so many other aspects imitative of those in Crete, it seems reasonable to expect the Spartan *syssitia* to parallel the Cretan in this regard. Perhaps, the similarities between the elements of the *agoge* of Sparta and those of other Dorian communities merely reflected their common tribal past (Forrest, 1968, p. 53; Oliva, 1971, pp. 30–31). Similar elements can be found in the training of warriors in tribal societies of the recent past, as well as those of today.

7. The ancient Greeks accepted human inequality as a basic fact of life and all poleis were divided into classes or orders according to what were believed to be natural differences among men (Finley, 1973, pp. 45*ff.*). Each class had a distinct political and social existence and, of course, "nobility of birth must be matched by nobility of conduct" (Hamilton, 1964, p. 58). This meant that it was a matter of common belief that only the "best men" (*aristoi*) could be good men, and only good men could truly enjoy the good life—a life not possible for the *demos*, the commoners. As in the multitudinous class-based societies that have existed since that time, whatever the rationale for dominance, membership in the aristocracy was basically decided by masculine bloodlines from beginnings lost in myth. It was retained by wealth and brute force, although not usually obtainable by those methods once a ruling aristocracy existed.

8. According to Aristotle (*Politics*, 2, 1270a19–21), the *homoioi* could bequeath or give their *kleroi* away but not sell them.

9. See Ridley for an argument that they were not restricted to this sphere, but also farmed, fished, and herded.

10. Sparta certainly earned its reputation as the most bellicose of the Greek poleis in its periodic suppression of helot revolts, in wars against its neighbors, as well as in military meddling in the politics of sixth-century Athens. After the Lykourgan reforms, Sparta institutionalized a commitment to courage as the highest virtue and, especially after the Messenian wars, possessed a well-trained and supplied standing army. Consequently, the marginal cost of warfare as a method of dispute-resolution could be expected to be lower than that of other poleis not having such institutions or armies—with predictable results. For a pioneering use of economic analysis to explain the transition from peaceful to violent means for dispute resolution among whites and Indians in late nineteenth-century North America—emphasizing the role of the Civil-War-enhanced standing army in lowering the marginal cost of war for whites—see Anderson and McChesney (n.d.).

11. Huxley (1962, pp. 49*ff.*) compares the strife-ridden period of the early and middle seventh century, with the period beginning at the end of that century and including the whole of the sixth. He points out the contrast between the martial poetry of Terpander, Thaletas, and Tyrtaios from the earlier period, and the poetry of Alkman, Stesichoros, Theognis, and Pindar from the later. The later poetry reflects a more open, tranquil, prosperous, and cultured society than that implied in the works of the earlier poets. The archeological evidence (*ibid.*, p. 63) seems to support this interpretation. See also Jaeger (vol. I, 1945, pp. 97–98) for

a contrast between the "richer and fuller life" of Sparta in both these earlier centuries with that of the Sparta contemporary to Plato.

12. Sources differ on the question of the extent to which coined precious metal circulated internally in Sparta. Some agree with Plutarch (*Lycurgus*, n.d., p. 55) that there was an absolute ban on such in archaic and classic Sparta, while others (Jones, 1967, p. 39) maintain that foreign coins were used even as part of the mess contribution. It should be noted that the famous iron spit money attributed to Sparta circulated in other poleis in antiquity prior to the introduction of coined money in the seventh century. Unlike Athens, Sparta lacked a domestic source of precious metal and a significant foreign trade sector. Just as Spanish dollars circulated freely in colonial America, Athenian owls, Aeginetan obols, and other currencies may have circulated in Sparta in place of a domestic currency. The supposed proscription against an internal precious metal coinage may be a myth invented to explain the absence of any Spartan coinage until the early third century.

13. The lack of any Spartan system of public finance (see below) and the resultant inability to anticipate the cost of the war, as well as the factors mentioned in note 10, may also help explain why war became the only option. See Gunderson (1974) on the war cost miscalculations by both sides that may have contributed to the outbreak of the American Civil War.

14. On the tendency for historical governing aristocracies to self-interestedly enforce endogamy to preserve or increase its share of social output, see Olson (1982, pp. 67–69).

15. Using the method of the counterfactual in a computer exercise, Hodkinson argues that the existence of some sort of female inheritance rights in Sparta would have reduced the degree of wealth and landholding inequality that could develop through time, as compared to what it would have been without such rights. Given the relative longevity and stability of the actual Spartan system, and the concentration by Aristotle's time of two-fifths of the land in the hands of women, he speculates that Spartan women may have had such rights.

16. The latter might be explained using Olson (1971, pp. 37–44). The *homoioi* were competitors for the "exclusive collective good" represented by the right to *kleroi*, while retention and defense of their common domain was an "inclusive collective good" to them. Consequently, there was a tension between the stimulus the first provided for restriction of the franchise, and the stimulus provided by the second for its expansion. The second would be the weaker stimulus because the existence of the standing army made it possible to coerce *perioikoi* and helots (whose respective populations were expanding throughout the whole period) to fill any deficiency in the military resulting from a declining population of *homoioi*—and without granting the franchise. The removal of the franchise, and therefore of the right to *kleroi*, as the penalty for failing to contribute appropriately to one's *syssition* can be seen as the outcome of the need to discipline the colluding *homoioi* so that no one might enjoy the benefits of collusion without bearing a portion of the costs, in the absence of any system of public finance. This could also (*ibid*., pp. 61–63) have been the purpose of the "selective incentives" of the cult of fear, the exaltation of the virtue of courage, the punishment of cowardice, and the burial customs of the *homoioi.*

17. Jaeger (1945) argues that it was Plato who first formulated the balance of powers theory of stability in government. Also, compare Plato (*Laws*, 712e–713a and 832c) in his reluctance to admit as "constitutional" any regime named or denoted merely by the social location of the central coercive element.

18. I use the word *ascetic* in the Christian, self-punishing sense. The word *ascetic* or *askesis* is, of course, Greek, and its classical meaning was "one who follows a discipline," e.g., gymnastic training.

19. The content of the ideal of *arete* changed from Homeric times to the heighth of classic Athenian culture in the fifth century. Homeric *arete* emphasized physical excellence, where

courage in battle meant glory and reputation (Starr, 1977, pp. 6–7), while by the fifth century excellence of character was implied by the term (Prentice, 1940, pp. 89–90). Plato's Socrates would have reduced the four cardinal virtues to the one of wisdom, as it contained all the others (Jaeger, vol. 1, 1945, pp. 106, 173–174).

20. The achievement of sufficient leisure by means of which *arete* could be sought in historical poleis, as opposed to the polis of the ideal, has been attributed by Bowra (1959, p. 86) and others to the widespread institution of slavery. Kitto (1951, pp. 131–134) considers and rejects this explanation in favor of an intentionally sought simple standard of life. Certainly, such a standard would exhibit the virtue of temperance; however, Athenians scarcely demonstrated the desire for a simple standard of life in their use of the tribute received during the period of the Delian League. In addition, Spartans inhabited the richest agricultural area of ancient Greece and their system of helotry was established to provide the income and leisure for the Spartan *homoioi* to train for their virtually continuous wars, and to pursue the particular Spartan concept of *arete* (Kitto, 1951, p. 95).

21. My use of the terms *ideal* and *practical realization* conforms to current colloquial usage. They are not the terms Plato would use, as Jaeger (vol. III, 1945, p. 215) reminds us. *Republic* would belong to the realm of the "intelligible" or of being or truth, while *Laws* would represent that of the "visible" or of becoming or opinion.

22. Jaeger (vol. II, 1945, p. 243, n. 213) argues that Plato's (416e) use of the word *syssitia* for the common meals of the guardians shows his adaptation of the Spartan custom. The Cretan common meals were called *andreia*; however, in contrast to the Spartan custom, and in apparent agreement with Plato's intention, the Cretan messes were maintained at public expense (Hammond, 1986, p. 99). See also David (1978) on the *syssitia* in *Laws*.

23. This is not to say that extensive market activity existed in ancient Greece. Polanyi (1968, pp. 103–104) notes the hot-house character of local markets, which often had to be encouraged by Spartan and other armies to provide supplies and dispose of booty. See also Hasebroek (1965, p. 84).

24. Thus, Winspear (1940, p. 199) is incorrect in finding the account of the founding of a polis in *Republic* incompatible with the account in *Laws*. Plato's emphasis was hypothetical in the first and historical in the second. Each account suited his respective purposes in the two books: the *Republic* presenting his ideal regime, the *Laws* his vision of the second-best—and the one possible to the nature of man as revealed in history.

25. See also *Letters*: VIII, 354b–c.

26. The influence of Dorian Crete is also clear but will not be treated here. Sparta, not Crete, is linked with Plato's alleged communism or socialism by the authorities referenced earlier.

27. On the possible political necessity of Spartan pederasty, see Cartledge (1981).

28. Lacey (1968, pp. 194–208) is especially valuable for bringing consistency into the accounts of Spartan family life given by all the main ancient authorities, showing the importance of the family in that society as against the view that view that it was merely an instrument for the breeding of soldiers.

References

Anderson, Terry L., and Fred S. McChesney. (n.d.). "Raid or Trade? An Economic Model of Indian-White Relations," Political Economy Research Center Working Paper 93–1.

Aristotle. (1947) *Nicomachean Ethics*. W.D. Ross, trans. in Richard McKeon (ed.), *Introduction to Aristotle*. New York: The Modern Library.

Aristotle. (1984). *Politics*. Carnes Lord, trans. Chicago: University of Chicago Press.

Austin, M.M., and P. Vidal-Naquet. (1977). *Economic and Social History of Ancient Greece: An Introduction*. Berkeley and Los Angeles: University of California Press.

Barnstone, Willis, trans. (1988). *Sappho and the Greek Lyric Poets*. New York: Schocken Books.

Beer, Max. (1957). *The General History of Socialism and Social Struggles*. New York: Russell & Russell.

Bowra, C.M. (1959). *The Greek Experience*. New York: New American Library Mentor Book.

Brann, Eva T.H. (1979). "Introduction." In Raymond Larson (ed. and trans.), *The Republic*. Arlington Heights, Ill.: Harlan Davidson.

Cartledge, Paul. (1981). "The Politics of Spartan Pederasty." *Proceedings of the Cambridge Philological Society* (27):17–36.

David, Ephraim. (1978). "The Spartan Syssitia and Plato's *Laws*." *American Journal of Philology* (99):486–495.

David, Ephraim. (1989). "Laughter in Spartan Society." In Anton Powell (ed.), *Classical Sparta: Techniques Behind Her Success*. Norman, OK, and London: University of Oklahoma Press.

Durkheim, Emile. (1962). *Socialism*. (Alvin W. Gouldner, ed.; Charlotte Sattler, trans.) New York: Collier Books.

Ekelund, Jr., Robert B., and Robert F. Hebert. (1990). *A History of Economic Theory and Method*, 3rd ed. New York: McGraw-Hill.

Ferguson, W.S. (1918). "The Zulus and the Spartans: A Comparison of Their Military Systems." *Harvard African Studies* (II):197–234.

Finley, M.I. (1970). *Early Greece: The Bronze and Archaic Ages*. New York: W.W. Norton.

Finley, M.I. (1973). *The Ancient Economy*. Berkeley and Los Angeles: University of California Press.

Fisher, N.R.E. (1989). "Drink, *Hybris* and the Promotion of Harmony in Sparta." In Anton Powell (ed.), *Classical Sparta: Techniques Behind Her Success*. Norman, OK, and London: University of Oklahoma Press.

Forrest, W.G. (1966). *The Emergence of Greek Democracy: 800–400 B.C.* New York: McGraw-Hill World University Library.

Forrest, W.G. (1968). *A History of Sparta: 950–192 B.C.* New York: W.W. Norton.

Gide, Charles, and Charles Rist. (n.d.) *A History of Economic Doctrines*, 2nd English ed. (R. Richards, trans.) Boston: D.C. Heath and Company.

Gittler, Joseph B. (1941). *Social Thought Among the Early Greeks*. Athens, GA.: University of Georgia Press.

Gomme, A.W. (1945). *A Historical Commentary on Thucydides*, Vol. I. Oxford: Clarendon Press.

Gray, Alexander. (1968). *The Socialist Tradition: Moses to Lenin*. New York: Harper Torchbooks.

Gunderson, Gerald. (1974). "The Origin of the American Civil War." *Jour. Economic History* 34(4):915–50.

Hamilton, Charles D. (1979). *Sparta's Bitter Victories: Politics and Diplomacy in the Corinthian War*. Ithaca, NY: Cornell University Press.

Hamilton, Edith. (1964). *The Greek Way*. New York: W.W. Norton, The Norton Library.

Hammond, N.G.L. (1986). *A History of Greece to 322 B.C.*, 3rd ed. Oxford: Clarendon Press.

Haney, Lewis H. (1949). *History of Economic Thought*, 4th ed. New York: The Macmillan Company.

Hasebroek, Johannes. (1965). *Trade and Politics in Ancient Greece*, Reprint of the 1933 English edition. New York: Biblo and Tannen.

Herodotus. (1972). *The Histories*. (Aubrey de Selincourt, trans.) Harmondsworth: Penguin Books.

Hesiod. (1977). *Theogony* in *Hesiod, The Homeric Hymns and Homerica*. (Hugh G. Evelyn-White, trans.) Cambridge, MA: Harvard University Press.

Hodkinson, Stephen. (1989). "Inheritance, Marriage and Demography: Perspectives upon the Success and Decline of Classical Sparta." In Anton Powell (ed.), *Classical Sparta: Techniques Behind Her Success*. Norman, OK, and London: University of Oklahoma Press.

Huxley, G.L. (1962). *Early Sparta*. Cambridge, MA: Harvard University Press.

Jaeger, Werner. (1945). *Paideia: The Ideals of Greek Culture*, 2nd ed., 3 vols. New York: Oxford University Press.

Jones, Arnold Hugh Martin. (1967). *Sparta*. Oxford: Basil Blackwell.

Kitto, H.D.F. (1951). *The Greeks*. Baltimore, MD: Penguin Books.

Lacey, W.K. (1968). *The Family in Classical Greece*. Ithaca, NY: Cornell University Press.

Laidler, Harry W. (1968). *History of Socialism*. New York: Thomas Y. Crowell.

Lenin, V.I. (1965). *The State and Revolution*. Moscow: Progress Publishers.

Marx, Karl. (1964). "Economic and Philosophical Manuscripts." In T.B. Bottomore (ed. and trans.), *Karl Marx: Early Writings*. New York: McGraw-Hill.

Marx, Karl. (1972). "Communism and the Augsburger Allgemeine Zeitung." In David McLellan (ed. and trans.), *Karl Marx: Early Texts*. New York: Barnes & Noble.

Marx, Karl. (1978). "Critique of the Gotha Program." In Robert C. Tucker (ed.), *The Marx-Engels Reader*, 2nd ed. New York: W.W. Norton.

Marx, Karl and Friedrich Engels. (1971). *The German Ideology: Part One (with selections from parts two and three)*. C.J. Arthur (ed.). New York: International Publishers.

Michell, Humfrey. (1964). *Sparta*. Cambridge: Cambridge University Press.

Mises, Ludwig von. (1951). *Socialism: An Economic and Sociological Analysis*. (J. Kahane, trans.) London: Jonathan Cape.

Mises, Ludwig von. (1969). *Bureaucracy*. New Rochelle, NY: Arlington House.

Oliva, Pavel. (1971). *Sparta and Her Social Problems*. Amsterdam: Adolf M. Hakkert.

Olson, Mancur. (1971). *The Logic of Collective Action: Public Goods and the Theory of Groups*. Cambridge, MA: Harvard University Press.

Olson, Mancur. (1982). *The Rise and Decline of Nations: Economic Growth, Stagflation, and Social Rigidities*. New Haven and London: Yale University Press.

Plato. (1961). *The Collected Dialogues of Plato* (Edith Hamilton and Huntington Cairns, eds.) Princeton: Princeton University Press.

Plutarch. (n.d.) "Lycurgus." In John Dryden (trans.), *The Lives of the Noble Grecians and Romans*. New York: The Modern Library.

Polanyi, Karl. (1968). *Primitive, Archaic, and Modern Economies: Essays of Karl Polanyi*. (George Dalton, ed.) Garden City, NY: Doubleday.

Popper, Karl R. (1966). *The Open Society and Its Enemies*, Vol. I: *The Spell of Plato*. Princeton: Princeton University Press.

Powell, Anton. (1988). *Athens and Sparta: Constructing Greek Political and Social History from 478 B.C.* Areopagitica Press.

Prentice, William Kelly. (1940). *The Ancient Greeks*. Princeton: Princeton University Press.

Ridley, R.T. (1974). "The Economic Activities of the Perioikoi." *Mnemosyne* (27):281–292.

Roll, Eric. (1974). *A History of Economic Thought*, 4th ed. Homewood, IL: Richard D. Irwin.

Schumpeter, Joseph A. (1954). *History of Economic Analysis*. (Elizabeth Boody Schumpeter, ed.) London: George Allen & Unwin.

Shafarevich, Igor. (1980). *The Socialist Phenomenon*. New York: Harper & Row.

Spiegel, Henry William. (1991). *The Growth of Economic Thought*, 3rd ed. Durham & London: Duke University Press.

Starr, Chester G. (1977). *The Economic and Social Growth of Early Greece: 800–500 B.C.* New York: Oxford University Press.

Thucydides. (1951). *The Peloponnesian War*. New York: The Modern Library.

Welles, C. Bradford. (1948). "The Economic Background of Plato's Communism." In *Journal of Economic History*, supplement *The Tasks of Economic History* (8):101–114.

Winspear, Alban Dewes. (1940). *The Genesis of Plato's Thought*. New York: Dryden Press.

Xenophon. (1942). "The Constitution of the Spartans." In Francis R.B. Godolphin (ed.) and H.G. Dakyns (trans.), *The Greek Historians*. New York: Random House.

Xenophon. (1942). "Ways and Means: A Pamphlet on Revenues." In H.G. Dakyns (trans.) and Francis R.B. Godolphin (ed.), *The Greek Historians*. New York: Random House.

Zimmern, Alfred. (1961). *The Greek Commonwealth: Politics and Economics in Fifth-Century Athens*, 5th ed. New York: Galaxy Book, Oxford University Press.

2 SIR JAMES STEUART ON THE MANAGED MARKET

Anastassios Karayiannis

> *. . . my point of view is, to investigate how a statesman may turn the circumstances which have produced this new plan of oeconomy to the best advantage for mankind, leaving the reformation of such a plan to time and to events.*
>
> —Sir James Steuart, 1767 (1966), pp. 75–6

Steuart was a creature of his time (the beginning of the Industrial Revolution), experienced in European political and economic situations. He worked on his *An Inquiry into the Principles of Political Economy* at the peak of the transitional period—in the world of ideas—from mercantilism (old order) to liberalism (new order). His attempts to synthesize these two streams of thought is evident from his attitude toward the function of the market and the role of the statesman.

Steuart justified and built a managed-market system as follows. At first, he used an evolutionary and historical approach to describe the possibilities and capabilities of a country to achieve and sustain an adequate level of economic development. Then followed his positive analysis of how some fundamental economic phenomena resulted in crucial market failures which, according to his view, could not be corrected by any internal mechanism. Last, he based most of his arguments on the assumption of the existence of a "perfect" statesman, whose role would be fundamental in the correction of those failures. All these reasons led him to the development of the concept of a managed economy that contained some elements very relevant to our time.

The purpose of this chapter is to analyze Steuart's ideas and arguments on behalf of the managed market. In order to do so, the significant views and arguments of Steuart on this issue, scattered throughout his "inquiry," are gathered and systematized. The subsequent analysis is also conducted, as far as possible, "from the shadow of [Adam] Smith's reputation," as Skinner has rightly suggested (1985, p. 19).

The chapter is composed of four sections. In the first section Steuart's views of the content and object of political economy and the characteristics of the statesman are examined. In the second section the cases where the operation of the free market fails to guarantee full employment with an adequate living standard are analyzed, and the ways and means with which the statesman must intervene in order to correct such failures are examined. The third section presents the means employed by the statesman to stimulate an underdeveloped economy to reach and maintain a high level of development and a favorable balance of trade. In the final section the main differences between Steuart's and Adam Smith's attitudes on the function of the free market and their beliefs regarding to the existence and operation of a perfect statesman are examined.

Political Oeconomy and the Statesman's Objects and Characteristics

Steuart, from the very beginning of his inquiry, makes clear that the role of the statesman is fundamental to political economy. The statesman's role is not only stimulative and preventive but also regulatory and corrective through indirect and direct intervention. Steuart begins his inquiry with the definition of economy as the art of household management exercised by the hand of the family (1.15).[1] He uses a broader but similar definition for *Political Oeconomy*, stressing its "paternalistic" substance: "Oeconomy and government, even in a private family, present . . . two different ideas, and have also two different objects. What economy is in a family, political economy is in a state" (1.16)—an idea advanced in pseudo-Aristotle's *Oeconomica* (343a, 1–5, 15–17) and developed later by Rousseau (1758, pp. 117–118).

Steuart, as he himself declares, wanted to take up his pen upon the subject of political economy toward "preparing the spirit of a people to receive a good plan of economy, than a proper representation of it" (1.18). Therefore,

> . . . although it seem addressed to a statesman, the real object of the inquiry *is to influence the spirit of those whom he governs*; and the variety of matter contained in it, may even suggest useful hints to himself. But his own genius and experience will enable him to carry such notions far beyond the reach of my abilities (1.12; emphasis added).

He employed both induction and deduction in his work and tried to verify his conclusions by an appeal to observation and experience (1.17, 1.142). Moreover, he stressed the relativity of conclusions regarding the principles of economic phenomena, which is ultimately related to the differences between times, countries, and institutions (1.4–5, 1.16, 2.339; see also Karayiannis, 1992, p. 288).

The character of Steuart's "inquiry" is both positive and normative (1.16, 1.74). Only after the positive analysis of any economic situation or problem does Steuart reach normative conclusions with respect to specific situations or problems. He states that his intention is to show what ought to be and not what is the statesman's economic intervention and policy (2.708).

Steuart used his various methodological tools together with his views on the scope and character of political economy to describe the evolutionary and interrelated processes of economics and politics. The influence of economics on politics and vice versa is a noticeable element of Steuart's historical and evolutionary approach (see, for example, 1.71–72, 74, 76, 181, 209–216; see also Skinner, 1962, pp. 20–21; Hirschman, 1977, pp. 82–83).

The basic principles of political economy depend on the assumptions made with respect to the behavior of individuals. Steuart makes clear that the motive of self-interest (1.20), though not the only "universal spring of human actions" (1.143; see also Khalil, 1987, p. 126), is used

> . . . as a general key to this inquiry; and it may, in one sense, be considered as the ruling principle of my subject, and may therefore be traced throughout the whole. *This is the main spring, and only motive which a statesman should make use of, to engage a free people to concur in the plans which he lays down for their government* (1.142; emphasis added; see also 1.143).

His second behavioral assumption is related to the statesman's self-interest. This motive according to Steuart, is simply the promotion of public good, and thus the statesman must judge everything in accordance with the public interest which is nothing more than the product of a collection of private interests (1.88, 142–144). Steuart, contrary to the early mercantilists who thought the statesman's ultimate goal was the increase of the power of the state, believed that the statesman's fundamental purpose ought to be the increase of the welfare of "his subjects":

> As we have taken for granted the fundamental maxim, that every operation of government should be calculated for the good of the people (1.21).

The statesman, in doing his best in promoting the public interest, must sacrifice the interest of some people for the general good (1.248), particularly when this interest is contradicted by the public good (2.363). Thus, the statesman, "in order to cement his society, should know how to engage every one, as far as possible, to turn his attracting pole towards the particular center of common good" (2.394).

Steuart does not stress that the interest of the public is higher than of individuals, that is, he does not favor an authoritarian system, neither a "despotic" nor a "popular" one (1.279, 304; see also King, 1988, p. 23). As he makes clear from the beginning,

> ... my natural partiality in favour of individuals had led me to condemn, as Machiavellian principles, every sentiment, approving the sacrifice of private concerns in favour of a general plan (1.10–11; see also 1.18, 293–294).

Although not a champion of individualism, neither does he follow the Aristotelean dictum, according to which: "the State is by nature clearly prior to the family and to the individual, since the whole is of necessity prior to the part" (*Politica*, 1253a, 15–20). On the contrary, he mentioned that individuals must avoid actions that may be turned against their welfare; thus, they will be forced to ask the statesman to intervene, *viz*:

> I must observe, that nothing would have been so easy as to soften many passages, where the politician appears to have snatched the pen out of the hand of the private citizen: but as I write for such only who can follow a close reasoning, and attend to the general scope of the whole inquiry, I have, purposely, made no correction; but continued painting, in the strongest colours, every inconvenience which must affect certain individuals living under our free modern governments, whenever a wise statesman sets about correcting old abuses. ... The more any cure is painful and dangerous, the more ought men carefully to avoid the disease (1.11).

Steuart's central figure in his inquiry is an imaginary statesman[2] or "an abstraction" (Skinner, 1985, p. 10), rather than a real one. He has endowed this figure with the following qualities and characteristics that are very rarely concentrated in a man or group of men who constitute the government in any state. An efficient statesman who will be able to undertake all those actions and responsibilities necessary for the promotion of the general welfare must: sacrifice his personal interest for the common good (1.11); have "virtue and justice" (1.20); be a cool administrator not having a man's "passions, vices and weaknesses" (1.217); be "constantly awake" (1.64); have a particular talent "to dispose the minds of a people to approve even of the scheme which is the most conductive to their interest and prosperity" (1.25); "gain the confidence of his people, so far as to impress them with a firm belief that he will consult their good, and nothing else, in what he undertakes" (2.656); be "sagacious" (1.291); have adequate knowledge on economic matters (1.333); and be impartial in regard to the interest of some of his citizens (2.389).

Steuart was well aware that the statesman's impartiality is crucial (1.26). Thus, he stressed that the statesman must not favor the interest of some of his people, that is, "by constituting a particular advantage in favour of some individuals of the same class above others" (1.273), nor obey any organized interests with a "strong . . . influence in parliament" (2.625). On the contrary: "When any one interest becomes too predominant, the prosperity of the state stands upon a precarious footing. Every interest should be encouraged, protected, and kept within due bounds" (2.637), and therefore, "I infer, that it is dangerous to the common interest, to permit too close an union between the members of any subaltern society" (2.394–395).

Steuart, in analyzing the ways and means by which the failures of the free market system could be corrected and/or avoided, introduced the following assumptions in regard to the statesman's decision making: (1) "a statesman at the head of government, who makes every circumstance concur in promoting the execution of the plan he has laid down" (1.238); (2) "every statesman to have good reasons for doing what he does, unless I can discover that his motives are bad" (2.625); (3) "a statesman at the head of government, systematically conducting every part of it, as to prevent the vicissitudes of manners, and innovations, by their natural and immediate effects or consequences, from hurting any interest within the commonwealth" (1.122); and (4) "Let not . . . a statesman regulate his conduct upon suppositions, nor conclude any thing from theory, nor from arguments *a priori* . . . but let him have recourse to information and experience concerning the real state of the matter" (2.693).

Steuart was well aware that the above assumptions in regard to the qualities and efficiency of the statesman are chimerical, he said: "I might safely say, there is no form of government upon earth so excellent in itself, as, necessarily, to make the people happy under it" (1.23). However, he used the statesman's intervention as the necessary role for the establishment of a well-functioning economy. He does so because he does not recognize any other role in its place (as, for example, the "invisible" hand of Smith) and he wanted the government to work and act only for the welfare of the citizens. In order to enforce his desire in regard to the efficient and proper statesman's intervention, he proposed the punishment of every civil servant for the abuse of public money (1.257; see also Eltis, 1986, p. 62) and he repeatedly noted the vices and the wrong decisions that must be avoided by the statesman.[3]

Market Failures and the Statesman's Intervention

Steuart believed that a free market economy it is possible to fail in the long run to achieve a state of full employment. The disequilibrium that would emerge would not automatically be restored. For the restoration of equilibrium the statesman's intervention through direct and indirect means is imperative.

Steuart is much more concerned with the idea that the statesman must be active mainly by influencing and preventing rather than prohibiting the actions of individuals (1.278). He was against every sudden introduction of new economic institutions or measures on the part of the statesman (1.292) because it could prove hurtful for the economy (1.89; see also Ohmori, 1983, p. 186). For Steuart, the statesman must intervene in economic matters gradually and must "model the minds of his subjects so as to induce them, from the allurement of private interest, to concur in the execution of his plan" (1.17). Thus, Steuart's economics could be characterized first as *economics of direction and stimulation* and then, when the conditions of the economy still remain unfavorable, as *economics of prevention and control.*

Steuart is mainly engaged with the long-run rather than the short-run effects of the free market.[4] His main interest was to show in which cases the free market fails to achieve full employment and what must be done in preventing and/or correcting such a situation (Sen, 1957, p. 130; Meek, 1958, p. 297; Skinner, 1981, p. 29). He makes clear from the beginning that the main principle to be followed by the statesman is the long-run equilibrium between the supply of and demand for goods and services (1.67, 86). He emphasized the long-run equilibrium as he considered that the short-run disequilibrium or the "gentle alternate vibrations" (1.200) between the demand for and supply of goods and services "may favour both sides of the contract" (1.201) and the level of output can be increased (1.194–195).

Steuart is primarily concerned with unemployment and conceived the objects of "Political Oeconomy" to be the achievement of full employment with an adequate living standard for all the people (1.17, 28). Thus, he treated unemployment as the main problem that a "modern" economy has to solve. He regarded it as a "load" on individuals and the state (1.73) and a situation that cannot be supported for long "because no power whatsoever in a statesman can go so far as to preserve numbers at the expense of the whole riches of his people" (1.294). If there were unemployment, Steuart was against any direct regulation and prohibition to human propagation being imposed by the statesman (1.80). Instead, he proposed the direct intervention of the statesman for the immediate relief of the unemployed when other measures and policies prove inefficient, by recommending "... hospitals for foundlings over all the country; and still more strongly the frugal maintenance of children in such hospitals, and their being bred up early to fill and recruit the lowest classes of the people" (1.80), and the collection of "the children of the wretched into workhouses" (1.249).

Steuart analyzed the following causes of involuntary unemployment:

First is that produced by the sudden introduction of machines as labor-saving innovations (1.122). In this case the statesman must find employment for the unemployed workers as he does for his soldiers after the end of a war (1.122–3). He can employ the unemployed laborers in public works, or in the army, or send them to the colonies (1.202–203).

A second cause of unemployment is produced by the diminution of "effectual demand." The diminution of effectual demand could be produced by (1) a permanent disequilibrium between the market prices of goods and their "intrinsic" values; (2) a permanent disequilibrium between the supply of and demand for goods and services; and (3) an increase in the rate of hoarding. Let us analyze more broadly those causes of unemployment and the remedies suggested by Steuart.

Steuart, by distinguishing between the market price and the "intrinsic" value of goods,[5] showed where the permanent disequilibrium between those two rates caused the emergence of unemployment. More specifically, where the supply of goods is higher than demand for a significant time, prices will decrease and "the workman fall into distress, and ... industry suffer a discouragement" (1.192). In that case the supply price (i.e., cost of production) becomes higher than the market price and "the reasonable profits" are diminished (1.192).

Steuart suggested that the remedy for such a situation was the adoption of two policies: (1) of managed supply and (2) of managed demand. The first policy has to do with the diminution of the level of supply, that is, "the statesman should diminish the number of hands, by throwing a part of them into a new channel" (1.191), which is a "forced" restoration of general equilibrium (1.229). The second policy can be realized through the increase of demand, by manipulating the level of taxes,[6] of public expenses, and of the money supply (see also the excellent analysis by Akhtar, 1979, pp. 293–297).

By extending taxes and public expenditures, the regulation of demand and production is made possible (1.332). More specifically, by taxes the production of public services and the employment of public servants are made possible (1.321). Thus, a portion of the taxes will, through the public expenditures, be returned to the individuals since it will be spent for domestic purposes (1.320). Generally speaking, through the imposition of taxes and the use of the public revenues, "effectual" demand and production will be increased while unemployment will be diminished (2.709, 725). Moreover, if the revenues from taxes are used on public investments, the level and efficiency of production will also be increased and thus unemployment will decrease:

> . . . if, for example, in consequence of the roads made, any inhabitant shall incline to remove from place to place in a chariot, instead of riding on horseback, or walking, he must engage somebody to make the machine: this is a farther extension to occupation, on the side of those who labour (2.378); [therefore,] . . . Expensive public works, are . . . a means of giving bread to the poor, and of advancing industry, without hurting the simplicity of manners (2.387).

If anyone argues that, by the imposition of taxes, resources are withdrawn from the citizens and their level of demand and production decreased,

> [t]he answer is, that it might be so, or not: whereas when the state gets it, it will be spent undoubtedly. Besides, had it been spent by individuals, it would have been laid out for the supply of private wants, which are not near so extensive as those of the public: and farther, when money is so taken from rich individuals, it obliges them to find out a way of procuring more, out of their solid property (2.726).

Thus, for Steuart there is no internal mechanism in the system that will guarantee that the citizens will spend all their income.

On the other hand, the statesman is able to diminish unemployment by using the supply of money as an instrument of economic policy. In order to increase domestic consumption the statesman increases the supply of money (1.323–324). And in the case where there is a shortage of metallic money, the statesman must put into circulation paper money in order to increase demand and production (1.327–328; see also Sen, 1957, p. 94).

Steuart does not pay attention to the possibility of inflation produced by an increase in the money supply, arguing that an increase in the quantity of money and its velocity of circulation in the main increases demand (1.303, 2.356–357); and if supply responds (2.354, 2.376), then production and employment also increase (2.344). Steuart, in criticizing the Humean quantity theory of money—though in an incomplete and incorrect manner (see Karayiannis, 1988b, pp. 542–544)—emphasized that the increase in money supply increases the demand and the supply of goods. Then, Steuart called on the statesman to help in the promotion of the circulation of wealth by introducing paper money in order to increase the circulation of goods, the multiplicity of wants among the industrious, and therefore the increase of supply through the increase of work effort and demand of individuals (1.316; 1.328; 1.330). In other words, Steuart supported a monetary policy of "cheap money" in order to increase, or at least to postpone the diminution of, the level of effective demand, production, and employment (Karayiannis, 1988a, pp. 44–46; 1991b, p. 332).

Steuart recognized also that there are some cases where the market is prevented from functioning competitively and thus permanent disequilibrium is produced between the market prices and the "intrinsic value" of goods. He was against any monopolistic and/or monopsonistic situation that would eliminate competition and prove hurtful for the general welfare because of the artificial increase in the rate of prices. In particular, he called on the statesman to punish those who are activated at first as monopsonist of a good but later become its monopolists and thus gain super-normal profits (1.175). He was also against the privileges given to some trading companies "farther than the public good necessarily requires it should be" (2.389). He further considered that when a privilege has been given to a company, the statesman must inspect all the affairs of the company "in order to be able to take measures which may effectually prevent bad consequences to the general interest of the nation" (2.394). Moreover, when there exist in the state "brotherhoods of labourers," that is, "confraternities, which prevent competition, and raise profits" in the production of necessary goods, it "is a point deserving the attention of a statesman" (1.273; see also 1.288, 2.390). Steuart was against all those collusions of producers because, among other things, people's manners and industry have changed in the "modern" economy and the individual "demands still more liberty" (1.288–289).

Effectual demand can also be diminished in the case where demand is higher than supply and the market price is increased. If this disequilibrium persists for quite a long period of time, then the real value of commodities will be increased because the extraordinary profits will be consolidated in it (1.192–193; see also Karayiannis, 1991a, p. 181). The consolidation of profits into the real value of goods causes a downward inflexibility of prices, and Steuart emphasized the likelihood and importance of such inflexibility. At the same time, a price increase in one sector of the economy will cause prices to rise in others, and hence an increase in the general price level will take place (2.II.221). For Steuart, the general diffusion of high prices is hurtful to the economy, because the absolute advantage of the country in international trade is lost and thus exports and total demand are decreased, a situation that causes unemployment (1.248). By omitting the role of the entrepreneur, Steuart disregarded the possibility that the increase of labor and capital productivity would counterbalance the increase of the real wage rate (increasing living standard) and so the level of prices would be diminished instead of being increased by the consolidation of profits. Since Steuart did not recognize any self-adjusting market mechanism in this case, he called for the statesman's intervention to prevent or to correct such a situation (1.193–194, 204, 251) and to maintain or restore an equilibrium consistent with the natural intrinsic values (Karayiannis, 1991a, p. 182). In order to prevent the consolidation of profits, the statesman can use the following specific policies:

First, he can increase the supply of labor and competition from the side of production to those branches of industry in which the profits have been consolidated (1.250).

Second, he can discourage the consumption of luxury goods among his people (1.250). The statesman is able to regulate directly the consumption of his people through taxation.

In Steuart's time the scientific environment was in favor of the imposition of taxes only upon luxury goods (see, for example, Montesquieu, 1748, vol. I, p. 209; Hume, "Of Taxes," ed. 1970, p. 85; Rousseau, 1758, pp. 147–148, 152). Steuart followed this line and justified the imposition of those taxes in the form of *ad valorem* on every stage of production (2.681) on the following grounds[7]:

1. Only the surplus income over and above the consumption of necessary goods is a suitable object for taxation: all taxes "ought to impair the fruits and not the fund; the expenses of the person taxed, not the savings; the services, not the persons of those who do them" (2.674) and "the load of all impositions may be equally distributed upon every class of a people who enjoys superfluity, and upon no other" (2.641; see also 2.675–676 ft. 3, 686, 690, 719, 733).
2. By the taxation of luxury goods the statesman is able to manipulate the consumption patterns of individuals (2.711, 719)—an idea also introduced by Rousseau (1758, p. 153).

3. By the taxation of luxury goods hoarding is decreased if the idle-rich consumer wants to enjoy the same living standard as before the imposition of the taxes (2.703–704, 724–725).
4. By the taxation upon luxury goods a redistribution of wealth is produced, "throwing a part of the wealth of the rich into the hands of the industrious poor" (1.334).

Effectual demand can also be decreased in the case where large profits have induced an increase in the rate of hoarding and "consumption and the demand for work would diminish in proportion to the part of the income withheld" (2.649).

He insisted on the deleterious effect hoarding has on effective demand as he clearly emphasized the use of money not only as a unit of account and a medium of exchange but also as a store of value (see Karayiannis, 1988a, p. 28, ft. 3). For Steuart, only increased "circulation of money" could eliminate hoarding, redistribute wealth, and increase the work effort of individuals (1.325–326). The "miser," by hoarding, diminishes the circulation of money, and thus the statesman "ought at all times to maintain a just proportion between the produce of industry, and the quantity of circulating equivalent, in the hands of his subjects, for the purchase of it" (1.323). In realizing this goal the statesman "must examine the situation of his country, relatively to three objects, *viz.* the propensity of the rich to consume; the disposition of the poor to be industrious; and the proportion of circulating money, with respect to the one and the other" (1.324).

Steuart considered interest to be an instrument for the diminution of hoarding, as "no money is to be suffered to remain useless to the proprietor of it" (2.444), and thus for the increase of consumption and employment (Karayiannis, 1988a, p. 40). Steuart was opposed to any direct regulation by "statute" of the market rate of interest (2.457, 459).[8] He maintained that since the market rate of interest is determined by the demand for and supply of loanable funds (mainly for consumption purposes) (2.455), the statesman can influence its rate by regulating the supply of money (2.462).

Steuart did not recognize the classical thesis that hoarding is eliminated because all savings become investments through the movement in the level of interest. He also did not relate the expectation of capitalists and entrepreneurs to the rate of profit and its influence on their investment plans. Instead he recognized the class of idle consumers who hoard their surplus if it is not consumed in luxury goods. Thus he called for the statesman's intervention with specific policies and measures for the elimination of hoarding and increase in "effectual demand."

In addition to the instrument of the money supply and the rate of interest in regulating effectual demand in the economy, Steuart also suggested the use of public debt for the accomplishment of the same goals (see also Stettner, 1945, pp. 456–457). This public debt can play a positive role by increasing public expenses and hence effective demand and employment, *viz*:

> Credit is in proportion to the capacity of paying the interest of money borrowed. Having abundantly insisted on the advantages of industry in providing for the poor, I next come to consider the permanent effects of it, after the first end has been accomplished. If a thousand pounds are bestowed upon making a fire-work, a number of people are thereby employed, and gain a temporary livelihood. If the same sum is bestowed for making a canal for watering the fields of a province a like number of people may reap the same benefit, and hitherto accounts stand even: but the fire-work played off, what remains, but the smoke and stink of the powder? Whereas the consequence of the canal is a perpetual fertility to a formerly barren soil (2.II.260–261).

Steuart considered that the rate of hoarding in an economy is decreased by the public debt and effectual demand is increased (2.642–644).[9] For Steuart the public debt does not decrease the consumption and investment of individuals by absorbing capital. Instead, the public debt supplements the effective demand of individuals, by giving an opportunity for the employment of capital which otherwise is hoarded:

> ... loans are filled by money stagnating, which the owner desires to realize: if he cannot do better, he lends it to government; if he can do better, he will not lend it (2.643).

Steuart did not give credence to the possibility that the increase of public credit could cause inflation in the economy. The extent of the public debt, according to Steuart, is regulated by the consequences of increased taxation for the repayment of capital borrowed. That is, the extent of public debt could be increased to the point where the increase of effective demand produced by the increase of public expenditures is outweighed by the decrease in effective demand caused by the decrease of private spending because of the increased taxation (2.640–641).

Induced Development

Although Steuart recognized the positive effects produced by the principle of "self-interest" and the accomplishment of "wants" as "a spur to industry," these motives are not his only base. In addition, he called on the statesman to intervene in order for these motives to function more completely for the achievement of a higher stage of economic development and the maintenance of a favorable balance of trade. The intervention of the statesman is helpful in the following cases of historical development: (1) when an underdeveloped country is driven to the stage of development and from infant trade to foreign trade; (2) when a country is competing in foreign trade with more advanced countries; (3) when a country has lost its absolute advantage in foreign trade; and (4) when a country is in the island trade (i.e., isolated country). Let us examine in more detail the ways and means by which the statesman intervenes in these cases.

In the first case, the transition of an underdeveloped economy to the stage of modern economy can be facilitated through the statesman's stimulation and intervention. More specifically, the statesman must create reciprocal wants among the producers "in order to bind the society" (1.40, 1.39).[10] This can be achieved by promoting the circulation of money and by helping to increase luxury consumption among individuals (1.43–44). Luxury consumption in the case of infant trade, that is, when foreign trade does not exist, could be introduced only through the statesman's intervention. According to Steuart, an individual's consumption pattern is determined by the effect of "imitation" or "fashion" and "conspicuous" consumption" (1.60–61, 243–244) and thus the statesman is able to influence the consumption pattern mainly of the idle-rich consumers who have a "taste for dissipation" (1.243). The statesman is able to influence this kind of consumption (1.281) by two means: indirectly through his own example and consumption pattern (1.244, 298, 309) and directly by the taxation of luxury goods (2.712).

The statesman, by extending luxury consumption, is able to increase in the absence of foreign trade the domestic demand, supply, and employment (1.151, 244, 261). This is made possible through the working of the "aspiration effect," namely through the increase of work effort produced by the multiplicity of wants and the imitation of luxury consumption (on this effect see Eagly, 1961; Akhtar, 1978, pp. 68, 70). However, the decisive factors that will make possible the transition of the economy to a higher stage of development are the establishment and increase of trade and money in circulation (1.156).[11]

For the accomplishment of the above goals the statesman must encourage the "vibration" (i.e., the redistribution) of wealth among the citizens, and particularly "between the rich and the industrious" (1.264). By the vibration of wealth economic inequality among citizens is diminished (1.282) and the operation of the aspiration effect is strengthened. Also, "as money is introduced into a country it becomes . . . an universal object of want to all inhabitants" (1.156). The circulation of goods and the vibration of wealth are made possible (1.304, 314) and the work effort of laborers is increased (1.157; see also Akhtar, 1978, p. 59).[12] Thus, the wants of the industrious will multiply as their wage is increased, and the total supply and demand will also be increased:

> The desires of the rich, and the means of gratifying them, make them call for the services of the poor: the necessities of the poor, and their desire of becoming rich, make them cheerfully answer the summons; they submit to the hardest labour and comply with the inclinations of the wealthy, for the sake of an equivalent in money (1.310).

The statesman is able to increase the work effort of individuals through the following additional practices: (1) by setting wages according to piece rates rather than time rates (1.169); (2) by the imposition of an expenditure or "proportional" tax on necessary goods in cases where the positive relationship between wage rate and work effort does not hold because of consumption saturation (2.691); and (3) by exercising an economic policy not "falling unequally upon individuals of the same condition" (1.212–213; see also Karayiannis, 1988a, pp. 34–35).

When a country is at the stage of foreign trade, Steuart's interest is mostly concentrated on the following issues: the way by which a country can gain an absolute advantage in some exportable industrial goods; the techniques and measures by which a country can maintain a favorable balance of trade; and the effects of free and nonfree trade on the economic development of the trading countries. Let us see how Steuart elaborates these issues.

In cases where the statesman must help the economy to obtain a favorable balance of trade, Steuart bestows him with many energetic and complicated interventions (1.262; see also Kobayashi, 1992, pp. 61–63):[13] "He must, as before, be attentive (1) to provide food, other necessaries and employment for all his people" (1.231); (2) to engage "the strangers to furnish articles of the first necessity, when the precious metals cannot be procured" (*ibid.*); (3) "to accept, in return, the most consumable superfluities which industry can invent" (*ibid.*); and (4) to "inspire his own people with a spirit of emulation in the exercise of frugality, temperance, oeconomy, and an application to labour and ingenuity" (1.231–232).

In justifying the intervention of the statesman in helping an underdeveloped country to gain an absolute advantage in foreign trade, Steuart has developed the infant industry argument (Hutchison, 1988, p. 349). He rationalized this argument because of the small profits at the beginning of some branches of production that discourage its development (1.204). Thus he stated that the statesman must permit a short-run, higher-than-normal rate of profit in the infant and protected branches of industry (1.236, 240) in order to gain dexterity and knowledge in this kind of production (1.106, 199, 262).[14] In order for those profits to be gained by the protected branches of industry, the statesman must prohibit or put duties on importation of such commodities produced at lower prices abroad (1.262). However, Steuart recognized that this kind of protection must not last for long:

> He [i.e., the statesman] must keep constantly an eye upon the profits made in every branch of industry; and so soon as he finds that the real value of the manufacture comes so low as to render it exportable, he must . . . put an end to these profits he had permitted as the means only of bringing the manufactures to its perfection (1.263).

The statesman also is able to support some branches of the economy by subsidizing and giving premiums. If a surplus of products exists in the country, the statesman "himself become[s] the purchaser, if others will not; or, by premiums or bounties on the exportation of the surplus which lies upon hand, promote the sale of it at any rate, until the supernumerary hands can be otherwise provided for" (1.241, see also 1.299). The statesman, by buying this surplus, is able to sell it in another country at a lower price "at the loss to himself" (1.257) (i.e., the loss will be paid from the revenues from taxes) and in this way prevent the emergence of unemployment. Steuart was well aware that there is a possibility for the subsidized sector of the economy to remain in the same state because of the unwillingness of producers to improve their production capacity:

> . . . premiums are often abused. It belongs to the department of the coercive power of government to put a stop to such abuse (1.257).

When a country has an absolute advantage in certain manufactured goods, the statesman must do what he can in order to sustain such an advantage. In addition, he can help the country to hold a positive balance of trade by encouraging the exportation of manufactured goods (labor-intensive goods) and the importation of raw produce (1.291).[15]

In the case where a country has lost its absolute advantage because of an unavoidable decline, Steuart called on the statesman to intervene. Steuart, under his growth-decay thesis in foreign trade (1.195–196),[16] attributed many duties to the statesman. He stressed some natural causes that direct the economy toward decay, and thus he asked the statesman to intervene in order to prevent decay from happening (2.637). He also noted that the remedies must be scheduled according to the relative circumstances that prevail in any economy (2.700).

Four things cause the stage of decay in foreign trade to begin, that is, where an absolute advantage is lost: (1) an increase of prices of the exportable commodities caused by the consolidation of profits; (2) an increase in the price of exportable goods caused by an increase of the "intrinsic" value of commodities because the price of necessary goods has been increased; (3) "the natural advantage of other countries" who can export goods at a lower price because of their natural endowments; and (4) the higher productivity of other countries and their more advanced and well-administrated economy (1.246–247).

In regard to the first cause of decay in foreign trade, Steuart suggested the following strategy of recovery: the statesman must intervene by diminishing the luxury consumption of producers and thus causing the intrinsic value of commodities to be decreased, *viz*:

> If manufacturers become luxurious in their way of living, it must proceed from their extraordinary profits. . . . To re-establish then the foreign trade, these consolidated profits must be put an end to, by attacking luxury when circumstances render an augmentation of people inconvenient, and prices will fall of course (1.250; see also 1.192–193, 239).

However, Steuart finds it preferable for the statesman to prevent the consolidation of profits by encouraging supply in sectors where demand is higher than supply (particularly of exportable goods) (1.240, 251).

Another natural cause of the increase in the intrinsic value of commodities is produced by the unbalanced growth of agriculture and population. In the case where population increases faster than agriculture (1.252)—as agriculture functions under diminishing returns (1.197–198)—then the price of subsistence goods will be increased. In such a case the statesman must encourage the importation of subsistence goods (1.198) or assist "agriculture with his purse" (1.200).[17] Indeed, "These appear to be the most rational temporary expedients to diminish the price of grain in years of scarcity" (1.255). The statesman may also exercise some regulatory activities in order to "keep the prices of grain in as just a proportion as possible to the plenty of the year" (1.254). Steuart also noted that placing premiums upon exportation is a good measure for the decrease of the agricultural surplus "when prices fall too low" (1.233).

For Steuart, the statesman's intervention and his remedies for the re-establishment of foreign trade are "difficult, and sometimes dangerous" (1.259); therefore, he suggested that the statesman must do what he can to "preserve" a beneficial balance of trade (1.260).[18]

In regard to the other two causes of the loss of absolute advantage in foreign trade, Steuart suggested that the statesman must encourage exportation—when the country is competing in foreign trade with more advanced countries—even by giving premiums (1.258).

When a country has already lost its absolute advantage in foreign trade by trading with a superior country, the statesman can intervene by introducing the following three measures:

> First, To renounce this branch of commerce entirely, and to take the commodities wanted from foreigners, as they can furnish them cheaper. Secondly, To prohibit the importation of such commodities altogether. Thirdly, To impose a duty upon importation, in order to raise the price of them so high as to make them dearer than the same kind of commodity produced at home (1.284).

Steuart disputed the second measure because he considered it to be "too violent a remedy ever to be applied with success" (1.290). Instead of that, the statesman must impose duties on the importation of goods which will be gradually augmented (1.292). What, then, will be the optimum rate of duties imposed on importations? Steuart argues that this rate must be such as "to allow such commodities to be imported, with a duty which may raise their price to so just a height as neither to suffer them to be sold so cheap as to discourage the domestic fabrication, nor so dear, as to raise the profits of manufactures above a reasonable standard, in case of an augmentation of demand" (1.285).

Steuart turned against the sudden prohibition of imported goods because it will increase the price of those goods in domestic industry:

> A sudden stop upon a large importation, raises the prices of domestic industry by jerks, as it were; they do not rise gradually; and these extraordinary profits engage too many people to endeavour to share in them. This occasions a desertion from other branches of industry equally profitable to the state (1.291).

Here Steuart regards the profit motive as the main influence on the allocation of capital and labor to the most profitable enterprises. However, he did not use this mechanism for the explanation of the market phenomena and their solution.

Steuart suggested the statesman at first do what he can by examining the causes and the remedies for regaining a profitable foreign trade and not to stop it altogether (1.293). However, he was well aware that international trade stagnates if the same policies on foreign trade are followed by all countries (1.296).

The establishment of free trade, according to Steuart, can prove beneficial to the trading countries only if they have the same level of development and individuals share the same consumption preferences, *viz*:

> Were industry and frugality found to prevail equally in every part of these great political bodies, or were luxury and superfluous consumption every where carried to the same height, *trade might, without any hurt, be thrown entirely open. It would then cease to be an object of a statesman's care and concern* (1.296; emphasis added).

Steuart recognized that through international trade, world production would be increased by the increase in the work effort of individuals:

> . . . trade has an evident tendency toward the improvement of the world in general, by rendering the inhabitants of one country industrious, in order to supply the wants of another, without any prejudice to themselves (1.119; see also 120).

Through exports, "effectual" demand is increased, and if supply responds, "the whole industrious society will grow in vigour, and in wholesome stature" (1.182). But if supply does not respond to the augmented demand, extraordinary profits will emerge and exports will decrease (*ibid.*).

In the case of island trade, the statesman's main duty is the promotion of domestic consumption when the country has not reached its full-capacity level of production (1.300). Also in this state the statesman must prevent fraud by merchants and promote the distribution of grain to all parts of the country (1.255).

One can clearly deduce from the above analysis that for Steuart, the main failures of the market that statesman must cure in the above four cases of a country's developmental process are the increase in unemployment and the avoidance of a negative balance of trade. There is no internal mechanism or internal factor to treat such market failures. Therefore, according to Steuart, it is only through the statesman's indirect and direct intervention that the crisis produced in the free market can be overcome.

Steuart and Smith

It is natural to make a comparison between two famous economists of the eighteenth century, Steuart and Adam Smith. If we proceed to the core of their different solutions to economic problems, we find that the former stressed the negative possible outcomes of the free market, while the latter, the positive ones. On the other hand, when we compare Steuart's and Smith's assumptions on the existence of a perfect statesman and his crucial and necessary role in the economy, we come to another critical difference.

Contrary to Steuart, who assumed the theoretical existence of a perfect statesman, Smith rejected such a possibility. Smith was extremely hostile to politicians and spoke very caustically about them. In *The Wealth of Nations* he called the statesman or politician an "insidious and crafty animal . . . whose councils are directed by the momentary fluctuations of affairs" (ed. 1976, p. 468). In *Lectures*, he also says, "They whom we call politicians are not the most remarkable men in the world for probity and punctuality" (ed. 1978, p. 539). Smith did not suppose the existence of a perfect statesman like the one introduced by Steuart. On the contrary, he comments that "[t]he violence and injustice of the rulers of mankind is an ancient evil, for which, I am afraid, the nature of human affairs can scarce admit of a remedy" (*The Wealth of Nations*, ed. 1976, p. 493).[19] He believed that the statesman did not have an adequate and appropriate knowledge to direct the economic actions of individuals so as to maximize their welfare (*The Wealth of Nations*, ed. 1976, pp. 456, 687). Moreover, for Smith, the statesman was also "by nature extravagant, and prone to maldistribution" (Eltis, 1986, p. 67), while bureaucrats were inefficient (Reisman, 1982, p. 217).

We are not claiming that Steuart's and Smith's different approaches to the subject of the statesman's intervention gave rise to their different analyses of the market. Rather it seems that because they stressed different market forces as the predominant one (the former, the adequacy of demand; the latter, efficiency of production) as well as different roles (the former, the small producer; the latter, the capitalist-entrepreneur), they reached different conclusions on the function of the free market. Steuart stressed the possibility of crises and the long-run disequilibrium of the market, while Smith emphasized the smooth operation of the system and the tendency to long-run equilibrium. Or, to put it differently, Steuart's analysis was addressed toward showing how the emergence of economic crises could be avoided or prevented, while Smith's was directed toward demonstrating what the general framework of the system would be that would guarantee the minimum emergence of crises. Moreover, the difference of opinion between the two authors in regard to the purposes and qualities of the statesman does seem to influence their different attitudes toward the function of the free market. Their differences on the subject of the statesman's intervention also brings to mind a similar differentiation of opinions that took place in ancient Greece between Plato and Aristotle.

Plato entrusted to the statesman many activities in intervening in the economic actions of individuals (see, for example, *Laws*, 632 B; see also Karayiannis, 1990, pp. 34–36). Moreover, he stressed that the statesman must be educated in the "art of government" in order to increase the necessary qualities and characteristics for the execution of his duties (*Laws*, 250 B, 292 B; *Statesman*, 261 D, 293 A, D).

Aristotle, on the other hand, did not rely much on the statesman's qualities for the smooth operation of the economy, but rather considered the statesman to be inefficient in the direction and control of human actions. Moreover, he noted that the majority of politicians seek to satisfy their private interest and not that of the general good. As he comments:

> ... the majority of those engaged in politics are not correctly designated politicians, for they are not truly political, since the political man is one who purposely chooses noble actions for their own sake, whereas the majority embrace that mode of life for the sake of money and gain (*Eudemian Ethics*, 1216, a20–30).

Therefore, if we want to draw a parallel between these two pairs of scientists, we can say that Steuart displayed a similar attitude to Plato[20] on the efficiency of the statesman's intervention, while Smith followed Aristotle's approach more closely.

Conclusions

From the foregoing analysis it could be deduced that Steuart's attitude toward the managed market and his policy suggestions came from his analysis of cases of market failure. We cannot say with certainty that his belief in the powers of the wise statesman forced him to schedule a market analysis with visible cases of failure of whether the contrary was the case.

However, it is very difficult to deny the similarity of Steuart's views about the necessity of the statesman's intervention with the economic policies introduced by Keynes and the Keynesians and followed by various countries in the twentieth century. The various economic policies for the avoidance of unemployment, for increases in effective demand, and for the protection of domestic production, and so on, are similar to those developed by Steuart. Despite his neglect of some mechanisms and behaviors that would produce, under definite assumptions, a general equilibrium, Steuart showed a lack of realism in regard to the efficiency of the statesman's intervention (Hutchison, 1988, p. 350). This lack of realism is not very profound in regard to the instruments of economic policy as it is in regard to the abilities of the statesman.

It is not necessary to go through mercantilism, socialism, and economics of control in order to find economic policies that are similar to those suggested by Steuart. By abstracting from the characterizations and parallels[21] of Steuart's "inquiry" with older or later developed economic ideas, policies, and arguments, it is difficult to deny evidence that may prove that Steuart was born either too late or too soon. In the twentieth century, most of the countries of the Western world have at one time or another followed policies similar to those suggested by Steuart. The great weakness of Steuart is his assumption of a perfect statesman to handle all the problems that need a solution. As experience has shown, the existence of such an entity is extremely rare.

Acknowledgments

I would like to thank Ray Petridis (Murdoch University) for helpful comments on an earlier draft. The usual caveats apply.

Notes

1. All references cited to 1805 edition of Steuart's *Works* are as follows: volume, book, page (e.g., 1.I.257). For Skinner's edition of *Principles*, we cite volume and page only (e.g., 1.152).

2. In his work Steuart used the term *statesman* as "a general term to signify the legislature and supreme power, according to the form of government" (1.16).

3. For example, Steuart noted the case in which some statutes of the king of France in 1720 destroyed the public credit (2.441–442).

4. For an excellent analysis of microeconomics before Smith, see Rashid (1986, pp. 844–851).

5. Steuart regarded the "intrinsic" value of a commodity as being measured by the cost of production and particularly by the level of real wages. However, he stressed also that the level of wages is mainly determined by the demand for labor, that is, by the consumption patterns of rich individuals and not by the price of necessary goods. That is why in our article (1991a, pp. 168–174) we spoke of Steuart's "quasi labour theory" of value.

6. Taxes, as Steuart made clear, must not be imposed on individuals arbitrarily and unequally (1.213). Also the individual must recognize that taxes "are paid for the advantage of the public, not for that of private people" (2.708–709).

7. Steuart was against direct taxation on wages, profits and capital; he stressed that such taxation would prove hurtful for the economy, because:

(a) Direct taxation on wages decreases the living standard of workers (2.675–676, ft. 3.).
(b) Taxes levied on necessary goods will increase the rate of wages and the general level of prices in the economy (2.694–695) and thus exports and "effectual" demand will be decreased. However, Steuart recognized one case where the taxation on necessary goods would be beneficial to the economy. This is the case where the laborers enjoyed a luxurious living and their work effort had been decreased (2.691–692, 695). Thus Steuart not only stressed the demand side effects of taxation but also the supply effect (Eltis, 1986, p. 61).
(c) By the direct taxation on income and profits, the incentives of individuals for increasing their productive effort could be decreased (2.687–688). Steuart suggested direct taxes be imposed only on the interest received from the public dept (2.722).
(d) Taxes on capital will decrease the surplus of the economy that is directed to investment (2.687–688, 705, 712, 723).

8. Steuart observed that if the statesman must regulate the rate of interest directly by law it must be done by establishing a legal level of interest above the rate that could be established in the market (2.457, 460–461).

9. Steuart was opposed to the foreign debt not only because of fear of the country becoming dependent on foreigners but also because of the loss of capital to foreign countries

through the payment of interest (2.636, 644–645). For the ways that, according to Steuart, a public debt could be repaid, see Sen (1957, p. 112).

10. Steuart goes so far as to regard the spatial distribution of the units of consumption and production as partially influenced by the activities of the statesman (1.60–61, 64).

11. Steuart considers trade to be a time-saving operation and a branch of product distribution according to the dictates of demand and supply (1.156). He also makes clear that the merchants have the power to introduce in underdeveloped countries a taste for superfluities (1.163).

12. The introduction and extensive use of money in the economy, according to Steuart, produces some beneficial effects: it (a) expands economic growth; (b) increases the effectiveness of the tax system; and (c) produces a more equal distribution of wealth (Karayiannis, 1988a, p. 28, ft. 3).

13. For a more developed economy the statesman should have great delicacy of touch. Steuart used the metaphor of the watch to show that the statesman must very carefully intervene in the "modern" economy, and mostly with long-run targets (1.217; 278–279).

14. Steuart, in developing his thesis for the protection and encouragement of infant industry, mentioned that the statesman "must likewise spare no expense in procuring the ablest masters in every branch of industry; nor any cost in making the first establishments, in providing machines, and every other thing necessary or useful to make the undertaking succeed" (1.263), and he "ought to multiply the numbers of scholars" (1.263). Is Steuart suggesting here that the statesman must offer public education in bettering the "master" of enterprises, or encourage the competition from the side of supply in order that only the most able producers survive in the market? He does not make clear which one of those policies is being suggested.

15. Steuart was an advocate of a favorable balance of trade. However, in contrast to the old mercantilists who considered the surplus of foreign trade as consisting of precious metals, Steuart emphasized its real terms and in particular measured it by the net amount of labor value added. He recognized that only when a country imports lower labor cost, or lower labor value-added commodities than are exported, does it have a favorable balance of trade (1.291, 294).

16. Steuart strengthened his growth–decay thesis by considering history (1.195; for this thesis see also Low, 1952, pp. 323–324; Skinner, 1981, pp. 32–33). This thesis had been put forward first by Plato who, philosophically speaking, wrote: "since for everything that has come into being destruction is appointed" (*Republic*, 546 A). In the eighteenth century Hume was the writer who before Steuart stated this thesis in his letter to Lord Kames (4th March, 1758, ed. 1932, pp. 271–272).

17. Steuart proposed also the establishment of a granary scheme by which the real wage rate and the level of production of grain will be secured (Campbell, 1953, pp. 50–51; Skinner, 1985, p. 12; Eltis, 1986, p. 56).

18. For the policies suggested by Steuart for dealing with disequilibrium in the balance of payments and capital mobility, see Perlman (1990).

19. Smith was against the statesman's intervention because he considered there to be no such being as an "impartial" statesman. He argued that statesmen usually make laws for their material and other benefits (*Lectures*, ed. 1978, p. 181). He also stressed that the capitalists by their money and power are able to influence and "corrupt the members of parliament" (Pack, 1991, p. 149). Moreover, he was opposed to the statesman's intervention in the economy because he considered that the British government in the past had done more harm than good (Reisman, 1982, p. 219).

20. The resemblance between Plato and Steuart is also obvious in regard to the capability

of the statesman to influence the "spirit of people." The philosopher stressed that "by further laws and institutions you expel illiberality and commercialism from the souls of those who are to pursue them thoroughly to their profit" (*Laws*, 747 B). Steuart, on his side, considered that "[t]he spirit of a people is formed upon a set of received opinions, relative to three objects; morals, government, and manners" (1.22). This spirit changes naturally between generations (1.24–25), but change is also affected by the government (2.638; see also Khalil, 1987, p. 121). It seems that Steuart used the model of Spartan economy primarily to show how Lycurgus prepared the "spirit of the people" (1.219, 227) in order to establish such a system of economy which, as he said, "I readily grant, is not likely to take place" (1.227).

21. Steuart has been variously characterized by early (see King, 1988, pp. 32–33) and modern commentators as mercantilist (see, for example, Kobayashi, 1967, p. 3; Anderson and Tollison, 1984, p. 459) and as a predecessor of Keynes (Sen, 1957, p. 151).

References

Akhtar, M. (1978). "Sir James Steuart on Economic Growth." *Scottish Journal of Political Economy* 25(1):57–74.

Akhtar, M. (1979). "An Analytical Outline of Sir James Steuart's Macroeconomic Model." *Oxford Economic Papers* (July): 283–302.

Anderson, C., and R. Tollison. (1984). "Sir James Steuart as the Apotheosis of Mercantilism and his relation to Adam Smith." *Southern Economic Journal* 51: 456–468.

Aristotle. (1935) *Eudemian Ethics*, English trans. by H. Rackham. Cambridge, MA: Loeb Classical Library, Harvard University Press.

Aristotle. (1926). *Politica*, English trans. by W.D. Ross. Oxford: Oxford at the Clarendon Press.

pseudo-Aristotle. (1921). *Oeconomica.* English trans. by E.S. Foster. Oxford: Oxford at the Clarendon Press.

Campbell, R. (1953). "Sir James Steuart—A Study in the Development of Economic Thought." Unpublished doctoral thesis, University of California.

Eagly, R. (1961). "Sir James Steuart and the Aspiration Effect." *Economica* (February): 53–61.

Eltis, Walter. (1986). "Sir James Steuart's Corporate State." In R.D. Collison Black (ed.) *Ideas in Economics.* London: Macmillan Press, pp. 43–73.

Hirschman, Albert. (1977). *The Passions and the Interests, Political Arguments for Capitalism before its Triumph.* Princeton, NJ: Princeton University Press.

Hume, David. (1970). *Writings on Economics*, edited with an introduction by E. Rotwein. Madison: The University of Wisconsin Press.

Hume, David. (1932). *The Letters of David Hume*, edited by J. Creig, Oxford: Oxford at the Clarendon Press.

Hutchison, Terence. (1988). *Before Adam Smith: The Emergence of Political Economy, 1662–1776.* Oxford: Basil Blackwell.

Karayiannis, Anastassios D. (1988a). "James Steuart on Distribution." *Quaderni di Storia dell' Economia Politica* 6(2):25–50.

Karayiannis, Anastassios D. (1988b) "Early Critiques on the Humean Quantity Theory of Money." *Spoudai* 38(3–4):534–547 (in Greek).

Karayiannis, Anastassios D. (1990). "The Platonic Ethico-economic Structure of Society." *Quaderni di Storia dell Economia Politica* 8(1):3–45.

Karayiannis, Anastassios D. (1991a). "Sir James Steuart on Value and Prices." *Spoudai* 41(2):167–190.

Karayiannis, Anastassios D. (1991b). "Coin and Paper Money in the Late pre-Smithian Economics: A Controversy." In *Festschrift in Honour of Lazaros Th. Houmanidis*. Piraeus: University of Piraeus, pp. 310–339.

Karayiannis, Anastassios D. (1992). "Pioneers of Economic Methodology." In *Festschrift in Honour of Professor Athanasios Kanellopoulos*. vol. I. Piraeus: Univerity of Piraeus, pp. 274–302.

Khalil, Elias. (1987). "Sir James Steuart vs Professor James Buchanan: Critical Notes on Modern Public Choice." *Review of Social Economy* 45(2):113–132.

King, J.E. (1988). *Economic Exiles*. London: Macmillan Press.

Kobayashi, Noboru. (1967). "James Steuart, Adam Smith and Friedrich List." *The Science Council of Japan, Division of Economics, Commerce & Business Administration*, Economic Series No. 40, pp. 1–37.

Kobayashi, Noboru. (1992). "The First System of Political Economy—An Essay on Political Oeconomy of Sir James Steuart." *Keizai Ronshu*, Daitobunka University, 55:47–88.

Low, J.M. (1952). "An Eighteenth Century Controversy in the Theory of Economic Progress." *The Manchester School of Economics and Social Studies*: 311–330.

Meek, R. (1958). "The Economics of Control Prefigured by Sir James Steuart." *Science and Society*: 289–305.

Montesquieu, C. (1893). *The Spirit of Laws* (1734–48), trans. by T. Nugent. London: J & W. Clarke.

Ohmori, Ikuo. (1983). "A Methodological Approach to Sir James Steuart's Political Oeconomy." *Waseda Business Review* (9):181–203.

Pack, J. Spencer. (1991). In Hants Aldershot (ed.), *Capitalism as a Moral System: Adam Smith's Critique of the Free Market Economy*. England: Edward Elger.

Perlman, Morris. (1990). "Sir James Steuart's Absorption and Wealth Approach to the Balance of Payments." *History of Political Economy* 22(1):125–136.

Plato. (1963). *Laws*. trans. by A.E. Taylor. In E. Hamilton, and H. Cairns (eds.), *The Collected Dialogues, of Plato*. Princeton: Princeton University Press.

Plato. (1963). *Republic*. trans. by P. Shorey. In E. Hamilton, and H. Cairns (eds.), *The Collected Dialogues, of Plato*. Princeton: Princeton University Press.

Plato. (1963). *Statesman*. trans. by J.B. Skemp. In E. Hamilton, and H. Cairns (eds.), *The Collected Dialogues, of Plato*. Princeton: Princeton University Press.

Rashid, S. (1986). "Smith, Steuart, and Mercantilism: Comment." *Southern Economic Journal* 52(3):843–852.

Reisman, David. (1982). *State and Welfare: Tawney, Galbraith and Adam Smith*. London: Macmillan.

Rousseau, J.J. (1973). *A Discourse on Political Economy* (1758) in J.J. Rousseau (ed.), *The Social Contract and Discourses*. London: J.M. Dent & Sons, Ltd.

Sen, S. (1957). *The Economic of Sir James Steuart*. London: G Bell & Co.

Skinner, A. (1962). "Sir James Steuart: Economics and Politics." *Scottish Journal of Political Economy*: 17–37.

Skinner, A. (1981). "Sir James Steuart: Author of a System." *Scottish Journal of Political Economy*: 28(1):20–41.

Skinner, A. (1985). "Sir James Steuart—A Perspective on Economic Policy and Development." *Quaderni di Storia dell' Economia Politica* 3(2):3–24.

Smith, Adam. (1978). *Lectures on Jurisprudence*, edited by R. Meek, D. Raphael, and P. Stein. Oxford: Clarendon Press.

Smith, Adam. (1976). *An Inquiry into the Nature and Causes of the Wealth of Nations* (1st ed. 1766), edited by R. Campbell and A. Skinner. Oxford: Oxford at the Clarendon Press.

Stettner, W. (1945). "Sir James Steuart on the Public Debt." *Quarterly Journal of Economics*: 451–476.

Steuart, Sir James. (1966). *An Inquiry into the Principles of Political Economy* (1st ed. 1767), edited by A. Skinner. London: Oliver & Boyd.

Steuart, Sir James. (1967). *The Works, Political, Metaphisical & Chronological of Sir James Steuart*, in six volumes (1st ed. 1805). New York: A.M. Kelley.

3 ECONOMIC THEORY AND POLICY: AN INTRODUCTION TO JOHN STUART MILL'S POLITICAL ECONOMY

Samuel Hollander

Introduction

This chapter outlines some implications for economic policy of John Steuart Mill's position on the nature and function of abstract economics. It is designed as a sort of introduction to his theory of economic policy rather than a statement of that theory as such.[1]

Mill's methodological pronouncements are of prime importance in our exercise. The second section is concerned with constraints on the applicability of economic theory flowing from its character as a specialized science of "wealth" (throughout read "income") based on maximizing behavior and, accordingly, pertinent to particular institutional frameworks. Special problems arise from the "progressive movement of society" at play. The indispensability of theory as the sole means of dealing with causality and avoiding misleading surface appearances, and various cautions regarding the "art" of applied economics, are examined in the third section. A concern with theory testing prior to application is a further consideration. It emerges furthermore, in the following section, that economics does not allow positive historical prediction; its function, rather, is to recommend measures that encourage "beneficial" and counteract "injurious" *tendencies*.

The fifth section considers Mill's position that the scientific character of economics flows from the *competitive* principle. This generalization must be fully appreciated, since taken literally it severely limits the applicability of theory. The declaration in fact excludes only small-number cases rather than monopolistic competition or monopoly. Mill's enthusiastic championship of both the efficiency and the dynamic cases for competition is summarized in the sixth section. A companion discussion in the subsequent section broadens the relevance of competitive theory, considering the "universality" of the *method* of economics. This extends the coverage of theory to institutional structures other than capitalist-exchange provided that maximizing behavior is at play (precluding custom, gift, or force) and the absence of the small-number problem assured.

Mill's contrast between the laws of production and distribution—the former supposedly "immutable" and the latter "malleable"—is of obvious relevance for any theory of economic policy. The contrast, taken up in the next section, is shown to be built on sand, the inflexibility of the first category turning on given knowledge, while the amenability of the second to social choice neglects the *consequences* of such choice, consequences revealed by economic theory. Mill's distinction is only meaningful in a weak sense involving the contrast between problems of efficiency and of value judgment. In the subsequent section the impact of productive organization on productivity (and also on population growth) illustrates the fact that the choice of particular institutional arrangements has consequences amenable to theoretical treatment in terms of the competitive model.

The pre-conditions required to assure that competition is the appropriate policy for manpower allocation is the subject of a later section. Here are encountered Mill's elaborations of the Smithian analysis of the wage structure. It was acceptable as yielding an equitable pattern—even acceptable for Socialists—subject to (1) correction of certain irrational forms of behavior, (2) removal of barriers to mobility created by education costs; and (3) assurance of full employment in the labor market as a whole, introducing a link between micro-economic and macro-economic analysis of the very first importance to labor policy.

The aggregate labor market is dealt with more fully in the latter part of the chapter, with particular reference to the population problem. Competition again provides the key. Although Mill did not accept the competitively determined general wage as necessarily "equitable," especially considering the nonequitable distribution of property, he sought means to strengthen the relative strength of labor in the market, theory demonstrating that competition need not act against labor's interests. That was the moral insisted upon, coupled with the belief that the solution to low wages lay with labor itself, not with government or varieties of paternalism. A concern with the "free-rider" problem emerges in the discussion of prudential population control opening up a potential for legitimate social (even legal) control of population growth.

I suggest in the next-to-last section that Mill's celebrated recommendation for a stationary state—the logical limit to population control—should not be taken too seriously. Too many social *desiderata* turn on growth, and stationariness might be dangerous from the perspective of labor displacement, capital loss abroad, resource misallocation, social conflict, and prospects for new technology. On balance, Mill gave a *positive* answer to the question of whether growth is desirable.

The final substantive section illustrates the impact of changing empirical circumstances on the policy implications derived from the classical growth model and the Law of Markets. Specifically, it concerns the linkage of economic cycles with an unprecedented buoyancy of capital accumulation and the consequential justification for socially desirable government expenditure. That all this is consistent with the Law of Markets illustrates the flexibility of the theory-policy relation in Mill's hands, and provides a case study of his methodological caution against simple-minded applications. The new perspective extends to public finance, and here a contrast emerges between Mill's new radicalism with respect to government expenditure and his long-standing and continued concern with the disinsentive effects of progressive taxation.

Specialization in Social Science: Constraints on the Applicability of Economic Theory

Mill distinguished the "science" from the "art" of political economy, the indicative from the imperative mood: "Science takes cognizance of a *phenomenon*, and endeavours to discover its *law*; art proposed to itself an *end*, and looks out for *means* to effect it" (CW, IV, p. 312). The science is perceived generally as treating "the production and distribution of wealth, so far as they depend upon the laws of human nature" (p. 318); and, more narrowly, as "concerned with [man] solely as a being who desires wealth, and who is capable of judging of the comparative efficacy of means for obtaining that end" (p. 321). The specifications are finally formulated as wealth maximization subject to "two perpetually antagonizing principles . . . aversion to labour, and desire of the present enjoyment of costly indulgences," which "do not merely, like other desires occasionally conflict with the pursuit of wealth, but accompany it always as a drag, or impediment, and are therefore inseparably mixed up in the consideration of it" (pp. 321–322). The science is, therefore, based on a specific behavioral pattern and the social phenomena under investigation are themselves limited in range to the production and distribution of "wealth."

An intimate connection is drawn between the wealth-maximization hypothesis and the limited range of subject matter treated by political economy. The supposed circumstance that different classes of social fact depended "immediately and in the first resort . . . on different kinds of causes," allowed for "distinct and separate, though not independent, branches of sociological speculation" (VIII, pp. 900–901). In political economy, the relevant class of social phenomena is that

> . . . in which the immediately determining causes are *principally* those which act through the desire of wealth; and in which the psychological law *mainly* concerned is the familiar one, that a greater gain is preferred to a smaller. I mean, of course, that portion of the phenomena of society which emanate from the industrial, or productive operations of mankind; and from those of their acts through which the distribution of the products of those industrial operations takes place *insofar as not effected by force or modified by voluntary gift* (emphasis added).[2]

Income maximization was, therefore, not one among roughly equal motives, but the *predominating* influence governing a specific range of social phenomena; and since "the law of the effect is compounded by the laws of all the causes which determine it" (IV, p. 322),[3] there was ideally to be an ultimate synthesis of the results of all the specialist branches of social science to form a general theory of wealth. Economics provided a *partial* theory of wealth, and a model based on the wealth-maximization hypothesis as the "sole end" of activity was only an approximation to be qualified in application to particular cases because of "disturbing causes," including conflicting behavioral patterns (p. 323).

For the specialist procedure to be legitimate, the range of study must accordingly encompass a sufficiently homogenous pattern of behavior; it further followed that the specialist exercise was "liable to fail in all cases in which the progressive movement of society is one of the influencing elements" (VIII, p. 906). The scope of the subject matter of political economy is thus restricted. Not only does the income-maximizing hypothesis require that we concentrate on a particular range of activity (the production and distribution of income) where such an assumption constitutes at least an excellent first approximation, but even this assumption only holds good (again as an approximation) in the context of a specified nation and period.

Mill's repeated references limiting the practical guidance to be derived from political economy to "any given state of society," to "any given condition of social affairs," to "any country or time the individual circumstances of which we are well acquainted" confirm the limited scope conceived for the propositions of the science—the fact that even the isolation of tendencies (as distinct from the making of specific predictions) requires the initial postulation of a constrained environment. Universally applicable propositions were, therefore, not in order because of the "eminently modifiable nature of the social phenomena, and the multitude and variety of the circumstances by which they are modified; circumstances never the same, or even nearly the same, in two different societies or in two different periods of the same society" (pp. 898–899). Far from being represented as being of "universal" relevance, the axiomatic foundation of political economy was pertinent only to well-defined environmental conditions, and even then subject to qualification considering the potential intervention of "disturbing causes."

Contrasting with his qualified championship of deductive theory in political economy is Mill's rejection of the Bentham school and its "interest philosophy." To base a *theory of government*[4] and make proposals for reform on the assumption of self-interest was "unscientific" (p. 892). His strictures did not relate to irresponsible policy applications but rather to the supposed predominance of the Benthamite interest philosophy throughout time and space, its *universality* (IV, p. 333). This criticism did not apply to political economy envisaged as a science of relatively narrow scope and not of universal relevance even as a first approximation; the procedure of distinguishing between income maximization and other behavioral patterns reflected a quest for practicality given the problem of "composition of causes," and was valid only in the light of the empirical relevance of the maximization hypothesis in that temporal and geographic environment which the model was designed to treat. And even in the advanced competitive capitalist system for which the model is designed, other motives may be at play in special cases so that the applied economist must be ever on the alert.

Apart from political ethology Mill seems hesitant to specify the particular specializations that would ideally complement political economy. Conceivably, by the distinction between competition and custom and the constraint that "only through the principle of competition has political economy any pretension to the character of a science" (II, p. 239), he intended the character of an *independent* science, the case of custom being the subject of a complementary science based upon an alternative axiomatic basis. An investigation of wealth based on altruistic behavior might provide a second example.[5]

Contemporary political economy is actually less severely constrained than it is formally represented to be. For its axiomatic foundation in fact included some behavioral assumptions conflicting with income maximization: "in a few of the most striking cases (such as the important one of the principle of population)" corrections "are . . . interpolated into the exposition of Political Economy itself; the strictness of purely scientific arrangements being thereby somewhat departed from, for the sake of practical utility" (p. 323).

The relaxation of the formal constraints on the scope of political economy also emerges in the treatment of knowledge (and elementary education and health). In the case of speculative activity in general, the "material fruits, [of thought], though the result, are seldom the direct purpose of the pursuits of savants," and to that extent does not fall within the economist's domain (p. 43). Mill, however, proceeds to qualify himself:

> But when (as in political economy one should always be prepared to do) we shift our point of view, and consider not individual acts, and the motives by which they are determined, but national and universal results, intellectual speculation must be looked upon as a most influential part of the productive labour of society, and the portion of its resources employed in carrying on and remunerating such labour, is a highly productive part of its expenditures.

Yet the proposed incorporation of activities governed by other than income-maximizing motivation does not indicate what *professional* competance the economist has to bring to bear. The incorporation into economics of the determinants of pure science was largely a proposal flowing from a realization that though maximization motives may be irrelevant, the subject was too close to home to be safely relegated to "another science."

What we actually do have from Mill is not always consistent with the initial presumption of an absence of profit maximization.[6] But to the extent that our comprehension of the system is extended beyond mere empirical relationships, the potential role of deductive theory in policy recommendation is enhanced.

The Indispensability of Economic Theory and Further Cautions Regarding Policy Application

Thus far I have referred to limitations imposed on the scope of economic theory, particularly in policy application. But Mill's harshest criticism was reserved for the "experimental" method. The "infant state" of the social sciences he blamed on a failure to appreciate that scientific methods "to accomplish anything worthy of attainment, must be to a great extent if not principally, deductive" (VII, p. 384). In discussing "fallacies of observation" (VIII, p. 781), Mill contrasted surface manifestations of apparent causal linkages and a deeper undercurrent of causation moving in a very different direction (a distinction made much of by Marx). Conspicuous examples include the notion that lavish state expenditure provides a stimulus to industry, an error corrected by the Law of Markets; the common case against free trade, corrected by the comparative cost theory with further light cast by the classical theory of growth; the explanation of inflation in terms of upward wage pressure corrected by the *inverse* wage-profit theorem which itself turns on the theory of allocation (cost of production theory of value),[7] coupled with the quantity theory approach to the price level; and the notion that expansion of the currency is stimulatory which erroneously presumes that inflation is unanticipated.

The requirement for theory does not, however, pertain to the technological level of conception. For example, an observed downward trend of agricultural costs over several decades would have to be analyzed by an empirical investigation of the impact of diminishing agricultural and increasing manufacturing returns, innovation, changing work attitudes, labor relations, health, skill, business organization, and so forth, with the "abstract" science of economics scarcely entering the picture. Indeed, the empirical investigation contributes toward a specification of the axioms required by economic theory. The function of the science is rather to explain the data at the more profound level involving human decision making, for which reason precisely economic models were restricted to particular behavioral patterns. Taking the Ricardo–Malthus–Mill growth model as an example, we have a relation linking falling agricultural productivity to the return on capital (a relationship that entails the inverse wage-profit mechanism and thus the competitive pricing mechanism in labor and commodity markets) and hence to savings decisions, and a reverse relationship brought into play by certain categories of innovations. Theory tells us that the imposition of Corn Laws sets in motion the former tendency and is thus adverse to the growth of wealth, a matter easily disguised by the statistical data.

The theoretical constructs mentioned above turn on a specific set of behavioral and institutional axioms. And this limitation on the scope of the specialist social science rendered it unlikely that empirical laws pertaining to specific policy changes, such as the effect of Corn Laws on "wealth," could ever be obtained. Given the social and institutional environment relevant to legislation, there were likely to be too few observations to reveal any pattern whatsoever, since different conflicting causes acting on wealth would be at play in each specific case, some acting positively and some negatively (pp. 908–909).[8] Even in the unlikely event of a large number of observations relating to Corn Laws in a given environment, at best all that could ever be yielded is a generalization stating that in a majority of cases such laws were accompanied by a particular outcome, and such generalizations would be of little use since it would still remain necessary to interpret them by reducing them to the underlying causal forces at work. It is "from theory" only that the effects on wealth specifically due to Corn Laws could be appreciated; to base recommendations on apparent empirical regularities might prove disastrous.[9]

The absence of genuine empirical laws precluded direct verification of theory against the results of "*a posteriori* observation" in the specialist branches of social science (p. 896). Nonetheless, responsible use of theory in policy recommendation required at a minimum *indirect* verification—the political economist's knowledge "must at least enable him to explain and account for what *is*, or he is an insufficient judge of what ought to be" (IV, p. 335). He must allow for "the disturbing influence of unforeseen causes," but also "carefully watch the result of every experiment, in order that any residuum of facts which his principle do not lead him to expect, and do not enable him to explain, may become the subject of a fresh analysis, and furnish the occasion for a consequent enlargement or correction of his general views" (pp. 335–336). If we cannot account for the existing state of social phenomena in terms of our model, allowance made for disturbing causes, "we are not, in the present state of our knowledge, fully competent to draw conclusions, speculative or practical, for that country . . . we must turn back, and seek the explanation by an extension and improvement of the theory itself" (VIII, pp. 909–910).

Even after satisfying the foregoing conditions, the "guidance of practice" remained a hazardous exercise. The intervention of unforeseen disturbing causes was always a possibility: "Effects are commonly determined by a *concurrence* of causes. If we have overlooked any one cause, we may justly reason from all the others, and only be further wrong. Our premises will be true, and our reasoning correct, and yet the result of no value in the particular case" (IV, p. 337). This problem was compounded by the fact that, by its nature, the art of political economy involved more than the application of the corresponding specialist science:

> One of the strongest reasons for drawing the line of separation clearly and broadly between science and art is the following—That the principle of classification in science most conveniently follows the classification of *causes*, while arts must necessarily be classified according to the classification of the *effects*,

> the production of which is their appropriate end. Now an effect, whether in physics or morals, commonly depends upon a concurrence of causes, and it frequently happens that several of these causes belong to different sciences (p. 331*n*).

Because of the characteristic interdisciplinary nature of art, it followed that the "mere political economist, he who has studied no science but Political Economy, if he attempts to apply his science to practice, will fail" (p. 331). In these terms we can appreciate Mill's appeal for broadmindedness, notwithstanding his insistence on the legitimacy of specialization. For the necessity of a detached discipline of political economy did not gainsay that its practitioners, like all other scientists, might be narrow minded, "regarding, not any economical doctrine, but their present experience of mankind, as of universal validity" (X, p. 306). The only security against this narrowness was "a liberal mental cultivation, and all it proves is that a person is not likely to be a good political economist who is nothing else." Unfortunately, the qualities required of a good theorist mitigated against those required of a good applied economist (IV, p. 333).

On the Preclusion of Secular Prediction

There could in fact be no practical maxims of general applicability even if social phenomena conformed to *known* causal relationships, precluding the problem of "disturbing" causes. The dilemma was that of weighing in the balance the relative force of the numerous causal influences (even if we suppose them to be known, which they are not) *playing on the condition and progress of society*—influences "innumerable, and perpetually changing; and though they all change in obedience to causes, and therefore to laws, the multitude of the causes is so great as to defy our limited powers of calculation" (VIII, p. 878). Worse still, "the impossibility of applying precise numbers to facts of such a description would set an impassable limit to the possibility of calculating them beforehand, even if the powers of the human intellect were otherwise adequate to the task." At best, the laws of human nature applied to the circumstances of a *given* state of society might suggest "that a particular cause will operate in a certain manner unless counteracted"; but "we can seldom know, even approximately, all the agencies which may coexist with it, and still less calculate the collective result of so many combined elements" (p. 898). There is the further complexity, of course, that "great men" or governments can *influence* social progress, including the intellectual development of the race (pp. 936–937).

Social science was for these reasons unable to generate specific secular predictions, and to this extent had to be distinguished from astronomy, the data of which were relatively few and stable. The limitation extended to population growth and living standards:

> . . . all generalizations which affirm that mankind have a tendency to grow better or worse, richer or poorer, more cultivated or more barbarous, that population increases faster than subsistence, or subsistence than population, that inequality of fortune has a tendency to increase or to break down, and the like, propositions of considerable value as empirical laws within certain (but generally rather narrow) limits, are in reality true or false according to times and circumstances (p. 791).

Mill had in mind socialist critics of contemporary society (see below on 'The Population Problem'). He also rejected predictions by socialists of an increasing tendency toward monopoly (V, p. 730).[10]

Mill, it is true, did perceive certain regularities relating to "the progressive change in the condition of the human species" (VIII, p. 925). But the problem was that of connecting those regularities "with the laws of human nature, by deductions showing that such were the derivative laws naturally to be expected as the consequence of those ultimate ones." Until such linkage was established, they were "applicable only within the bounds of actual observation"; and "without any means of determining their real limits, and of judging whether the changes which have hitherto been in progress are destined to continue indefinitely, or to terminate, or even to be reversed."[11] Similarly, until an empirical relation "could be connected with the psychological and ethological laws on which it must depend, and, by the consilience of deduction *a priori* with historical evidence, could be converted from an empirical law into a scientific one, it could not be relied on for the prediction of future events, beyond, at most, strictly adjacent cases" (p. 915), or, so it is implied, used as a reliable basis for long-term policy.

Nevertheless, Mill based policy recommendations on secular generalizations derived from observed facts rather than any specific theoretical model. These generalizations relate differences in productivity between countries and over time to natural advantage, security, knowledge and co-operation, work habits, savings propensities, and so forth—characteristically inductive materials. Statistical generalizations as the basis for policy recommendations such as Corn Law legislation were unavailable as we have seen earlier; theoretical models were indispensible. But the individual influences acting on wealth are supposedly discernable in the historical record by close inductive analysis. And Mill's institutional recommendations frequently involve measures designed to act on the individual components thus obtained, thereby reinforcing positive "tendencies" and counteracting negative tendencies generated in the course of "Progress":

> We must seek our objects by means which may perhaps be defeated, and take precautions against dangers which possibly may never be realized. The aim of practical politics is to surround any given society with the greatest possible number of circumstances of which the tendencies are beneficial and to remove or counteract, as far as practicable, those of which the tendencies are injurious (p. 898).

For this, a knowledge of tendencies "without the power of accurately predicting their conjunct result [sufficed] to a considerable extent." The perception of which tendencies are "beneficial" or "injurious" raises the issue of value judgment with which we are not now concerned.

Economic Science and Competition

We turn now to Mill's celebrated declaration that "only through the principle of competition has political economy any pretension to the character of a science" (II, p. 239), or the caution that the analysis of exchange or price formation *presumes* competition, for "only so far as [prices] are thus determined, can they be reduced to any assignable law" (III, p. 460).[12]

The analysis of competitive price, which turns on "the axiom . . . that there cannot be for the same article, of the same quality, two prices in the same market," is in fact limited to the wholesale sector, for Mill represents individual consumers as typically failing to act in maximizing fashion:

> For [retail purchases] there often are not merely two, but many prices, in different shops, or even in the same shop; habit and accident having as much to do in the matter as general causes. . . . Either from indolence, or carelessness, or because people think it fine to pay and ask no questions, three-fourths of those who can afford it give much higher prices than necessary for the things they consume; while the poor often do the same from ignorance and defect of judgement, want of time for searching and making inquiry, and not unfrequently, from coercion, open or disguised.

This provides a perfect instance of counteracting forces to income maximization, limiting the applicability of economic models even in advanced capitalism.[13]

The domain of economic theory extends to the treatment of *monopolistic competition* in the modern sense of the term—namely markets subject to unrestrained freedom of entry, yet in which competition does not act on price (II, p. 243). This situation characterized the retail trade: "the price paid by the actual consumer seems to feel very slowly and imperfectly the effect of competition; and when competition does exist, if often, instead of lowering prices, merely divides the gains of the high price among a greater number of dealers." More specifically, "custom" indicated a particular markup over the wholesale price and what competition there was avoided price cutting (pp. 409–410).[14]

Mill recognized efficiency losses flowing from the excess capacity of retail firms, today identified with monopolistic competition: "the share of the whole produce of land and labour which is absorbed in the remuneration of mere distributors, continues exhorbitant; and there is no function in the economy of society which supports a number of persons so disproportioned to the amount of work to be performed" (p. 410). His concern with inefficiencies due to excessive numbers is a pervasive theme of his critique of contemporary society: ". . . the class of mere distributors, who are not producers but auxiliaries of production, and whose inordinate number, far more than the gains of capitalists, are the cause why so great a portion of the wealth produced does not reach the producers" (III, p. 791; *cf.*, p. 983).[15]

A major source of the problem (in addition to the degree of rigidity imposed by custom) was seen to lie in the ability to differentiate by location if not by product—an ability already weakened in the "great emporia of trade" (II, p. 410). For an increasing "intensity of modern competition", which encouraged a policy of "great business at low prices, rather than high prices and few transactions, "was observable in major cities offering "a sufficient inducement to large capitalists to engage in retail operations"; these "generally found [it] a better speculation to attract a large business by underselling others, than merely to divide the field of employment with them" (p. 253).[16]

A word on simple monopoly. Mill recognized that increasing returns mitigated against competition; in the context of increasing returns he observed that "where competitors are so few, they always end up agreeing not to compete. They may run a race of cheapness to ruin a new candidate, but as soon as he has established his footing they come to terms with him" (p. 142). Public utilities provide a case in point; it is to gas and water that Mill alludes in referring to trades which "from the nature of the case, [are] confined to so few hands, that profits may admit of being kept up by a combination among the dealers" (p. 405). Though he justified regulation of public utilities, governments were also charged with unjustifiable encouragement of barriers-to-entry (III, pp. 927–928).

A "strict or absolute" monopoly—a single seller—was easily dealt with as the limiting case, with Mill providing a nice statement of the total revenue function, which implies revenue rather than profit maximization as the objective: "The monopolist can fix the value as high as he pleases, short of what the consumer either could not or would not pay; but he can only do so by limiting the supply" (p. 468). While Mill formally restricted the scientific treatment of pricing to the competitive case and designated monopoly, whether natural or artificial, as a "disturbing cause," it was in fact a structure that had "always been allowed for by political economists" (II p. 239), and Mill made use of the tools of economic analysis in its treatment.

The Advantages of "Competition" Summarized

Mill regarded competition as providing "the best security for cheapness," that is, for efficiency (V, pp. 731–732), and he welcomed policy measures encouraging the development of an institutional framework and pattern of behavior most conducive to its effective operation. At the same time, he conceded to Socialists that competition provided no assurance of *quality*; here socialists had "really made out the existence not only of a great evil, but of one which grows and tends to grow with the growth of population and wealth."[17] For

> [e]ven in commerce properly so called—the legitimate province of self-interest —where it is enough if the ruling motive is limited by simple honesty . . . the vastness of the field, the greatness of the stakes now played for, and the increasing difficulty to the public in judging rightly of transactions or of character, are making the principle of competition bring forth a kind of effects, the cure of which will have to be sought somewhere else than in the corrective influence of competition itself (V, p. 625).

Mill expressed concern with probity; he was not starry-eyed about competition where the institutional framework was inappropriate.

Mill's competition is not of the modern price-taking variety; it allows firms a price-making ability and might be satisfied merely by the possibility of free entry. And there is competition as a *discovery process* to be considered.[18] The *dynamic* role of competition is much emphasized as a stimulus to innovation:

> When relieved from the immediate stimulus of competition, producers and dealers grow indifferent to the dictates of their ultimate pecuniary interest; preferring to the most hopeful prospects, the present ease of adhering to routine. A person who is already thriving, seldom puts himself out of his way to commence even a lucrative improvement, unless urged by the additional motive

of fear lest some rival should suplant him by getting possession of it before him (III, p. 928).

In a reaction to socialist claims, Mill insisted on competition as a discovery process and essential source of progress into the foreseeable future:

> It is the common error of Socialists to overlook the natural indolence of mankind; their tendency to be passive, to be the slaves of habit, to persist indefinitely in a course once chosen. Let them once attain any state of existence which they consider tolerable, and the danger to be apprehended is that they will thenceforth stagnate; will not exert themselves to improve, and by letting their faculties rust, will lose even the energy required to preserve them from deterioration. Competition may not be the best conceivable stimulus, but it is at present a necessary one, and no one can foresee the time when it will not be indispensable to progress (p. 795).[19]

The same emphasis on *pressure* stimulating innovatory measures—in fact, it is extended to invention—emerges also in the discussion of the falling profit-rate tendency. While technical change is frequently treated as an exogenous disturbance (e.g., II, pp. 98–99; III, pp. 942–945), allowance is made for *induced* technology and its application: "The curtailment of profit, and the consequent increased difficulty in making a fortune or obtaining a subsistence by the employment of capital, may act as stimulus to invention, and to the use of them when made" (III, p. 827). The treatment of technical progress purely as a "disturbing cause" is clearly inappropriate. Indeed, Mill himself speaks of the profit-technology relation as a "tendency," thus according it the same status, with all its implications, accorded the pressure on profits of scarce land: "the artificial abstraction of a portion of profits would have a real tendency to accelerate improvements in production."[20]

The Universal Method of Political Economy

Mill's own conception of political economy eschewed all universalist connotations. The false perspective of contemporary political economists who suggested that their subject, founded on axioms reflecting contemporary conditions, was of universal relevance, Mill hoped would weaken with a better appreciation of ethology (VIII, p. 906). At the same time, he insisted on the utility of the subject constructed on a relatively narrow axiomatic base, and this because "its method of investigation is applicable universally . . ." (p. 904). Thus in the course of his criticism of English economists who "attempt to construct a permanent fabric out of transitory materials," and suppose that output is shared among three distinct classes (laborers, capitalists, and landlords), all "free agents, permitted in law and fact to set upon their labour, their capital, and their land, whatever price they are able to get for it" (IV, pp. 225–226), Mill added a qualification that withdraws the barbs as far as concerns the method itself: "Though many of its conclusions are only locally true, its method of investigation is applicable universally" (p. 226).

The so-called "universal" applicability of the method of political economy does *not* conflict with the position that "only through the principle of competition has political economy any pretension to the character of science." Mill was quite explicit regarding the specific range of institutions intended:

> The conclusions of the science, being all adapted to a society thus constituted, require to be revised wherever they are applied to any other. They are inapplicable where the only capitalists are the landlords, and the labourers are their property; as in the West Indies. They are inapplicable where the universal landlord is the State; as in India. They are inapplicable where the agricultural labourer is generally the owner both of the land itself and of the capital, as in France; or of the capital only, as in Ireland. We might greatly prolongue this enumeration.

Mill adds that "whoever has mastered with the degree of precision which is attainable the laws which, under free competition, determine the rent, profits, and wages, received by landlords, capitalists, and labourers, in a state of society in which the three classes are completely separate, will have no difficulty in determining the very different laws which regulate the distribution of the produce among the classes interested in it, in any of the states of cultivation and landed property set forth in the foregoing extract" (VIII, p. 904), a reference to the range of specific institutional arrangements outlined above.

The general applicability of the method of political economy does not, therefore, extend maximization principles to all possible cases including those involving custom or gift or force, which were not amenable to economic analysis and would have to be dealt with by "some other" science. Mill was pointing rather to the working out of the maximization hypothesis within a wide variety of institutional arrangements in addition to the capitalist-exchange system but involving something akin to a competitive frame of reference.[21]

The Laws of Production and Distribution

Mill's famous distinction between the *immutable* "laws of production" and the *malleable* "laws of distribution," if tenable, would be profoundly significant for a theory of economic policy. As for the "laws and conditions of the production of wealth"—such as the constraint imposed on industry by capital, diminishing agricultural returns, the differential effects on capital of productive and unproductive consumption (savings vs. consumption)—these "partake the character of physical truths. There is nothing optional or arbitrary in them" (II, p. 199). Production is given priority in the sequence of production, distribution, and exchange to convey the notion of universally applicable constraints on social policy. In particular, on the "laws of production" was based the need for *population control*, the simple moral being that "a greater number of people cannot, in any given state of civilization, be collectively so well provided for as a smaller. The niggardliness of nature, not the injustice of society, is the cause of the penalty attached to over-population" (p. 188). The error of confounding "necessities arising from the nature of things, and those created by social arrangements" was responsible for two sorts of misconceptions, causing some economists "to class the merely temporary truths of their subject among its permanent and universal laws," and others "to mistake the permanent laws of Production (such as those on which the necessity is grounded of restraining population) for temporary accidents arising from the existing constitution of society—which those who would frame a new system of social arrangements, are at liberty to disregard" (pp. 455–456). This latter error, characterizing what was to be the Marxist perspective on Malthusianism, Mill intended to undermine by according priority to production. But his target extended to paternalist Conservative apologists for the status quo who, for their own self-interested reasons, rejected population control (XIII, p. 641).

The formal categorization of laws implies that political economy can generate not even a tentative explanation of wealth differentials geographically or temporally, since it considers the narrowest range of determinants—allocative efficiency and changing labor and capital supply in the presence of decreasing and increasing returns—relegating various qualitative determinants (knowledge, physical energy, organization) to the ceteris paribus pound as the subject matter of other sciences. In fact, it is only if the state of knowledge—the same holds for physical energy and organization—is placed on a par with the "properties of nature" that the distinction between production and distribution can be made, since once knowledge is recognized as an endogenous variable from the perspective of political economy the notion of "physical" laws of production is untenable. Fortunately, Mill by no means adopted in practice the narrow perspective implied by the categorization. Consider the following statement on the scope of political economy:

> In so far as the economical condition of nations turns upon the state of physical knowledge, it is a subject for the physical sciences, and the arts founded on them. But in so far as the causes are moral or psychological, dependent on institutions and social relations, or on the principles of human nature, their investigation belongs not to physical, but to moral and social science, and is the object of what is called Political Economy (II, pp. 20–21).

The dependence of the "economical condition of nations" on "institutions and social relations" alludes to the notion that productive organization—and thus productivity—is in very large part an institutional and social matter. The analyses of the impact on productivity of the joint-stock arrangement, of different systems of land tenure, of inheritance law, of poor relief systems, of civil protection, all demonstrate that production *is* "malleable." Moreover, as we shall see, Mill is clear that its "malleability," as far as it turns upon organization, actually *does* fall within the domain of the economist. And the same can be said of knowledge, as is apparent from the widening of the scope of political economy to cover activities not motivated by maximizing behavior, and the role accorded such behavior in decisions regarding innovation.

In addition to the neglect of the "universally" present phenomenon of land scarcity and its consequences, Mill complained of a typical failure to recognize features common to a wide variety of distributional arrangements, a failure resulting from excessive attention to the outward forms of the familiar capitalist-exchange system. Partly to counter this danger he placed distribution before exchange.

Mill thus adopted a Marx-like approach to the source of profits, rejecting the popular belief that profits depended on prices, reflecting a failure to look below "the outside surface of the economical machinery of society" (p. 410).[22] Profits arose rather from the fact that labor works for a longer time than is required to reproduce its own subsistence (p. 411), money constituting merely the *machinery* of the exchange process (pp. 71–72, 83, 86*n*; III, p. 455).

More generally, the laws of distribution were said to be "regulated by the same principles when paid in money, as they would be if apportioned in kind" under different social arrangements (III, p. 698). For example, wage-rate determination in terms of the "ratio between population and capital" would still hold good even "if all the capital in the world were the property of one association, or if the capitalists among whom it is shared maintained each an establishment for the production of every article consumed in the community, exchange of commodities having no existence" (pp. 695–696). And indeed, the inverse profit-wage relation was "a law of arithmetic" that necessarily holds true: "If the labourers really get more, that is, get the produce of more labour a smaller percentage must remain for profit. From this law of Distribution resting as it does on a law of arithmetic, there is no escape. The mechanism of Exchange and Price may hide it from us, but his quite powerless to alter it" (p. 479). The primary message Mill sought to convey is that even in a noncapitalist system the same basic distributional problems arise; a technical divorce of distribution and valuation within the context of an exchange system is not intended.

Profit, despite its source in "surplus labour time," emerges as a nonexploitative income required to assure the appropriate supply of capital, with Mill insisting on a regular positive relation between the surplus relative to the capital stock and the growth rate of capital: "[It is] an almost infallible consequence of any reduction of profits to retard the rate of accumulation" (p. 843). This regular functional relation applies also in a socialist system, the required interest rate there dictated by the chosen rate of growth of the national economy: "the renumeration for capital is to be such as is found sufficient to induce savings from individual consumption, in order to increase the common stock to such a point as is desired" (V, p. 747). Evidently, wage income cannot be allowed to consume the entire national income. Consistent with this perspective is Mill's isolation as the main problem of capitalism, not the payment of profits as a deduction from wage income but the excessive size of the class of distributors, a matter of *inefficiency* due to imperfections of competition.

The formal dichotomy between production and distribution represents the latter as "a matter of human institution solely. The things once there, mankind, individually or collectively, can do with them as they like. . . . The distribution of wealth, therefore, depends on the laws and customs of society" (II, pp. 199–200). This formal designation is in practice undermined by the distributive constraints common to various institutional arrangements just outlined. Distributive "rules" are, true enough, "what the opinions and feelings of the ruling portion of the community make them, and are very different in different ages and countries" but, given the state of opinion and the corresponding distributive system, there will be certain results that follow and that are as much "immutable" as are the laws of production: "We have here to consider, not the causes, but the consequences, of the rules according to which wealth may be distributed. Those, at least, are as little arbitrary, and have as much the character of physical laws, as the laws of production" (p. 200); and though governments or nations have the power of deciding what institutions shall exist, they cannot arbitrarily determine how those institutions shall work."

The distinction between the laws of production and distribution, understood literally, therefore proved a brittle one. The "inflexibility" of the laws of production applies only when key determinants of productivity are held constant; the "modifiability" of the laws of distribution does not apply to the consequences flowing from choice of particular distributive forms. But the mutually exclusive contrast was not in fact called for to convey Mill's message regarding constraints of a technical order that must be faced under all forms of social organization, and the dependence of such organization itself upon human will. Taken in this light we are close to the distinction between problems bearing only on efficiency and problems involving value judgment.[23]

Productive Organization and Motivation

Though the task of *rationalizing* empirical regularities—especially those relating to progress—remained to be undertaken, Mill sought wherever possible to provide some foundation for various empirical results in laws of behavior, thereby enhancing the significance of deductive theory as a basis for policy recommentation. We shall illustrate by the attempt to rationalize the observed impact of productive organization on efficiency and population control.[24]

Mill had a low opinion of the efficiency of *hired labor* (II, p. 137). As for hired managers, prudence required that they be somehow controlled by the capitalist *or that they be stimulated by a share in profits*, for "[m]anagement . . . by hired servants, who have no interest in the result but that of preserving their salaries, is proverbially inefficient" (pp. 401–402). Their "fidelity and zeal" were assured by fear of dismissal and by conscience in the case of routine tasks; but "to carry on a great business successfully, requires a hundred things which, as they cannot be defined beforehand, it is impossible to convert into distinct and positive obligations" (p. 137). Nonetheless, Mill maintained that Adam Smith's negative evaluation on similar grounds of the joint-stock organization entailing the divorce of ownership and control was exaggerated. For Smith had overlooked various countervailing considerations. Thus the disadvantages might be reduced by resort to some form of profit-sharing relating the "interest of the employees with the pecuniary success of the concern," and by attraction of "a class of candidates superior to the common average intelligence," opportunities enhanced in large concerns (p. 139). The net result of such devices and the careful selection of candidates "often raises the quality of the service much above that which the generality of masters are capable of rendering to themselves" (p. 140).

While, therefore, Mill, in discussing alternative methods of organization and proposing reforms, generally bases himself on apparent empirical regularities, when it comes to joint-stock organization he attempts to rationalize the observations in terms of more basic behavior characteristics. This applies equally to the impact on productivity (and on population control) exerted by alternative forms of agricultural organization. In both contexts decision making based on profit maximization provides a rationalization of empirical material, in an inverse deductive procedure.

Mill examined the qualifications required when cultivation is undertaken, not for profit by the capitalist but for subsistence by the laborer (peasant ownership, metayage, and allotment holding) who seeks "not an investment for his little capital, but an advantageous employment for his time and labour" (III, p. 499). Here many of the tools or theorems of competitive analysis prove indispensable, and Mill expressed the hope that "further adaptations of the theory of value to the varieties of existing or possible industrial systems" would be undertaken by "the intelligent reader" (p. 501). His analysis of various contemporary forms of land tenure reflects a preoccupation with the empirical validity of the maximization axiom in a wide variety of alternative institutional contexts. Appeal to "custom" often indicates an admission of ignorance; but there is a surprisingly little on custom in the analysis of land tenure and its impact on productivity (and population) where the principles of "competition" based on maximization axioms predominate. This same procedure again confirms the untenability of a strict distinction between laws of production and distribution in that the distributional arrangements are shown to play strategically upon production.

There is also the matter of population control: "supposing a peasantry to possess land . . . sufficient for their comfortable support, are they more, or less likely, to fall from this state of comfort through improvident multiplication, than if they were living in an equally comfortable manner as hired labourers?" (II, p. 283). There was direct and indirect empirical evidence of a negative impact of peasant proprietorship on population growth from Switzerland and Norway (pp. 285*ff.*). The rationale in terms of motivation offered is that "every peasant can satisfy himself from evidence which he can fully appreciate, whether his piece of land can be made to support several families in the same comfort as it supports one," evidence not available to the day laborer (p. 284).[25] Moreover, the positive impact of peasant proprietorship on productivity and accumulation created a presumption in favor of the behavioral axiom selected: "Is it likely that a state of economical relations so conducive to frugality and prudence in every other respect, should be prejudicial to it in the cardinal point of increase of population?" (p. 283).

The facts of the case thus vindicated or, rather, could best be accounted for by the axiomatic basis of the self-interest model. Even so, Mill warned against positive prediction in the application of the model to future cases, considering the possible intervention of disturbing causes; in the Belgian case, for example, there was the impact of the church to consider (p. 292). And the important theme that "Cultivation spontaneously finds out that organization that suits it best" (p. 293)—illustrating one aspect of the case for competition—justified Mill's further argument that if there exists in special circumstances excessive numbers under peasant proprietorship, it could not be presumed that the *technical* farming unit was too small: "a subdivision of occupancy is not an inevitable consequence of even undue multiplication among peasant proprietors."

Manpower Allocation and Competition

When operating effectively, competition assured a just structure of wages as well as prices: "In truth, when competition is perfectly free on both sides, its tendency is not specially either to raise or to lower the price of articles, but to equalise it; to level inequalities of remuneration, and to reduce all to a general average, a result which, in so far as realised (no doubt very imperfectly), is, on Socialistic principles, desirable" (V, p. 729). There was no tradeoff between efficiency and equity in this regard. Mill's charges against contemporary capitalism relate—apart from inefficiency due to market imperfections—to the lack of distributive justice and also to *dependency* on "the will of an employer," not to competition as such:

> No longer enslaved or made dependent by force of law, the great majority are so by force of poverty; they are still chained to a place, to an occupation, and to conformity with the will of an employer, and debarred by the accident of birth both from the enjoyments, and from the mental and moral advantages, which others inherit without exertion and independently of desert (p. 710).

Under these conditions rewards were divorced from either merit or effort; it was not the case that everyone "willing to undergo a fair share of . . . labor and abstinence could attain a fair share of the fruits" (pp. 714–715); birth, accident, and opportunity were the ruling determinants. The Socialist contention that much "crime, vice and folly" resulted from poverty in contemporary conditions was also justified.

As for policy implications, the impediments to a satisfactory competitive outcome had to be taken into account. It was required that certain irrational forms of behavior be corrected, that the *aggregate* labor market be in equilibrium, and that social and financial obstacles to upward mobility be removed.[26] In these respects the standard Smithian competitive wage analysis was inadequate; for it presumed the labor market as a whole to be in equilibrium, whereas in the event of general unemployment the differentials are distorted: "when the supply of labor so far exceeds the demand that to find employment at all is an uncertainty, and to be offered it on any terms a favour, the case is totally the reverse. Desirable laborers, those whom every one is anxious to have, can still exercise a choice. The undesirable must take what they can get" (p. 383). For this reason, and also because of various natural and artificial monopolies, wage differentials were "generally in an opposite direction to the equitable principle of compensation erroneously represented by Adam Smith as the general law of the remuneration of labor." This constitutes an original perspective on the linkage between macro- and micro-economics of the very first importance engendered by empirical observation.

The reference to "natural and artificial monopolites" involves a second major breakaway. Smith's allowances for educational costs (even when supplemented by allowance for legal restrictions on mobility) did not suffice to explain ruling differentials, for the costs even of a minimal education and of maintenance during the training period "exclude the greater body of the laboring people from the possibility of any such competition" as would reduce the "monopoly" return of the skilled (p. 386). Here we encounter the celebrated concept of *noncompeting industrial groups* reflecting social and financial obstacles to upward mobility. Despite broader educational opportunities, there was still "a much greater disparity than can be accounted for on the principle of competition" (p. 387). Various "customary" expenses attaching to some trades, such as the cost of maintaining clothes and appearance, further hindered entry.[27]

Notwithstanding the criticisms of Smithian analysis, Mill played down somewhat the implications of his allowance for noncompeting groups. He continued to emphasize in labor-market analysis the notion of an *average* wage and in price analysis that of competitive cost price turning on labor and capital mobility between alternative uses. It may well be that this reflects his confidence in an actual and prospective breakdown of barriers that promised to reinforce the relevance of orthodox competitive theory. As he phrased it, although "[i]n this country there are few kinds of labor of which the remuneration would not be lower than it is, if the employer took the full advantage of competition," competition "must be regarded, in the present state of society as the principal regulator of wages, and custom or individual character only as a modifying circumstance, and that in a comparatively slight degree" (p. 337).

The Population Problem

The formal definition of political economy incorporates reference to the "laws of human nature." Mill's aggregative theorizing, however, does not always require extension back to individual maximizing behavior. Such is the case of the "wage-fund" approach to the labor market in its simplest *static* version. On it he based a barrage of conclusions regarding labor policy, reflecting the position that the condition of the laboring class "can be bettered in no other way than by altering that proportion [between capital and population] to their advantage; and every scheme for their benefit, which does not proceed on this as its foundation, is, for all permanent purposes, a delusion" (II, pp. 340–343). In these terms he countered the view "that the government without providing additional funds, could create additional employment" by means of tariffs or other protective measures (p. 64). And in terms of this minimal theoretical structure he formulated the equilibrating function of wage movements—"Goods can only be lowered in price by competition, to the point which calls forth buyers sufficient to take them off; and wages can only be lowered by competition until room is made to admit all the laborers to a share in the distribution of the wages-fund" but no further (p. 356)—and applied it against minimum-wage proposals and also to emphasize that competition is not *necessarily* adverse to labor's interests.

Mill's perspective on labor policy is nicely captured in his belief that "the greater part of the good [government] can do [for the poor]" is "indirect, & consists in stimulating & guiding the energy & prudence of the people themselves" (XIII, p. 645). Similarly, Mill attacked the paternalism of the "young Englanders" (represented by *The Times*) as based on thin air, contrasting with "those fundamental principles which one did think had been put for ever out of the reach of controversy by Adam Smith, Malthus, & others, designed to persuade labor that it is the business of others to take care of their condition, without any self control on their own part" (pp. 643–644). His message was a positive one. The Malthusian doctrine "indicat[ed] the sole means of realizing that improvability by securing full employment at high wages to the whole laboring population through a voluntary restriction of the increase of their numbers" (I, p. 107); it did not, "as vulgarly supposed, imply that in one's opinions on social arrangements one looks only to amount of production & not to the producers" (XIII, p. 661).

Mill's position is best appreciated against a theoretical background that perceives of competition as potentially acting in labor's favor by assuring low prices and high wages in the appropriate market circumstances.

"Socialists generally," he complained, "and even the most enlightened of them, have a very imperfect and one-sided notion of the operation of competition" (V, p. 729). Mill did not actually consider the competitive wage as the *just* wage, and this largely because the contemporary distribution of property governing the framework of the market was itself not established on equitable principles. The competitive outcome was, however, acceptable *faute de mieux* in contemporary society and viewed as such by general opinion:

> I can conceive Socialism, in which the division of the produce of labor is made among all, either according to the rule of equality (Communism) or according to any other *general* rule which may be considered more just than absolute equality. But under a system of private property in past accumulations in which no general rule can be laid down, I think that to give any one the power of deciding according to his own views of equity without a general rule would only perpetuate & envenom instead of healing the quarrel between capital & labor. The only thing which people will in these circumstances submit to as final, is the law of necessity, that is, the demand & supply of the market, *tested* (when not otherwise known) by the result of a strike. All that I consider practicable in the present state of society is to strengthen the weaker side in the competition, which can only be done by the prudence, forethought, wise restraint, & habit of cooperation, of the working people themselves (XV, p. 749).

As for the legitimate steps "to strengthen the weaker side in the competition," one must keep in mind both Mill's support of unions and property-reform proposals.

The capital-population nexus, when extended to the *growth* context, provides the full-fledged basis for population control and in this dynamic context motivation proves to be of the essence with respect to both variables. That the growth model was not designed for positive prediction is clear from the obvious fact that Mill was engaged in an exercise in persuasion designed to play upon the key behavioral patterns. He in fact rejected the forecast by socialist critics of secularly falling real wages, tracing it to "ignorance of economic facts, and of the causes by which the economic phenomena of society as it is, are actually determined" (V, p. 727). Even population pressure was no longer an "irrepressable tendency" and an "increasing evil," considering increased prudence, the acceleration of capital accumulation, and easier emigration (p. 728). Mill insisted on the fact of rising living standards and also on the relatively limited effect that even a full-fledged redistribution of income would have in raising the lower paid (p. 736).

What, then, was intended by the so-called "tendency" of population to increase faster than subsistence? Nothing more than that, in the absence of technical change and with no slackening of population growth, a decline in marginal product and the real wage must occur. But "the progress of improvement has a counteracting operation, and allows of increased numbers without any deterioration, and even consistently with a higher average of comfort" (II, pp. 188–189). In arguing thus, Mill was following directly in Malthus's footsteps. But despite this common ground there are differences regarding the role of self-interest and the free-rider problem.

Allowance was made by Malthus for state-financed education programs designed to inculcate the principle of prudential control (*An Essay on the Principle of Population*, 1890 [1826], pp. 533–534). Beyond this nothing more was required of the state: "The happiness of the whole is the result of the happiness of individuals, and to begin first with them. No co-operation is required. Every step tells. He who performs his duty faithfully will reap the full fruits of it, whatever may be the number of others who fail" (p. 457). It was held against communism that resort might have to be made to legal control of family size and the age of marriage (p. 357).

Mill was at one with Malthus regarding the need to inculcate by state-supported education the principle that population control holds the key to living standards; and he emphasized the so-called problem of poverty—that to rise above it required the actual experience of significantly higher standards (CW, II, p. 342). He also emphasized the peculiar difficulties attached to the system of hired labor: "The parent who has land to leave, is perfectly able to judge whether the children can live upon it or not: but people who are supported by wages, see no reason why their sons should be unable to support themselves in the same way, and trust accordingly to chance" (p. 284). But he was exercised by the free-rider dilemma. Accordingly, behavior regarding family size, motivated by a sense of social responsibility, or at the least socially oriented behavior enforced by public opinion, was required. In these terms he answered the free-rider objection to Malthus that the greater the confidence in the general exercise of prudence, the less motive for any individual to behave responsibly. The objection was valid, but "what is wanted is, not that the good should abstain in order that the selfish may indulge, but such a state of opinion as may deter the selfish from this kind of intemperance by stamping it as disgraceful" (V, p. 449). The solution hinged on a reform of public opinion. Once the Malthusian idea had taken hold among workers, "every laborer [would look] . . . upon every other who had more than the number of children which the circumstances of society allowed to each, as doing him a wrong—as filling up the place which he was entitled to share" (II, p. 371). Here is added an important generalization regarding motive: "Any one who supposes that this state of opinion would not have a great effect on conduct, must be profoundly ignorant of human nature; can never have considered how large a portion of the motives which induce the generality of men to take care even of their own interest, is derived from regard to opinion—from the expectation of being disliked or despised for not doing it". Assuming widespread acceptance of the foregoing opinion except on the part of that minority "in the habit of making light of social obligations generally," a case might be made out for legal control, "just as in many other cases of the progress of opinion, the law ends by enforcing against recalcitrant minorities, obligations which to be useful must be general, and which, from a sense of their utility, a large majority have voluntarily consented to take upon themselves" (p. 372).

Control of population was one consideration in the evaluation of the relative merits of communism and private property. A potential problem existed under *all* institutional arrangements, and conceivably the case for communism might turn out strongest, considering its potential in stimulating and enforcing a sense of social responsibility in individuals (p. 205). For since the cause of falling standards would be crystal clear to all (there being no employers or privileged classes to blame), "opinion could not fail to reprobate, and if reprobation did not suffice, to repress by penalties of some description . . . culpable self-indulgence at the expense of the community" (p. 206).

Here, then, Malthus and Mill diverged. Mill occupied the middle ground between Malthus who saw in self-interest the solution to excess population, and in fact objected to communism precisely because it would have to resort to measures of enforcement and punishment; and those who found the solution in communism and only in communism. Mill did not finally commit himself. He had a horror of centralized systems, and his more positive comments on other forms of socialism were qualified, for the full potential of private property had not yet been revealed. Moreover, he himself declaimed against paternalism in matters affecting the labor market (IX, pp. 374–375).[28]

On the Desirability of Economic Growth

Starting out from stationariness, an increase in the "effective desire of accumulation"—a reduction in the minimum supply price of capital—would create the *potential* for new growth, as will technological improvement. The message of Mill's famous chapter "Of the Stationary State" is that any new potential for expansion should ideally be taken out in higher real wages, preeminently in the form of increased leisure: "A stationary condition of capital and population implies no stationary state of human improvement. . . . Even the industrial arts might be as earnestly and as successfully cultivated, with this sole difference, that instead of serving no purpose but the increase of wealth, industrial improvements would produce their legitimate effect, that of abridging labor" (III, p. 756).

But this new view on policy—actually intimated by Malthus and Chalmers long before—does not mean that Mill disposed of the old growth economics. The stationary state was that much closer with population control than without, and there is no gainsaying the new look at distribution. Yet Mill was thoroughly aware that accumulation and population were proceeding apace, so that stationariness was not in sight, rendering his recommendations purely academic. Indeed, in the Britain of his day a steady per capital wage and a constant return on capital were achieved without population control because of the extremely high rate of capital accumulation reflecting new technology: "There is room in the world, no doubt, and even in old countries, for a great increase of population, supposing the arts of life to go on improving, and capital to increase." In any event, the recommendation itself is riddled with internal weaknesses which we shall briefly consider.

Technical change in Mill's stationary state provides the source for increasing leisure; indeed, stationariness of population would enhance productivity by effacing diminishing returns: "Mankind would . . . have the full benefit of all improvements in agriculture, or in the arts subsidiary to it, and there would be no difference, in this respect, between the products of agriculture and those of manufactures" (p. 712).[29] But the presumption regarding ongoing technical progress is partly wishful thinking since a technologically progressive manufacturing had been specifically linked to *expansion*.[30] The extension of joint-stock and other forms of complex organization he saw as determined by the progress of wealth and reinforcing such progress (see the earlier section on "Productive Organization and Motivation").[31]

Even assuming ongoing technological advance in the stationary state, there are worrying possibilities. Capital-absorbing innovation necessarily has a negative effect on the global "wages fund" and, therefore, on either employment or per capita wages or both. That is the alpha and omega of the Ricardian analysis of machinery that Mill accepted. The whole problem would be "temporary" in the event of net savings sufficient to compensate for any shortfall in employment opportunities; the extent and speed of adoption of such technologies relative to the generation of new savings become the key issue. And here, Mill, like Ricardo, was optimistic. For a variety of reasons, the adverse impact of new technology involved "a case abstractedly possible [rather] than one which is frequently realized in fact" (II, p. 134). For one thing, the extent and rapidity of adoption was relatively slow compared with net accumulation in the progressive economies of the day (p. 97). Further reason for optimism lay in the positive stimulus to savings engendered by the effects of new technology—effects on both the "ability" and "motive" to save (p. 98). But these optimistic prognostications fall away in a stationary state; Mill was silent on the shadow of "conversion" with its potentially adverse effects on labor.

Furthermore, in stationary conditions, as far as net domestic investment was concerned, capital exportation portended trouble. Mill himself points to a case where a floor to the return on domestic capital is imposed by returns abroad above the minimum rate corresponding to zero net savings such that "all further accumulations would go abroad" (III, p. 746). This was not the issue in contemporary Britain only because there net domestic investment was proceeding apace, with the return on capital held roughly constant above the practical minimum.

The process of profit-rate equalization with its efficiency implications is said to be aided "[i]n a rapidly progressive state of capital" since this avoids the necessity for an actual contraction of sectors (II, p. 407). There is reference to potential class hostility in a stationary or slowly growing system. For "to work at the bidding and for the profit of another, without any interest in the work—the price of their labor being adjusted in hostile competition, one side demanding as much and the other paying as little as possible—is not, even when wages are high, a satisfactory state to human beings of educated intelligence, who have ceased to think themselves naturally inferior to those whom they serve" (III, p. 766). A working-class status might be tolerable in "a new country rapidly increasing in wealth and population" (such as Australia and North America) where upward mobility to the employing class was an option; but "something else is required when wealth increases slowly, or has reached the stationary state, when positions, instead of being more mobile, would tend to be much more permanent than at present, and the condition of any portion of mankind could only be desirable, if made desirable from the first."[32]

There is, then, no policy bias against the desirability of growth. There are too many potential disadvantages attached to stationariness to allow one to consider Mill's chapter on the stationary state as much more than day-dreaming. And his concern for a desirable pattern of distribution as an end in itself did not give the investigation of equilibrium conditions—for which *static* theory is appropriate—precedence over growth theory.

A New Perspective on Macro-Economic Policy

Mill's adherence to the Law of Markets did not preclude recognition of slack periods when available capital is kept idle.

> When there is what is called a stagnation . . . then work people are dismissed, and those who are retained must submit to a reduction of wages: though in these cases there is neither more nor less capital than before. . . . If we suppose, what in strictness is not absolutely impossible, that one of these fits of briskness or of stagnation should affect all occupations at the same time, wages altogether might undergo a rise or a fall . . . (II, pp. 338–339).

Similarly, "capital may be temporarily unemployed, as in the case of unsold goods, or funds that have not yet found an investment: during that interval it does not set in motion any industry" (p. 65). Idle capital in these contexts refers not only to unsold stocks of goods but also to money funds available for investment in wage payments or other disbursements. What is involved is a well-considered supplementing of the proposition that "industry is limited by capital," by a function describing the state of aggregate demand for final goods—or, what is equivalent, the net excess demand for money.[33]

The allowance for general excess commodity supply must be seen in proper context, namely the recognition of regular cyclical fluctuations—the fact that "[e]xcept during short periods of transition, there is almost always either great briskness of business or great stagnation" (IV, p. 275). As for to the "quiescent" period, "nothing [tends] to engender in any considerable portion of the mercantile public a desire to extend their operations. The producers produce and the dealers purchase only their usual stocks, having no expectation of a more than usually rapid vent for them"—in contrast with the "unusual extension" of the speculative or "expectant" state where there exists some stimulus which "exciting more than usual hopes of profit, gives increased briskness to business," such as short crops, import restrictions, or new foreign markets (III, pp. 662–663). But quiescence itself allows for expansion: "Each person transacts his ordinary amount of business, and no more; or increases it only in correspondence with the increase of his capital or connexion, or with the gradual growth of the demand for his commodity, occasioned by the public prosperity." And that a quiescent period entails expansion constitutes, in fact, the necessary condition for the generation of regular cyclical fluctuations. I allude to cyclical consequences flowing from the downward "tendency" of the profit rate. The relationship is a mutual one, for while the profit-rate trend engenders speculation and the cycle, various capital losses associated with the cycle play back on the profit rate itself.

That cyclical fluctuations are a direct outcome of the falling profit rate provides a fine instance of Mill's attempt to rationalize observed relationships in terms of individual behavior:

> [The] gradual process of accumulation . . . in the great commercial countries, is sufficiently rapid to account for the almost periodic recurrence of these fits of speculation; since, when a few years have elapsed without a crisis, and no new and tempting channels for investment have been opened in the meantime, there is always found to have occurred in those few years so large an increase of capital seeking investment, as to have lowered considerably the rate of interest . . . [which] tempts the possessor to incur hazards in hopes of a more considerable return (p. 651).
>
> . . . the diminished scale of all safe gains, inclines persons to give a ready ear to any projects which hold out, though at the risk of loss, the hope of a higher rate of profit; and speculations ensue, which, with the subsequent revulsions, destroy or transfer to foreigners, a considerable amount of capital, produce a temporary rise of interest and profit, make room for fresh accumulations, and the same round is recommended (p. 742).[34]

The falling profit rate provides a splendid illustration of the notion of tendency to reflect not a necessarily observable trend, but one force among other possibly conflicting forces playing on a particular variable: ". . . it would require but a short time to reduce profits to the minimum, if capital continued to increase at its present rate, and no circumstances having a tendency to raise the rate of profit occurred in the meantime. The expansion of capital would soon reach its ultimate boundary, if the boundary itself did not continually open and leave more space" (p. 739). Constancy of the profit rate and of the real wage despite extraordinarily rapid accumulation and population growth characterized contemporary Britain, precisely because of changes in ceteris paribus conditions on which the "trend" is predicated, namely improved technology and capital losses of various kinds *including losses relating to cyclical fluctuations*—unsustainable capital projects during speculation periods, and "unproductive" consumption during the depressions that follow (p. 741).[35]

Mill established that over recent decades the secular return on capital had remained unchanged at a little over 3%. Though technical change sufficed only partially to counteract the effect of land scarcity in the face of expanding capital, putting downward pressure on the return on capital, that pressure induced wastage and a resumption of the roughly constant trend path; capital exportation also contributed to prevent profits from reaching the minimum (p. 745). The emphasis in this latter respect is on an historically low level compared to the level ruling in foreign countries, such outflows treated as a "disturbing cause," whereby "the decline of profits in England has been arrested. . . . it does what a fire, or an inundation, or a commercial crisis would have done: it carries off a part of the increase of capital from which the reduction of profits proceeds" (p. 746). In the absence of such outflows the impact of technical progress would not have sufficed to balance that of land scarcity and allow "a tolerably equal struggle against the downward tendency of profits" (p. 741). The *net* outcome of the various conflicting tendencies actually at work assured a constant trend path of the return on capital with fluctuations about it of a cyclical order.[36]

The policy implications flowing from the foregoing analysis of contemporary Britain are remarkable: "The theory of the effect of accumulation on profits . . . materially alters many of the practical conclusions which might otherwise be supposed to follow from the general principles of Political Economy, and which were, indeed, long admitted as true by the highest authorities on the subject" (p. 747). Specifically, in the absence of capital loss of various kinds, the rate of accumulation would be so great on Mill's empirical estimate as to force down the return on capital since technical progress could not in practice be relied on to counteract such heavy pressure on scarce land. The first deduction Mill draws from the fact of a highly active "spirit of accumulation" is that "a sudden abstraction of capital, unless of inordinate amount," need not be feared, for "after a few months or years, there would exist in the country just as much capital as if none had been taken away." At most, "the abstraction, by raising profits and interest, would give a fresh stimulus to the accumulative principle, which would speedily fill up the vacuum" (pp. 747–748). But more likely "the only effect that would ensue, would be that for some time afterwards less capital would be exported, and less thrown away in hazardous speculation."

The conclusion altered entirely the perspective toward government expenditure. The standard warnings by orthodox writers against measures that might reduce the capital stock, or its rate of accumulation, were no longer pertinent. Mill writes indeed as if capital is no longer to be treated as a scarce factor:

> [In] rich, populous, and highly cultivated countries, it is not capital which is the deficient element, but fertile land; and what the legislator should desire and promote, is not a greater aggregate saving, but a greater return to savings, either by improved cultivation, or by access to the produce of more fertile lands in other parts of the globe. In such countries, the government may take any moderate portion of the capital of the country and expend it as revenue, without

> affecting the national wealth: the whole being either drawn from that portion of the annual savings which would otherwise be sent abroad, or being subtracted from the unproductive expenditure of individuals for the next year or two, since every million spent makes room for another million to be saved before reaching the overflowing point (p. 748).

Government funding of emigration is one of the most important of Mill's policy deductions. The capital required for "the most extensive colonization" was likely to be moderate (pp. 748–749); but even in the unlikely event of an absolute decline in the domestic capital stock, the fresh stimulus afforded savings would rapidly make up the deficiency.[37] The new perspective also removed fears flowing from the "conversion" of circulating into fixed capital: "Since even the emigration of capital, or its unproductive expenditure, or its absolute waste, do not in such a country, if confined within any moderate limits, at all diminish the aggregate amount of wages fund—the actual and potential increase in capital being so great—"still less can the mere conversion of a like sum into fixed capital, which continues to be productive, have that effect" (p. 749). These sums, applied, for example, to railways, "are mostly a mere appropriation of the annual overflowing which would otherwise have gone abroad, or been thrown away unprofitably, leaving neither a railway nor any other tangible result" (p. 750).

Mill's favorable attitude toward expenditure of public money "for really valuable, even though industrially unproductive purposes" carries no Keynesian overtones. He had not abandoned the Law of Markets. Any difference of opinion on that matter, he pointed out, "involves radically different conceptions of Political Economy, especially in its practical aspect. On the one view, we have only to consider how a sufficient production can be combined with the best possible distribution but on the other there is a third thing to be considered—how a market can be created for produce, or how production can be limited to the capabilities of the market" (p. 575); and in our present context the same position is reiterated—the downward "tendency" of the profit rate did *not* reflect lack of markets (pp. 739–740). As we have just seen, Mill distinguished between established "general principles of Political Economy" and the practical conclusions drawn therefrom by "the highest authorities," insisting that his new position related specifically to the latter. In brief, increased government spending was not conceived as absorbing otherwise unemployed resources, but rather as promoting desirable public at the expense of misconceived private projects—opera houses in place of a superfluous network of railways—and unproductive private consumption (the cyclical features) but in empirical circumstances entailing ongoing growth of the economy and a simultaneous expansion of the private sector.

The same positive approach toward government expenditure is reflected in the formal treatment of taxation. Where the magnitude of the surplus and the strength of the sociological forces defining the "spirit of accumulation" are high, the standard case against government expenditure is weakened; taxation merely draws on funds that would otherwise have been "wasted" in outflows abroad or in the course of cyclical movements so that both categories of loss are avoided or at least diminished:

> The amount which would be derived, even from a very high legacy duty, in each year, is but a small fraction of the annual increase of capital in such a country; and its abstraction would but make room for saving to an equivalent amount; while the effect of not taking it, is to prevent that amount of saving, or cause the savings, when made, to be sent abroad for investment (III, p. 823).[38]

A distinction, however, is made between forms of taxation that eat into funds potentially available for accumulation, and taxation that has an actual *disincentive* effect by reducing the return on capital. The distinction reflects the proposition that "in rich, populous, and highly cultivated countries . . . what the legislator should desire and promote, is not a greater aggregate saving, but a greater return to savings" (p. 748), for a greater return will automatically generate an increase flow of funds available for domestic investment. In these terms we can appreciate why Mill, notwithstanding his new positive approach toward government spending, still insisted on the need to avoid laying "a tax on industry and economy" by, for example, *progressive* income taxation (p. 811). Similarly, a tax impinging directly or indirectly on profits, he feared, would be "detrimental to the public wealth, and consequently to the means which society possesses of paying any taxes whatever" (p. 830).

Rapid capital accumulation thus remained an objective of policy and doubtless would so remain at least as long as population growth proceeded at a rapid pace. This latter qualification is important. For without it the criticism in the chapter on the stationary state of political economists for identifying "all that is economically desirable with the progressive state,"—"with McCulloch, for example, prosperity does not mean a large production and a good distribution of wealth, but a rapid increase of it; his test of prosperity is high profits . . ." (p. 752)—would be troublesome for he himself called for "a rapid increase of wealth."

Summary and Conclusion

A pervasive theme can be traced through much of the foregoing—the use of competitive pricing as template in approaching policy issues. But Mill never blindly applies the competitive model; on the contrary, he warns against inappropriate application, and his policy recommendations are frequently designed precisely to assure a framework such that the axioms of the model are satisfied. Given the fulfillment of that prerequisite, the competitive model provided the key to efficient resource allocation, and (when applied to the labor market) of an equitable structure of wages.

Competition was of the "classical" variety. It extended beyond statics and constituted a dynamic process encouraging the discovery and adoption of new methods, and guaranteeing the survival of the fittest as in the choice between different firm or farm sizes and organizations. Moreover, Mill was not making a case for the necessary preeminence of the capitalist-exchange system over other institutional arrangements. The competitive model in its static and its dynamic guises, appropriately modified, served in the analysis of a variety of *alternative* institutional frameworks—I allude to the "universality of the method of political economy"—and demonstrated in some cases their efficiency advantage over even an ideally operating capitalist-exchange system. (Though he himself had little to say on socialist pricing schemes, he gave an open invitation to economists to undertake such an investigation.) There are, of course, supplementary value judgments that enter any policy preference, but it would be unjustified to draw too sharp a distinction between the "scientific" objectivity of economic *analysis* and the "non-scientific" subjectivity of economic *policy*. Mill's policy recommendations were based squarely on a systematic body of scientific knowledge under alternative institutional arrangements.

Thus far I have alluded largely to allocation and efficiency issues. Mill also saw in competition applied to the aggregate labor market the best guarantee of working-class living standards, following along Malthus's "prudential" path. He perceived no satisfactory alternative to the free labor market given the system of private property since no "general rule" could be laid down equivalent to communist "equality"; but the impact on population control provided a further index in addition to that of efficiency for any choice between alternative institutional arrangements.

We closed our examination with a discussion of macro-economic considerations. It bears repeating first that Mill hit upon the fact that the desirable operation of competitive pricing is distorted by *general* unemployment. Second, while the Law of Markets throughout ruled supreme, evidence of an unprecedented rate of capital accumulation—itself partly responsible for cyclical instability—led Mill to a wholly new outlook on the merits of public expenditure. (This supplemented a long-held case favoring monetary intervention of a countercyclical order.) But though orthodox classical theory was shown to be extremely flexible in application, even in the context of this radical transformation of policy we find a reiteration of warnings against the potential disincentive impact of taxation measures, especially of progression.

Serious implications for the current training of economists emerge from Mill's theory-application nexus—presuming that policy is indeed our ultimate concern. It points to the necessity for a profound knowledge of actual conditions to allow estimation of the empirical appropriateness of particular models. For a model pertaining (let us say) to the capitalist-exchange system cannot be applied to that system without modification for specific circumstance; while the general appropriateness of the model selected will, of course, depend on the institutional arrangements under investigation, suggesting that exercises in theory must not be limited to games involving capitalists and hired labor. Second, there is the warning emerging in the analysis of the wage structure against a sharp macro-micro divide. And third, there is the requirement for some methodological sophistication to convey the fact that economics, unlike several of the physical sciences, does not have the predictive ability to allow one to say what *will* happen historically. In these respects Mill would have looked aghast at much of what today passes for economics.

Notes

1. The exercise might serve as a guide from Volume I of my *Economics of John Stuart Mill* (1985) on "Theory and Method" to Volume II on "Political Economy." The chapter in fact summarizes the first volume with specific reference to the conversion of economic theory into the real world of policy. I am not concerned in this exercise with the precise timing of Mill's pronouncements or other "scholarly" matters. All references CW are to the *Collected Works of John Stuart Mill*, University of Toronto Press, followed by volume number and page number.

2. On the implied *competitive* requirement see the section. "On the Preclusion of Secular Prediction."

3. The methodological principle involved is that of "composition of causes"—that each individual causal law is at work even if its effects are counterweighed by conflicting tendencies. Thus the law of diminishing returns is operative even when (uncorrected) cost data may not reveal it. This explains Mill's insistence on the law in the very context of a discussion of the "countervailing tendency" of technological progress acting in "habitual antagonism" to it (II, p. 182). It is in this sense that one must understand the phrase "tendency of the returns to a progressive diminution . . . a result of the necessary and inherent conditions of production from the land" (p. 187).

4. The theory of government involved two general principles: that the actions of the average ruler are determined solely by self-interest; and that the sense of identity of interest with the governed is producible only by accountability to the governed.

5. The objective *ideally* was a "synthesis" connecting together theorems relating to the production and distribution of wealth based upon a variety of different behavior patterns—

for example, "custom" as well as "competition"; linking the end of wealth creation with other ends of human activity; and developing the whole (which would amount to a theory of "social statics" or "the mutual actions and reactions of contemporaneous social phenomena") into a full-fledged theory of social progress.

6. Thus in the context of small-scale farming Mill conceded "an absence of science, or at least of theory; and to some extent a deficiency of the spirit of improvement, so far as relates to the introduction of new processes. There is also a want of means to make experiments, which can seldom be made with advantage except by rich proprietors or capitalists" (p. 147). Theoretical science (and not only experimentation and innovation proper) *is* thus to some extent undertaken in commercial undertakings, the expenditure governed by profit calculations.

7. Mill particularly emphasized the need to get the theory of value right (III, p. 456).

8. There is a further problem. The object of verification is to assure the adequacy of a theoretical model for purposes of policy proposal. But since the most appropriate case study for verification of the predictions of the theory is in all likelihood precisely that for which the proposals, based on the model's predictions, are being made "the verification comes too late to be of any avail for practical guidance" (p. 909).

9. Mill insisted that a priori or deductive method professes experience but not *specific* experience of economic facts. By "specific experience" we must understand such relationships as that between Corn Laws and wealth. It cannot refer to the individual axioms, since Mill described the maximizing behavior characteristic of the contemporary commercial and industrial sphere as an "empirical law" albeit of "the lowest kind" and this, like all the axioms, *is* based on "specific" evidence (VII, pp. 454–455).

10. This was written in 1869. But in 1836 Mill had perceived Marx-like consequences of a low return on capital for industrial structure: "the fall of profits, consequent upon the vast increase of population and capital, is rapidly extinguishing the class of small dealers and small producers, from the impossibility of living on their diminished profits, and is throwing business of all kinds more and more into the hands of large capitalists" (XVIII, p. 136).

Also relevant are Mill's observations regarding prospects for cyclical stability (see the section "A New Perspective on Macro-Economic Policy).

11. Here we must bear in mind the so-called "inverse deductive method." The complexity of the quest for a dynamic science of society, extending as it does over the full range of human history and all human activities, and entailing pre-eminently changes in behavior patterns, precluded the direct derivation of laws of progress from the elementary principles of human nature, even in the limited sense of tendencies. Required were preliminary observations of series of effects portraying regularities, that is, the discovery of "empirical laws" of progress, which only at a subsequent stage would be related logically to principles of human nature. This reverses the sequence characterizing the specialist branches of social science where a ratiocinative analysis can often be undertaken on the basis of assumed behavioral, institutional, and technological axioms—actually provisionally assumed axioms, since they are continually subject to verification.

12. One formulation of the subject matter of political economy explicitly incorporates the *competition* requirement. It encompasses the accumulation of wealth and its use in production; the determinants of labor productivity; the legal protection of property; and distribution, or "settling the division of the produce by agreements, under the influence of competition . . . and employing certain expedients (as money, credit, &c.) to facilitate the distribution" (IV, p. 322).

13. The same perspective emerges in a discussion of "Competition and Custom," where it is reiterated that the single-price axiom turning upon pecuniary interest does not apply at the retail level because of the failure of consumers to act as maximizers (II, pp. 242–243).

14. The monopolistic competition model emerges also in the discussion of professional remuneration where "competition operates by diminishing each competitor's chance of fees, not by lowering the fees themselves" (II, p. 243). Medical services and banking, too, are said to fall into the category at least to some extent, competition acting to keep the return on capital on a par with opportunities elsewhere in part by reducing market shares (IV, pp. 306–308).

15. The efficiency losses in retailing extend to a failure of prices to reflect new technology, although where a major change occurs the effect is likely to filter through belatedly. Here the properties of demand elasticity emerge—for prices are more easily maintained in the case of a "rich" clientele (III, p. 460).

16. The desirable trends were likely to be further undermined by the transport revolution that breaks down the dependency of consumers on local dealers (p. 243).

17. On the benefits for labor deriving from competition, see the section on "The Population Problem."

18. That competition also serves to assure that the preservation of the fittest emerges in the context of scale economies:

> Whether or not the advantages obtained by operating on a large scale preponderate in any particular case over the more watchful attention, and greater regard to minor gains and losses, usually found in small establishments, can be ascertained, in a state of free competition, by an unfailing test. Wherever there are large and small establishments in the same business, that one of the two which in existing circumstances carries on the production at greatest advantage will be able to undersell the other (II, p. 133).

19. Though Mill believed that monopoly impeded the adoption of new technology, he justified patent protection, since the patent merely "postpon[es] a part of the increased cheapness which the public owe to the inventor, in order to compensate and reward him for the service" (p. 927). The essence of the allowance lies in the temporary character of the protection, without which only the "very opulent or the public-spirited" would undertake inventive effort and "bring [an] idea into a practical shape."

20. One final matter. Mill rejected the commonly held view that cyclical instability could be attributed to "increased competition." He related it rather to the downward trend in the profit rate. (On this, see "Summary and Conclusion.")

21. In all this nothing is said formally of the empirical justification for the hypothesis in the systems in question. But we know that for economics to be of any great practical service there must be evidence that the maximizing axiom does reflect the "predominating influence" governing behavior in the particular sphere of activity and locale under investigation.

22. This perspective reflects the methodological proposition that (to use Marx's terminology) "appearance" must not be confused with "essence."

23. For example, Book I, ix of the *Principles* is devoted to large- and small-scale farming "as a question of production, and of the efficiency of labor"; examination of the issue "as affecting the distribution of the produce, and the physical and social well-being of the cultivators themselves" was postponed (II, p. 152). Similarly, Mill in Book I applauded large-scale industrial marketing "[w]ith a view merely to production, and to the greater efficiency of labor," conceding "drawbacks, rather social than economical . . ." (p. 141).

24. Drawing upon observations of the record, Mill spelled out three major "tendencies" that characterize the "progressive economical movement of civilized nations," namely advances in technology, in security, and in "cooperation" (III, pp. 705–706). The progress of wealth and industry is said also to encourage the propensities toward freer trade and emigration (pp. 711–712).

Mill envisaged good prospects for a great extension of the joint-stock and other forms of complex organization determined by the progress of wealth and reinforcing such progress. There is an objective argument, that the introduction of large establishments is facilitated in a *growing* economy (II, pp. 140–141). And the "progress of modern society" played on the capacity for industrial cooperation in a more subjective sense. While "economical progress" had a debilitating effect upon intelligence and efficiency of the *individual*—his/her ability to adapt means to ends—*collective* intelligence and efficiency increases because of an increased capacity for cooperation reflected in better industrial discipline, adherence to plan, subordination of individual caprice, and so forth (III, p. 708), a capacity that improves with practice, "and becomes capable of assuming a constantly wider sphere of action."

25. *Cf*: "[I]t is much more obvious how many mouths can be supported by a piece of land, than how many hands can find employment in the general labor market" (VI, p. 529). Malthus had expressed the same opinion.

26. In addition, there was the possibility of a structure set around an unacceptably low general level; but, as we shall see, the notion of "justice" does not extend to the *general* level of wages.

27. The foregoing perspective governs the approach to women's earnings. It was the competitive market mechanism on which Mill relied for at least part of the solution to their relatively low earnings, considering the fact that "occupations which law and usage make accesible to them are comparatively so few" (p. 395). Thus alluding to restrictions on female factory labor, Mill protested: "it should . . . be an object to give them the readiest access to independent industrial employment, instead of closing, either entirely or partially, that which is already open to them" (III, p. 953).

28. The growth model on which the recommendation for population control is based entails a regular functional relation between capital accumulation and the return on capital, and between population growth and the real wage. But there is some evidence of a possible (partially absorbed) change in position in Mill's later writings pertaining to the *motive* governing accumulation and perhaps population, too.

A second modification emerging late in Mill's career also has major policy implications, namely a new concern with wage-induced substitution against labor.

29. One of Mill's arguments for a stationary state relates to its greater potential in encouraging population control: "If it were evident that a new hand could not obtain employment but by displacing, or succeeding to, one already employed, the combined influence of prudence and public opinion might in some measure be relied on for restricting the coming generation within the numbers necessary for replacing the present" (p. 753).

30. Mill saw self-interest as a positive driving force only in the more mundane task of assuring small gains and savings, but as mitigating against truly innovatory ventures. He placed his faith rather in hired management of above-average intelligence, a solution available only to large-scale enterprises. This in turn implies a rationalization of the relationship between scale and innovation (possibly even invention). See also the comments on small-scale farming in the section on "Productive Organization and Motivation."

31. Mill realized that natural resource exhaustibility rendered the theoretical stationary state—zero growth of population and capital at unchanged wage and profit rates—an impossibility. Innovation and new mining discoveries would be *essential* to counteract this sort of diminishing returns (II, pp. 171, 184–185).

32. There is also a suggestion (in the first edition only) that *custom* impeding competitive wage determination is reinforced in a stationary state (II, p. 337).

33. The Law of Markets is understood by Mill as an equality not an identity; in disequilibrium excess commodity supply (excess demand for money) is allowed. The full analysis requires reduction to manifestations of individual maximizing behavior.

34. Mill expressed some doubt whether social progress would "moderate" price fluctuations arising "from the alternations of undue expansion and excessive contraction of credit. . . . Such vicissitudes, beginning with irrational speculation and ending with a commercial crisis, have not hitherto become less frequent or less violent with the growth of capital and extension of industry. Rather they may be said to have become more so: not in consequence, as is often said, of increased competition; but as I prefer to say, of a low rate of profits and interest, which makes capitalists dissatisfied with the ordinary course of safe mercantile gain" (p. 718). But in evidence given in 1867 Mill denied that the cyclical problem was worsening in terms either of depth or frequency (V, p. 601).

35. A "tendency" which itself encourages the counteracting force renders questionable the designation of the latter as a "disturbing cause" bearing as it does a connotation of independence.

36. For the most part the argument proceeds as if technical change constitutes a purely exogenous disturbance. Yet allowance is sometimes also made for induced technology rendering inappropriate its designation as "disturbing cause."

37. One aspect of Mill's support for colonial activity turns on the check to any reduction in the domestic profit rate due to pressure on scarce land by providing a source of cheap wage goods (p. 746).

38. Mill reacted similarly to proposals to pay off the national debt. See also his evidence before the Select Committee on the Income and Property Tax (V, pp. 493–494). Although he favored savings over consumption expenditure, on the grounds that by saving a "fund in perpetuity [is created] for maintaining labor," a still better choice would be endowing a school.

4 CHURCH, STATE, AND MARKET: ACCENT ON THE SOCIAL

Thomas Nitsch

If Man is social by nature, he will develop his nature only in society, and the power of his nature must be measured not by the power of the separate individual but by the power of society. . . . The reason for this [enhanced productivity via simple cooperation] is that man is by nature . . . a social animal—dass der Mensch von Natur . . . ein gesellschaftliches Thier ist.

—Karl Marx, *Die heilige Familie*, 1845; *Das Kapital*, 1867–1883

It is this natural propensity [springing from their mutual dependence] which moves men to join together in civil society, and likewise into particular associations of citizen with citizen which, while certainly lesser and imperfect, are true societies . . . . Civil society exists for the common good—il bene comune.

—Leo XIII, *RN:DCO/DQO*, 1891

Prominent among these [rights which are inalienable and proper to the human person] is the "natural human right" to form private associations; [and,] because the right of association is a natural right of the human being, [it] therefore precedes his or her incorporation into political society.

—John Paul II, *CA:OHA*, 1991, #7

Introduction

Modern society (the social system) conceived structural-functionally is constituted of four basic institutions (or subsystems) designated as follows: ideology (the meaning system), polity (the organization system), economy (the adaptation or provisioning system), and family (the belonging system). Each of these, in turn, may be analyzed and further described in terms of its (1) general symbolic medium (GSM), (2) sanction, (3) symbolled value, (4) structural components, and so on.[1] Thus, for example, focusing on polity versus economy, we have here, respectively, (1) power versus wealth, (2) coercion versus inducement, (3) effectiveness versus utility, (4) collectivities versus roles, (5) force versus dominion, and (6) sovereignty/submission versus prestige/respect. In the case of the ideology or meaning system, of which institutional religion is a subset, we have (1) influence, (2) persuasion, (3) solidarity, (4) norms, and (5) consent (concensus)/(normative) intractability (see Fig. 1).[2]

In the above societal system, the economy constitutes what is often called the "social economy," to distinguish it from "individual," "personal," or other types of economy, that is, from the management or administration of the family, or "private" (versus the national or global) household.[3] But there is another specific and narrower conception of the social economy, in what may be referred to as the Franco/Roman-Catholic paradigm of *l'économie nationale*. Here, the latter is institutionally divided into the private, public, and social sectors. The first (*l'économie individuelle ou privé*) consists in the individual, privately owned and operated households and firms interacting with one another on a self-interested, individualistic basis; the second (*l'économie d'état ou public*), in state enterprises, general-government operations (regulatory, legislative, etc.), and national defense; and the third, in what has recently been described as that "dynamic third sector," *l'économie sociale*, composed of various forms of voluntary associations, vocational groups, intermediate bodies, and the like, as exemplified by trade unions, employers' associations, mutual benefit societies, charitable endowments, cooperatives, and so on.[4] In the earlier days, the institutional church filled in the hiatus between the ("negligent") private and public sectors with its own alms-houses, orphanages, hospitals, and so forth, some of which remain today under Catholic auspices, still performing the so-called "corporal works of mercy." This is what the social economy exhibits were all about at the International Expositions of the second half of the last century.[5]

In developing this chapter, we shall employ both of these paradigms: the (essentially) Parsonian/modern-sociological (P/M-S) and the Franco/

Figure 1 Basic institutions of human society (subsystems of the social system)

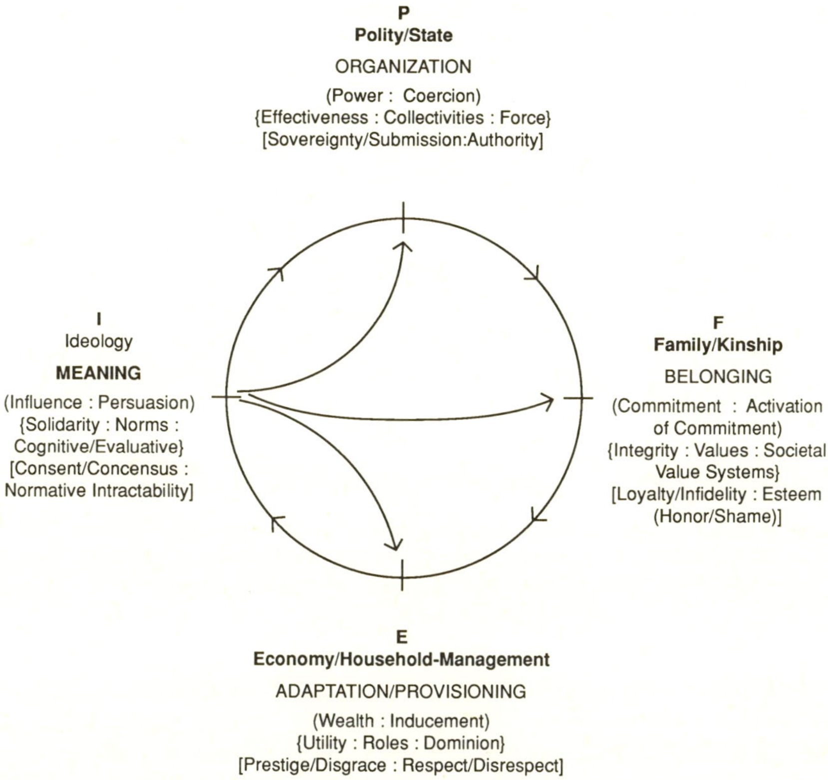

Note: Initial for Basic Institution or Subsystem (E = Economy, etc.); *Popular Designation*; FUNCTIONAL DESIGNATION; (General Symbolic Medium: Sanction); ⟨Value Symboled: Structural Components: Encoded(s)⟩; [Success/Failure Indicator: Rating Index.].
Source: Adapted from Malina and Nitsch (1991a).

Roman-Catholic (Fr/R-C), in perhaps an "overlay" if not integrative fashion; and, whichever, at varying levels of abstraction depending on the purview—that is, national, regional-bloc, global economy/society. Also, to the extent that P/M-S fits within our Fr/R-C framework (Fig. 2), we shall have it submissive to the traditional Mediterranean family analog of society: state or polity = father, private-sector = mother, and the "middle entity between the individual and the state" (Mulchay, 1952, p. 9)—intermediate bodies, voluntary associations, vocational groups, and so on—or *l'économie sociale* proper = the children (Malina, personal communication, July 10, 1992).

Figure 2 Modified Parsonian/Malina–Nitsch Model of the Social System

Modern Society

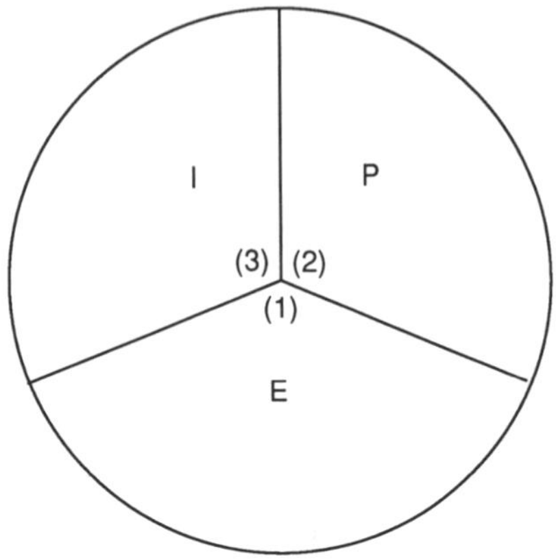

Basic Institutions/Subsystems

Note: (1) Economy: Adaptation/Provisioning, Wealth, Inducement, etc.
(2) Polity/State: Organization, Power, Coercion, etc.
(3) Ideology/Religion: Meaning, Influence, Persuasion, etc.
Source: Adapted from Figure 1, Malina and Nitsch (1991a).

It is notable that even the Fr/R-C paradigm thus far described is a much looser confederation and more of a "mixed bag" than corporat(iv)ism, or the corporate state proper, in the strict sense thereof (e.g., Schneider, 1959; and see Freeman, 1989, *passim*).[6] Ideally, there would be a clear and distinct, free-standing network of these socioeconomic institutions, with functional ties drawn (yet borders remaining) between that network and the public (or state) and private (or individual) economies as they stand equally free and distinct. The ideal model (in the Weberian sense) would take the form of a pyramid, with the individual economy at the base, the social economy in the middle, and the state forming the apex (Fig. 3). In the R-C case, the principle of subsidiarity governs the overall (national-economy) system, while that of solidarity is the glue of the social economy proper.[7]

The role of the church or institutionalized religion as a secular force in both its ideological and more material aspects has, of course, been prominently recognized in the history of economic thought. Wasn't the church the supranational impediment, in the same way that the manor and town were the infranational ones, which had to be overcome and superseded in

Figure 3 The Franco/Roman-Catholic Model of l'Economie Nationale

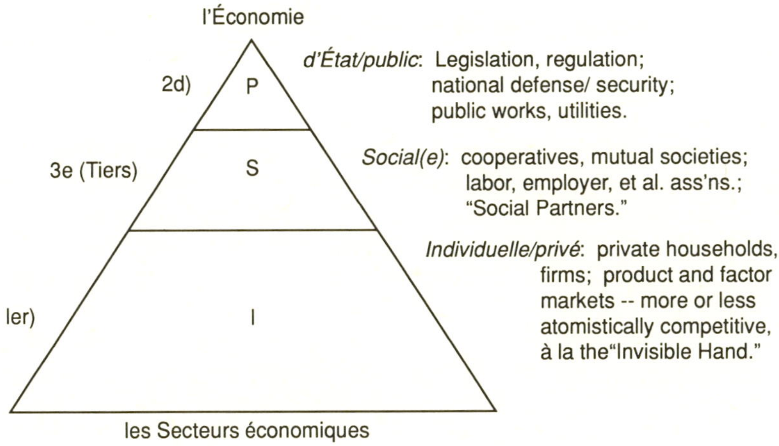

Source: Adapted from Desjardins (1983); Le Monde, Le Figaro—"Économi(qu)e."

the emergence of the nation-state and attendant mercantilist/cameralist *Oeconomie politique*, *Staatswirthschaft*, and so forth, as the dominant *isms*?[8] For those histories of economics that still deem to cover the ancient/early phases of Biblical/Graeco-Roman–Scholastic/Medieval thought, the institutional/ideological role of the church/religion is obvious. And, again, once secular society and economy had truly come into their own (albeit with the considerable, if not indispensable, support of the Weberian Protestant Ethic of Calvinism-Puritanism) with the ascendency of the industrial system,[9] the more the sovereign or state neglected its "social responsibilities," the more it befell institutionalized religion and its alms-houses, "People's Homes," or "*Solidarités*," to assume that mantle.[10] This, along with, and embracing, the aiding and abetting of labor associations and forms of "self-help" constituted the so-called corporal works of mercy in praxis—generic alias (in the Roman church at least), "Catholic action."[11]

When we turn our attention from economic history and the history of economics to the contemporary setting and comparative economic systems, we note, first of all, the scene—and various pertinent scenarios—that is currently Europe—Eastern, Central, and Western. There we have a mixed bag and general situation very much in flux. This includes, and not mutually exclusively or totally inclusively, the so-called "Socialist Economies in Transition," the decomposition or dissolution of the former Soviet Union (USSR) into the newly formed Confederation of Independent States (CIS);

the disintegration, deterioration or otherwise transformation of Yugoslavia (Bosnia-Hercegovina et al.) into God knows what; and, most recently (January 1, 1993), the separation of Czechoslovakia into Slovakia and the Czech Republic. Side by side, and partially overlapping these developments, is the reunification of Germany, or otherwise absorption of the German Democratic Republic by the Federal Republic of Germany, and the struggle of the latter and its partners to form a more perfect union. A full-fledged European Community (EC) is attempting to evolve from the transitional Common Market or EEC among socioeconomically disparate nations. Each step of the way, the EC seeks to overcome the tug-of-war between the negative political forces of not relinquishing all sovereignty and the (presumably, at least) essentially and mutually positive net present value of total economic integration. Surely our topic of church, state, and market is central to this scene, with the case of Poland as exemplary in this regard.

A "Third Way" or No: The Participatory Economy/ Workers' Self-Management, the Social Market Economy, Welfare Capitalism, or What?

Basically the Roman-Catholic church has striven (1891 to 1991–92) to navigate a middle course between the Scylla of unbridled/laissez-faire capitalism, on the one hand, and the Charybdis of monolithic state-socialism, on the other. We have already noted the Fr/R-C formation or institution of the *Tiers Secteur*—that middle or intermediate-body economy, *l'Economie sociale*—between the first and second (individual/private and state/public) sectors or economies. Recently, on reading *Centesimus Annus* and then the just-promulgated *Catechism of the Catholic Church* (John Paul II, 1992), an enthusiastic, right-wing cleric in this country (Sirico, 1992) has proclaimed—as fait accompli, once and for all—the official demise of any "third way" or mere compromise solution between classical socialism and classical capitalism. To him, it is now the (properly proscribed, of course) market economy—virtuous as victorious!

Intermediate types and mixed varieties, both theoretically and praxeologically, between the two extremes, as we know, are manifold, a mere sampling appearing in the heading of this section. Yet, the church itself, while rejecting *both* classical socialism/communism with rigorous central-planning *and* the unfettered pursuit of private profit with near-total reliance on the market mechanism for resource allocation and need satisfaction, presently and provisionally giving the nod to a properly circumscribed and supplemented market system (John Paul II, 1992, #2424–2425), continues to protest that it "has no models to present" (John Paul II, 1991a, #43); or, as an early apologist intermediating between *Rerum Novarum* (1891) and *Quadragesimo Anno* (1931) had declared, "Catholicism gives to the world no Economic system; it is not bound to any definite or fixed economic constitution, and binds to no fixed economic system" (Pesch, III, 1926, p. 547; *cf.* Nitsch, 1990, pp. 67–68, 88–89, *nn.* 74, 78).

Still, much to the dismay of many of the faithful and others outside the esoteric circles of social economics, social/moral philosophy and theology, the church—whose primary and exclusive focus is supposed to be the "Other World," the Kingdom to come—continues to poke its nose into the affairs of the "temporal order," the "things of this world," matters that "belong to Caesar" and—of course—the marketplace.[12] At the same time, to the consternation of others, the *magisterium* or "teaching office" of that church proceeds to explain all material evil—all adverse human-social conditions and developments—in terms of an initial offense against or separation (alienation) from God on the part of the individual or group, although moral responsibility is always personal, never collective or communal (Nitsch, 1987, pp. 13, 19, *op. cit. n.* 30; *idem*, 1986, pp. 61–62).

Yet, like it or not, and for better or worse, this institution has served and continues to serve as a significant, non-negligible force in the temporal order, the real (social/material) world; it is not, nor does it purport to be, *totally* or solely other-worldly, though that is its primary orientation and particular competence (John Paul I, 1978; see also Nitsch, 1986, pp. 58–59). Now, from the social-economic standpoint, there are two aspects of this fact: one, empirical or positive; the other, moral or normative. One is the subject of sociology or social analysis; the other, of normative or moral-philosophical/theological nuancing. We shall examine the latter first.

Does the Pope Have Models, If Not Armies as Well?

The key to the present question lies in both Pesch's post-*Rerum Novarum*/ pre-*Quadragesimo Anno* formulation in the first quarter of this century and John Paul II's recent disclaimer (*CA*, 1991, #43). The significant qualifier in the case of Pesch, as the present writer sees it at least, is *bestimmte(s)* in his original German (rendered above), to wit:

> Der Katholizismus gibt der Welt kein Wirtschaftssystem, er ist an keine *bestimmte* Wirtschaftsverfassung gebunden und bindet an kein *bestimmtes* Wirtschaftssystem (emphasis added).

As with so many German terms and contexts (including the Hegelian-Marxian *aufheben*, meaning to negate/abolish, affirm/preserve, *and* transcend/supercede!), it seems likely that several connotations apply here simultaneously: definite, fixed, preordained, definitive, and so on. Thus, in his recent "no models" affirmation of the church's position and role as articulated earlier by our so-regarded "commentator on *Rerum Novarum* [and] sourcebook of *Quadragesimo Anno*" (Mulchay, 1952, p. 8), John Paul II first declares and then explains (*CA:OHA*, 1991):

> 43. Ecclesia exempla non habet proponat; models that are real and truly effective can only arise *within the framework of different historical situations*, through the efforts of all those who responsibly confront *concrete problems* in all their social, economic, political and cultural aspects—aspectibus socialibus oeconomicis politicis et culturalibus—as these interact with one another (emphasis added).

In a word, the economy—the human household-management system—is, as the present writer noted some 30 years ago, "man-made"; there is no preordained or predestined "best" form or formulation, *de natura* or supernaturally (Nitsch, 1963).

But, instructively, to add meaning to his "responsibly" stipulation, the Holy Father continues here:

> For such a task the Church offers her social teaching as an *indispensable and ideal orientation*, a teaching which, as already mentioned, recognizes the positive value of the market and of [private] enterprise, but which at the same time points out that these need to be oriented towards the common good—in bonum intendi commune. This teaching also recognizes the legitimacy of workers' efforts to obtain full respect for their dignity and to gain broader areas of participation in the life of industrial enterprises so that, while cooperating with others and under the direction of others, they can in a certain sense "work for themselves" [*cit. LE:OHW*, 1981, #15] through the exercise of their intelligence and freedom.

The emphasis here is *not* added; but one is tempted to underscore "the common good' and "broader areas of participation," which the author himself might have done had he deemed it necessary by this point. At the same time, to begin to bring all of this together, let us call attention to some commonalities of language and thought, not between Karl Marx and John Paul II, but between Adam Smith (*WN*, 1776–1789), Leo XIII a century later, and John Paul II two centuries later. Thus, in referring to our second quotation opening the chapter, we note the Pontiff's allusion to the human-natural tendency "to join together in civil society"; Smith's term (adapted by Hegel, for example) was "civilized"—alternatively, "commercial," "civilized and commercial"—society (equal to Hegel's *buergeliche Gesellschaft*).[13] I refer here in particular to the so-called "alienation passage" (Smith, 1937, pp. 734–740) and opening paragraph of Book I,

Chapter IV, of the *Wealth*. Next, we move to the opening paragraph two chapters earlier, where we find the famous allusion by Smith to that "certain propensity in human nature . . . to truck, barter, and exchange one thing for another" (*viz*., the human-natural propensity to trade), followed by (1) an elaboration of the near-total interdependence of "man . . . in civilized society" in the subsequent paragraph (especially p. 14), whence (2) that opening paragraph of Chapter IV, where we are informed that "when the division of labour has been once thoroughly established, . . . every man . . . lives by exchanging, or becomes *in some measure* a merchant, and the society itself grows to be what is properly a commercial society" (p. 22; emphasis added). Here, we merely compare John Paul II's language regarding the workers' ability to "in a certain sense 'work for themselves'" (*CA:OHA*, 1991). Of interest is that this comes at the tail-end of a pronouncement that has just (qualifiedly) endorsed the market system (alias, commercial society); and one surely has to wonder if the worker today, and even in the system that the present Pontiff has in mind, is any more of a "merchant" or any more her/his own "employer" than two-plus centuries ago when Smith (d. 1790) was first-drafting and last-revising his famous *Wealth of Nations*. Wisely, one must remark, did they qualify "in some measure" and "in a certain sense."

Actually, it seems, as the present writer observed 29 years ago (Nitsch, 1964), it is difficult to accept that the church affirms or endorses no particular model or system when it (1) upholds private property as a natural right; (2) relatedly declares the socioeconomic classes as (super)naturally (pre)ordained; (3) opts for the marketplace over the central planning board; and here, for good measure, we add, (4) views the state as likewise (super)-naturally (pre)ordained. To Smith, Hegel, and Marx, this *was* a definite model, particular system, and so forth: "civilized and commercial society," "*buergerliche Gesellschaft*" ("civil Society"), and "*das kapitalische System*"—all quite interchangeably. That is to say, the system or model that may be clearly distilled from *CA* (1991) and the new *CEC* (1992) is no less specific and distinct than Smith's normative "obvious and simple system of natural liberty" *qua* "invisible hand [of] free and universal competition" circumscribed and supplemented by the "visible hand" of the Sovereign (*WN*, 1937, p. 651), Hegel's "*buergeliche Gesellschft*" *cum* "*politische Staat*," and Marx's socialism/communism, stages I and II. The only difference is, with Smith and Marx, perfection was achieved and further evolution/development would stop when commercial-society II and communism II (respectively) were reached[14]; the Pope(s) says (have said), no specific one forever. For the time being, however, the nod goes to reformed capitalism (Ref-Cap) and not to revised socialism (Rev-Soc).

The Church in the Social System: Positive Analysis

As Malina and Nitsch have presented the matter recently (1991b, especially pp. 52–57), the dynamic interaction between the several basic societal institutions or subsystems in the present type of connection begins with the church/religion in the I subsystem, and moves outward and around to P, F, and E. (see Fig. 1). Namely, we said that in their *Pastoral Letter on Catholic Social Teaching and the U.S. Economy* the National Conference of Catholic Bishops (1986) or (1) the church was drawing on its *influence* to *persuade* (2) the polity to exert its *power* in *coercing* desired changes in (3) the economy. This we regarded as the primary/direct routing of the thought and action. Surely, there was an intent and attempt as well to work circuitously down through the local ordinaries, deaneries, and parishes to engage (4) the family to participate in this process,[15] just as there was an intent to influence elements of the economy directly (as in Fig. 1), that is, to conscientize and convert "corporate execs" and others to a more just, Christian *modus operandi.* But, for reasons not articulated earlier (1991a,b), it must now be noted that, characteristically, the bishops would not address the family as an integral social unit or institution, but only individual members thereof. Remember, it is individuals, not groups, that are morally accountable, damned or saved, and so on. Thus, in the present social analysis, it does no damage to our positive model to suppress the family, or otherwise exclude it from explicit portrayal, as in Figure 3. Otherwise, perhaps, if we let F = families as the societal subtotals of the individual members thereof, we could now stipulate the indirect routing of I $\rightarrow$ F $\rightarrow$ P/E, as well as the short-circuited I $\rightarrow$ E; but nothing of significance is lost by focusing on the primary I $\rightarrow$ P $\rightarrow$ E thrust.

The reactionary response to the bishops' enterprise here, of course, would be that (à la M. Friedman et al.) the social cost of the suggested government intervention would exceed the social benefit thereof, both properly discounted. That is, if something in the economy needs changing, nature will take care of it; the government as "nightwatchman in the marketplace" is fine, also as mechanic and even reformer, but not as redesigner or reconstructor of the economy or *economic system* as such. That's a definite "no, no."

The U.S. Catholic bishops proposed no radical change in our extant "mixed economy" in their pastoral letter, no alternative to the market system here as regulated and supplemented by government, except for significantly more activism and progressivism in the latter case. In this, they have been affirmed by John Paul II in his latest social encyclical, where he was endorsing (qualifiedly) essentially such a system as a reasonable exemplar for the formerly socialist economies in transition. The pope, of course, defines and redefines social doctrines in exercising his *magisterium*, and as well in suggesting appropriate courses of action in more specific current situations in discharging his "pastoral" office (*pastorium*). The bishops, in conference or otherwise, only interpret and apply doctrine at their respective local levels; hence, their letter was a pastoral utterance. Yet, as such, they constitute a fixture in the (national) social order; there, they, and the (arch)diocesan pastoral councils, and others down through the hierarchy, constitute the church—under the eyes and authority of the "Holy See" (Vatican), the church *qua* fixture in the *universal* social order. And, of course, this is not to detract from the superior influence of the non-Roman national churches, such as the Church of England, Church of Norway, and so on.

Conclusion

The church (institutional religion), like the state or polity (of whatever form), and the market system (the economic form in question) are fixtures of the positive social order. The significance of the market economy is that it is essentially "free-standing". In the case of the United States, for example, it is regarded as the *dominant* basic institution or subsystem.[16] In the Soviet Union, as we knew it, the economy—by virtue of state ownership and central-command planning—was largely embedded in the polity, which, in turn, was and currently is dominant. Societies differ structural-functionally (see Fig. 1) according to the relative free-standingness of the basic institutions or subsystems featured here, and to the relative "top-sidedness" thereof.

For the foreseeable future (twenty-first century), the church will continue its free-standing existence and ongoing attempt to exercise its moral influence in the social order, and in particular on the economic sphere thereof, via its sanction of *persuasion*. This it has done and likewise will continue to do at both the loftier level of its *magisterium* or teaching office and that more mundane of its *pastorium* or pastoral solicitude, in the Roman case at least.

With the liberation and recrudescence of religion (the churches) in Eastern/Central Europe, and including "Mother Russia" itself, the analysis of Friedrich and Brzezinski some 40 years ago (1956, pt. VI) has been borne out. The churches, like the family, proved to be one of those "Islands of Separateness" that would withstand the test of time in its immunity from the power of the state. Dormant in appearance, perhaps, but insulated by nature, hybernative by force as well as by expediency, "inactive" but never inert, waiting. . . . What rightful place it will rise to occupy is, of course, another question, and will no doubt vary from country to country.

From the point of view of Rome, the church is the dominant or top-side institution in—if not of—the universal social order. This is what is meant by its two (presumably interchangeable) designations: catholic, from the Greek *katholikos*, meaning ubiquitous; and universal, from the Latin *uni* + *verti*, meaning (literally) to turn or rotate around one, specifically Rome, to (and from) which all roads lead. At the same time, this church recognizes itself and is recognized as a distinct or free-standing institution and valence in the world or temporal order, other-worldly or eternally oriented though it may be. Thus, while it may not view itself as embedded in this world in the Polanyian sense, in the same "eyes of the Holy See" ("*le Saint-Siège*") these other institutions—separate and distinct, and similarly "nonembedded" as they may be (perceived)—remain (nonetheless) "relative," and must bend to "Her," or else. This is what is meant by that church (the Vatican, Rome) *qua* "hieracracy" (Nitsch and Malina, 1984, p. 7; Malina and Nitsch, 1991b, pp. 42*ff.*); and, as opposed, for example, to theocracy, where there is total embedment of P, E, and F in I (church, religion).

No doubt the United States will remain a chremacracy (*ibid.*) or ploutocracy, with E (wealth) dominant or top-side, and the church(es) or religion playing essentially a tempering, restraining, nudging role. As the countries of Eastern Europe move in the direction of free private-enterprise/marketized systems, their economies perforce will become more disembedded from the polity; although, as the U.S. bishops themselves recognized, and as Marx had taught in his writings over the 40-year period of 1843–1883,[17] the state must initiate, orchestrate, and engineer any conversion, reformation, or revolution of and in the social economy, however fundamentally, simply, but completely *social* its "soul" must be. In this process, and that of the *Glasnost* accompanying the same *Perestroika*, the church emerges as both freer-standing and ascendent. This is virtually axiomatic, given the need for another religion to fill the void created by the decline of religious Marxism (Nitsch and Malina, 1984; pp. 3–13; 1989, p. 35).

Having confined our attention to the Northwestern world, we have not begun to address our question in terms of the less developed countries (LDCs) of the Third World, where church as integral and/or still missionary as well as state and market (embryonically, or at least economy) is surely as much of an issue as with the so-called advanced industrial nations treated here. These, essentially, Malina and Nitsch (1984, p. 8) have regarded as "patronacracies" or living models of "clientelism," with E, P, and I embedded in F or kinship, but certainly emergent and increasingly free-standing. Malina and Nitsch also say, that "one Holy, Catholic and Apostolic Church" has itself fractured, though not to the point of being two (or more). Here, the struggle is between the traditional (Roman) church and that "theology of liberation" which would sublate unto itself Marxian social analysis as Thomas Aquinas did Aristotelian social analysis. The former hold they can do so without joining Marx in his atheism, as did Aquinas without succombing to Aristotle's "paganism." But that is another chapter, to which John Paul II's *Solicitudo Rei Socialis* of 1987 more exclusively applies, although to which the present analysis is clearly *not* irrelevant.[18]

We have come nearly full circle, where we rest. For all of the above—North America, Western–Eastern Europe, Central and South America, and non-Muslim Africa—the Fr/R-C model discussed earlier, along with the accordingly adapted or Modified P-M/N paradigm of Figure 3, are pertinent. Again, the most pregnant question in this regard lies in the transitions and turbulences of Eastern Europe. How those scenes and their respective scenarios will play and be played out, while not exactly anyone's guess, is surely questionable. Suffice it to say, don't expect a Poland-to-come (apparently the real success story so far[19]) to be a U.S. clone or little chip off the old U.S.A. block. Social market economy, welfare-state capitalism, and so on, would seem the limit, while nothing would be more R-C, for example, than *genuine* workers' self-management or some solidaristic, "Social System of Labour" along Peschian lines, alias "corprat(iv)ism."[20]

The quest continues for a more just and benign world order, for healthier and happier peoples along with wealthier nations. From a social standpoint, this has to be a function of the several institutions on which we have focused here. The present writer was selected for this topic because of the work he has done in the area of social Catholicism and, presumably, also in relation to and as reconcilable (synthesizable?) with social Marxism. The death, survivability or revivability of the latter is a question that will provide ample grist for the mills of the students of economic thought and political theory as well as simply practitioners of social analysis far into the foreseeable future. Thus, similarly, one might inquire, "Is Aristotle dead, or merely sublated beyond recognition?" Is the "invisible hand" of Adam Smith, whence Hegel's "thousand-handed deity," defunct, or is it still alive and well à la Ronald Reagan's "magic of the marketplace" held out to non-believing, would-be achievers in his Caribbean Basin Initiative unveiled in October 1982?[21]

The present writer harbors a modicum of faith, or at least of hope, that the Roman Catholic church can and will serve as an instrument of improvement of the human social condition both globally and nation-specifically. Even with a Supreme Pontiff whom many regard as conservative-reactionary in matters of faith and morals (the area of competency to which the claim of infallibility pertains), there has been some noticeable attempt at sublation—if not plain cooptation—of otherwise regarded "radical" perspectives, including the Marxian conception of *homo faber*, the human being as subject and (co)creator, liberation theology's "preferential option for the poor," and so on. It seems encouraging that conservative apologists even adhere firmly to the recognition that the economic system is of human design, is object and instrument. It also seems encouraging that socialization of the means of production can be required by the common good, etc. (see Peschke, 1992, in these regards). It is further encouraging that faithful conservative apologists are also required to recognize, as one has most recently (Whitehead, 1992), that "Papal Social [i.e., economic] Teachings" are equally binding on the *Christifideles Catholici Orbis Universos* as "the Church's authentic but ordinary teachings on faith and morals" (p. 4), "e.g., birth control" (p. 8). That, to the present writer and to others, is some concession!

Perhaps, with the models that remain valid from that particular moral-theological stance, a viable and optimal middle way will be forthcoming; and, perhaps some day, a truly radical Third Way *qua* the *Aufhebung*—simultaneous abolition, preservation, *and* transcendence—of the two, still-vying, basic alternatives will be seized on and synthesized. Surely, from what is found in the last three social encyclicals of the present Pontiff (John Paul II, 1981, 1987, 1991) and the equally doctrinal *CEC* (1992), the Vatican would not frown on the adoption of the so-called "neo-" or "social corporatist" model recently described and proposed by Pekkarinen and colleagues (1992)—nor, similarly, on virtually the same under the aegis of "negotiated economy" of Angresano (1993)—as a workable eclecticism for both the reforming economies of Eastern and Central Europe and the developing ones of the Third World. In light of Petr's recent essay (1990), the affirmation of John Paul II (1991, #43) of the official Roman Catholic position of letting history decide the actual form, rather than to force it from an invariant worldly ideology, is the more prudent and humanly beneficial course.

Acknowledgments

As in many previous efforts, the author must acknowledge the input of his sometimes not so silent, but here essentially "limited," partner, Bruce J. Malina, Professor of Theology at Creighton.

Notes

1. The list continues: (e) encodeds, (f) success/failure indicator, and (g) rating index; see Fig. 1.

On the role of religion or the church in premodern-Western society, when economy and polity were still embedded, and then as they emerged as free-standing subsystems, see Clebsch (1979). On the religion-state-economy trichotomy of the "classical liberal theorists" of the seventeenth and eighteenth centuries (Locke–Smith), see Wiser (1986, pp. 99*ff*.).

2. For further explication, articulation, documentation, and application of this paradigm, see Malina and Nitsch (1991, pp. 3–5); Nitsch and Malina (1984, pp. 5–9, Fig. 3); and Malina (1986, pp. 69–87).

3. While the private, personal, domestic, family, and so forth, versus public, political, and so on, distinction in the mercantilistic sense dates back at least as far as early-Peripatetic antiquity and is repeated in very similar fashion by the "last of the mercantilists" in 1767, and further distinctions have been drawn between political and social economy, one might most instructively consult Elliott (1973, pp. 3, 13) for the generic social versus individual we have in mind here. (See Aristotle, ed./trans. Armstrong, 1935*ff*., pp. 323*ff*., 344–351; Steuart, 1767, pp. 1–3; Nitsch, 1980, 1990.)

4. See Desjardins (1983), Mulchay (1952, p. 9), Leo XIII (1891–1939, #36–44), Pius XI (1931–1939, #29–39), and John XXIII (1961, #84–103), whence "Teaching-Aid Outline" (by Wm. J. Bertsch and Wm. J. Gibbons, S.J.), p. 107. The articles cited (G.H., Lebaube, Noblecourt, Rollat; "Social") from the several 1985–88 issues of the two leading French dailies, *Le Monde* and *Le Figaro*, are particularly illustrative of this sectoring of (alternatively) *économie* and *La Vie Économique*, respectively: "Social," "Affaires," "Étranger," "Monnaies," "Marches Financiers," etc.; and, "Économie–Social–Entreprises–Bourse–Finances," under which, for example, are "Commerce," "Automobile," "Échanges," "Politique Économique," and the article "Social: etc." Thus, that last item in *Le Figaro* notes that, according to "a sounding of the *Nouvel Économiste*," some 63% of employers interviewed were in favor of maintaining the "interprofessional minimum wage growth." The latter, we are further informed, joined the National Council of French Employers in holding that the minimum wage should be determined by branches of industry or individual firms, "not by a state decision." Similarly, the earlier bylined article (Lebaube) in *Le Monde* makes reference to the "APEC" (Association for the Employment of Staff), as the (higher-echelon) "equivalent of the ANPE [National Agency for Employment]"; to the workers and employers, as represented by their individual and respective "*organisations syndicales et patronales*," as "'*the social partners*'"; and so forth. That same expression is employed in the earlier article of Noblecourt (1985), regarding "the new cantors of liberalism [who would] deregulate to the maximum the social and economic game" (opening paragraph). There we also note, significantly, by the subtitle, a suggestion of social-economic democracy—or "*économie sociale démocratique*"—at the grassroots level superceding the concentration of private-market power in the top- or senior-

management echelons (i.e., to paraphrase, challenging the private enterprise or managerial power structure). Finally, one cannot help noting here that the very terms of the labor-employer negotiations discussed there—employment, wages, and hours of work—come under the penumbra of "Social Policy" in the Maastricht Treaty of the integrating European Community (see Fig. 2).

5. The eminent economic sociologist and religious-reformative social economist Fr. Le Play was responsible for organizing several of these exhibits (see Nitsch, 1988, pp. 34, 203; Herbertson, 1946, pp. 100–102). Cummings (1890) provides an excellent description of the very Roman-Catholic nature of these exhibitions as that "'universal' exposition of 1889." Nothing could be more traditionally Roman-Catholic than the purpose of that exhibit, in that author's words, "to establish the relation of the material, intellectual, and moral advance of the worker to the advance in science, invention, art, and industry" (and see Nitsch, 1992a, *passim*). By way of content, the 15 enumerated sections were entitled as follows: Remuneration of Labor; Profit Sharing, Cooperative Production; Trade Organizations; Apprenticeship; Banks of Pension and Life Annuities; Insurance; Savings; Distributive (or Consumptive) Cooperation; Cooperative Loan Associations; Laborers' Dwellings; Workingmen's Clubs and Recreations; *Hygiène Sociale*; Institutions Created by Employers; and *Grande et Petite Industrie* (pp. 212–215). The "producer's point of view," as differentiated from but in combination with the "sociological standpoint" quoted earlier in the chapter, is indicative of the essentially Fr/R-C *patronisme*. Herbertson, in her account (p. 202), states regarding Le Play and the second Paris Exhibition (1867): "He was responsible for the addition of the famous Group X, consisting of 'objects intended to ameliorate the material and moral condition of the working-classes'"; whence, "The precedent thus set was followed in the Exhibition of 1889, which devoted a section to Social Economy." Boyd (1900, pp. 419–431) provides a similar description of "Social Economy, Hygiene, Public Charitable Relief" at the Paris Exposition of 1900. There, "the exhibits of the Palace of Congress and Social Economy, . . . constitut[ing] grand Group XVI of the Exposition," were organized in 12 classes labeled as follows: Apprentices—Protection of Child Workers; Labor and Wages—Profit Sharing; Large and Small Industries—Cooperative Associations of Production and Credit—Professional and Trade Associations; Farming . . . Large and Small . . . —Agricultural Unions, Agricultural Credit; Workmen's Dwellings; Cooperative and Provision Stores; Institutions for the Intellectual and Moral Improvement of Working Men; Provident Institutions; Public or Private Movements for the Welfare of the People; Hygiene; Public Charitable Relief (pp. 420–421). Finally, an examination of the contents of Book Five, "On the Amelioration of the Institutes of Charity and Welfare," of de Villeneuve-Bargemont's prominent work on *Christian Political Economy* (Paris, 1934) will provide a similar notion of this devout French/Roman Catholic's "*économie sociale*" in practice (pp. 676a, 409–462); whence, the eminent Bishop Wm. Em. von Ketteler of Mainz provides a German/Roman-Catholic slant, if one wants, of the church's historical mission of filling in any void between individual and state in addressing the great "social question" of the "condition of labour" down through the ages (1864, "The True and Practical Means of Helping the Working Class," pp. 97–148; 1981, pp. 381–419). These include church-operated institutions for the unable-to-work laborers, the proper moral and social formation and empowerment of workers for more efficacious participation in the various cooperative ventures and laborer associations, and the advancement of the producers' associations themselves via special means that only Christianity has at its disposal (pp. 138–148). A prime and living example of the sort of voluntary, social-help institution complying with this Fr/R-C model are the Societies of St. Vincent de Paul founded (1833) by Frédéric Ozanam, first-positor of the "Social Question" (1836) and early envisioner (along with de Coux, 1836–1840) of the "social revolution lying beyond the political revolution," and of St. Francis Xavier

(1840)—the former, to respond to the demands of charity and the latter, to fill in the void of "any Catholic-worker Society designed for adults" (Duroselle, 1951, Chs. III and V; Williams, 1950, pp. 14–17; and, Nitsch, 1992a, pp. 18–23, 37–48).

6. On the new social corporatism versus the classical state or politico-economic variety and the role of the Catholic church and Roman Catholic social thought therein, see Pekkarinen, Pohjola, and Rowthorn, (1992, Ch. 1, especially pp. 1–3; Ch. 2, especially pp. 24–29). Careful examination might reveal both fundamental similarities and specific differences between this "neocorporatist" construct and the tripartite Fr/R-C (and modified P/M-S) paradigm(s) advanced here. Thus, focus on corporatism as an economic system and as an objective instrument for understanding and explaining economic performance across countries results in a certain ostracism of church and religion, with seemingly the sole exception (by A. Guger, *ibid*, Ch. 11, p. 344) regarding its "important influence on women's attitude to employment and family" in Catholic versus Protestant countries. At the same time, the accent on social (versus state, and so on) corporatism suggests this conception's transcendence over the otherwise more compartmentalized political and economic focuses, and the integration of the two, as when "citizens' political rights [are extended] to cover economic activities in order to achieve social order in industrial and labour relations" (p. 3). Here, it is noted, "Solidarity is [the] natural concomitant" of the "non-exclusive and egalitarian nature" of social corporatism. Solidarity in this context is instructively compared with the same of John Paul II in his *LE* (1981, #8). The recommendation of the Scandinavian or Nordic-style corporatism to the favorable consideration of the countries of Eastern Europe in their conversion from centralized command planning to a market-based system should be compared with the independent works of Angresano (1990, 1992, Ch. 13; 1993, pp. 12–18) recommending essentially the same under the alias of "negotiated economy" as a "viable social economy."

7. Although it is the explicit function of the state to secure "the common good in the temporal order," this role is *subsidiary* to that of individuals and lesser bodies promoting their own interests to the extent feasible; that is, collective action should be conducted at the minimal necessary and sufficient level (John XXIII, 1961b, #20, 53; 1961a, pp. 406, 414; whence, Pius XI, 1931a, p. 203; 1931b, #79). On the "spirit of human solidarity . . . and bond of Christian brotherhood" which should guide the "social partners" (alias "workers and employers") in their mutual dealings, see John XXIII (1961b, #23; 1961a, p. 407); whence, the same among workers of different occupations, between labor and capital, and on the international plane, as per John Paul II (1981b, especially #8, 14, 17–18, 20). In both cases, the official operative term is *coniunctio(ne)*. The Latinized *solidarietas* first appears in the Vatican II document, *Gaudiam et Spes*, of Paul VI et al. (1965a, p. 1051; 1965b, p. 231). In respect to a contemporary, official articulation of *l'économie sociale*, attention is called to the "wide range of intermediate bodies (*corpora media*)" noted by John Paul II in the conclusion of his section on "Work and Ownership" (1981b, #14, p. 7b; 1981a, p. 616) along with the "labour or trade unions" sanctioned anew by the there-reaffirmed "right of association (*ius sese consociandi*)" (1981a,b, #20 in.).

8. The closest thing I have as a written source here is my own term paper on "Mercantilism" (Econ. 810, Ohio State University, Fall 1954, Robert D. Patton, Instructor), pp. 3–7. No doubt the parallels—if not the source—here were the universalism and particularism noted by Heckscher in his classic on the subject (1955, pp. 33–44).

9. See Gray (1933, pp. 65–73); and Patton and Warne (1963, pp. 23–26 and Pt. I, *passim*). It may be of further interest in the present connection to compare Thomas Mun's classic remark (*Englands Treasure by Forraign Trade* 1669, p. 2) that "the Merchant is worthily called The Steward of the Kingdoms Stock" with *Syriac Baruch*, 14:17: "You said You would make for Your world man [as] a Steward of Your Works. . . ." Contrary to Mun's attempt to

near-deify the merchant and justify his practices was Niccolò Machiavelli's (seemingly largely successful) effort totally to secularize the social; *viz*., the political, sphere, whence political economy. For, with his (originally) *De Principatibus* (*On Principalities* or *On the Authorities of the Prince*) of 1513 (ed., 1924; trans., 1985) not only was the sovereign (or state) relieved of any extra- or supra-political concerns and constraints (i.e., was "politics divorced from ethics"), but the polity would become the dominant or top-side social institution, and, if anything, religion would become imbedded in politics rather than vice versa. The reality and durability of this turn of the tables dawned on the present writer when, just recently, the media were informing how, almost handily, the three governing bodies of the Church of England had produced the requisite two-thirds majorities approving the ordination of women into the priesthood, effective pending the approval of the Queen and Parliament. (See Gray, 1931, p. 68; Mansfield, "Introduction," in Machiavelli, 1985, pp. vii, x–xi, xxi–xxii.)

10. The classic treatment of this subject is Gide and Rist (1947–48, pp. 602–618/526–540), here especially the sections on "Social Catholicism" and "Social Protestantism"—neither one to be confused with Catholic/Christian socialism—in Book V, Chapter. II, "Doctrines Inspired by Christianity." On the truly immiserated condition of the working masses—"the labouring poor, the great body of the people," who must have outnumbered the "rich" by at least 500:1—and the little that could be expected in the way of solution from state intervention and public relief in Marx's "homoeopathic doses," see Adam Smith, *WN*, Book. V, Chapter I (1937, pp. 734–740, 670) and Marx (1883, pp. 365–366; 1954, p. 342). No one chronicled better than Marx and Engels, of course, the extent to which the legislative and regulatory measures taken by the British government, for example, failed to achieve even the modest amelioration sought by Smith in his "obvious and simple system of natural liberty" as it came to pass in the ensuing century.

11. In this regard and, more particularly, the French scene at the time of *Rerum Novarum*, see especially Jannet (1893); also see Nitsch (1990a, pp. 57–58).

12. In the midst of a Mexican farm-workers strike (*huelga*) in a border area in south Texas in the later 1960s, the present writer remembers reading the remark of a local priest that he was ordained to administer the sacraments, not to intervene or take part in any labor dispute.

13. Smith, for some reason which the present writer has not yet established, preferred "civilized" [*sic*] over the (then) more usual "civil" (as per Ferguson, 1767, for example) society. At the hands of the first German translator of the *WN* (*viz*., "J.F.S.," *Nationalreichthuemern*, 2 vols., Leipzig, 1776, 1778), Smith's "civilized society (nations)" was usually rather transliterally rendered "*civilisirte Staate* (*Nationen*)"; but, on at least one occasion, we find "civilized society" (1937, p. 737) translated "*buergeliche Gesellschaft*" (II, 1778, p. 467), the rendering of choice of Chr. Garve (trans., *Nationalreichthums*, 4 vols., Breslau, 1794–1796), upon which Hegel (according to Hoffmeister) relied in citing Smith in his *Realphilosophie* of 1803–1804. Yet even with Garve's later version, there is one instance where Smith's "civilized . . . nations" (1937, p. lviii) is simply transliterated "*civilisirten . . . Nationen*" (I, 1794, p. 3). In a sense, Garve out-Adams Smith on two significant occasions (Book I, openings of Chapters IV and VI), by rendering the latter's mere "society" as "civil society," that is, "*buergeliche Gesellschaft*," bearing the implication that, *in posse*, "civil society," like its constituent classes and their respective shares, always was. The seeds of Hegel's social (and political) philosophy as found in those lecture-scripts I and II on *Realphilosophie* (1803–1804, 1805–1806*ff*.; ed. J. Hoffmeister, Leipzig, 1932/1931) would grow and blossom into the "System of Needs," "*buergeliche Gesellschaft*," "*politische Staat*," and so on, which highlight his more renowned *Rechtsphilosophie* of 1821 (ed. Hoffmeister, Hamburg, 1955; trans. T.M. Knox, *Philos. of Right*, Chicago, 1952). See Nitsch (1982, pp. 21–34; 1983–1984, pp. 30–31; 1985) and Wiser (1986, p. 100).

14. As we employ them here, Marx's socialism/communism stage/phase I is accomplished when the socialist state has succeeded in collectivizing the means of production (property); stage/phase II, when the state itself and as such has become "*aufgehoben*." (Marx, "Third Manuscript" [1844], as in *MECW*, III, 1975, especially pp. 296–306). Smith's C-S I and II denote, respectively, (1) the extant "Mercantile or Commercial System" as he detailed it in Book IV, and (2) his normative "system of natural liberty" *qua* that same with the visible hand of the sovereign retrenched and retracted as per the end of Book I and, again, the "invisible hand [of] free and universal competition" within and between nations prevailing by virtue of and as supplemented by "the sovereign."

15. Indeed, the present writer has participated in this particular process, as both (1) contributor to the "Implementation" column in the local archdiocesan newspaper, *The Catholic Voice*; and (2) member of the task force that drafted the Archbishop's pastoral letter on the local economy (see Sheehan, 1991).

16. See Malina and Nitsch (1991b, pp. 42–43). In addition to the two examples offered in support of this contention (which was challenged from the floor when the paper cited there [Malina and Nitsch, 1991a] was originally presented), the authors would here like to add the following: most white Americans—WASPS (White Anglo-Saxon Protestants) and WERCS (White Ethnic Roman Catholics) alike—will readily admit the responsibility of their forebears for the destruction of the Red Man's or Native People's culture(s) in the "settlement of the West." However, press the point that it was the RM's or NP's *economy(ies)* that was (were) really destroyed in that process, and tempers flare. As a specific example, white men felled many bison "just to watch them drop"; to the Lakota peoples of the plains, the buffalo meant food, clothing, lodging, and tools. Truly, in that and many other cases across the continent, "white economic development spelled red economic destruction"; and, again, "them's fightin' words where *whites* come from"! Today, most Native Americans would readily acknowledge that their culture has survived in much better shape than their economy has.

17. See Nitsch (1987, pp. 2–3 and accompanying *nn*. 7–9; 1992b, pp. 110–112).

18. The church divided in Latin America has manifested itself anew most recently, with Rome's "emendation" of the "Final Report" of CELAM (Consejo Episcopal Latinoamericano) IV held in Santo Domingo, Dominican Republic in October 1992. See Hebblethwaite (1993), whence Rodriguez (1992).

19. See Gregory and Stuart (1992, pp. 464–469), on "Poland: From Plan to Market via Shock Therapy," for the Polish approach in the present case; the *New York Times* (1992) item, whence Schnytzer and Weiss (1992) and Leven (1993), for a couple of opposing "failure stories" in Poland's transition.

20. Justice has not begun to be done here to the relevant literature, both generic and specific. Thus, the classic of Dahl and Lindblom (1953) entitled *Politics, Economics, and Welfare* (read: power, wealth, and human-social well-being) with its obviously dualist focus, nonetheless devotes explicit attention to Christianity, religion, and *Rerum Novarum*, for example, as per the Index (s.v., pp., 530b, 531a), while Lindblom's more recent *Politics and Markets* (1977), of (ostensibly, at least) the essentially same dualistic focus, devotes a chapter to "Preceptoral 'Education' and Moral Incentives" in comparing communism to previously articulated alternative systems (market, political-economic, etc.), and Friedland and Robertson's *Beyond the Market Place* (1990) is highlighted and interspersed with attention paid to family and ideology (in the form of "culture") by the various contributors. Most recently, the contributions by J.E. Elliott, W.J. Samuels, E. Raiklin, A.N. Rugina, B.S. Clark, L. Armour, and J.W. Barchfield (in O'Brien, ed., 1992) are most pertinent to the present study especially as regards the reforming social economies of Eastern and Central Europe, both ideologically and praxeologically. Finally, of particular interest and relevance here is the excellent study by

Freeman (1989), which, while it does not address the role of religion or the church or otherwise assumes it politicoeconomically "neutral," *inter alia*, distinguishes between "pluralist—private enterprise" (e.g., Britain), "corporatist—mixed" (Austria), "pluralist—mixed" (Italy), and "corporatist—private enterprise" (Sweden) forms of political economy today.

21. Ronald Reagan (Oct. 15, 1981), as quoted in Newfarmer (1984, p. 182).

References

Amuzegar, Jahangir. (1983). *Comparative Economics*. Cambridge, MA: Winthrop Publishers.

Angresano, James. (1990). "Sweden: An Example of a Viable Social Economy?" *International Journal of Social Economics* 17(4):12–31.

Angresano, James. (1992). *Comparative Economics*. Englewood Cliffs, NJ: Prentice-Hall.

Angresano, James. (1993). "The Efficacy of the Scandinavian Model of Negotiated Economy for the Transforming Central and Eastern European Economies." Paper presented at ASSA meetings, Anaheim, CA, January 4–7.

Boyd, James P. (1900). *The Paris Exposition of 1900*. N.p.: James P. Boyd.

Calvez, Jean-Yves, S.J., and Jacques Perrin, S.J. (1961). *The Church and Social Justice: The Social Teaching of the Popes from Leo XIII to Pius XII (1878–1958)*, trans. by J.R. Kirwan. Chicago: Henry Regnery Co.

Catholic News Service, Vatican City. (1992a). "World Peace Day Message: 'If You Want Peace, Reach Out to the Poor,' Pope Says." *The Catholic Voice* (Archdiocese of Omaha, NE) 91(16) (Dec. 18): 1, 22.

Catholic News Service, Vatican City. (1992b). " 'Place Economy at Service of Humans.' " *The Catholic Voice* (Archdiocese of Omaha, NE) 91(16) (Dec. 18): 22.

Clebsch, W.A. (1979). *Christianity and European History*. New York: Oxford University Press.

Coronado, Richard J. (1992). "*Centesimus Annus*: John Paul II's Encyclical on the Centenary of *Rerum Novarum*." *Forum for Social Economics* 22(1) (Fall): 22–34.

Cummings, E. (1890). "Social Economy at the Paris Exposition." *Quarterly Journal of Economics*, 4: 212–221.

Dahl, Robert A., and Charles E. Lindblom. (1953). *Politics, Economics, and Welfare*. New York: Harper & Row.

Desjardins, Nicole. (1983). "Rédecouverte de l'économie sociale." *Cahiers de l'actualité religieuse et sociale*, No. 260 (ler fév.): 89–96.

Devroy, Ann, and Al Kamen. (1992). "Social Policy Posts Filled by Clinton." *The Washington Post* (Dec. 12): Al, A10.

Duroselle, Jean-Baptiste. (1951). *Les Débuts du Catholicisme social en France*. Paris: Presses Universitaires de France.

Elliott, D.C. Bogert, and K. Huus. (1992). " 'Shock Therapy' for Yeltsin." *Newsweek* (Dec. 28): 40.

Elliott, John E. (1973). *Comparative Economic Systems*. Englewood Cliffs, NJ: Prentice-Hall.

European Community (EC). (1992). "Protocol/Agreement on Social Policy." *Maastricht Treaty on European Unity*, Feb. 7, 1992. Washington, DC: International Legal Materials, pp. 357–359.

European Communities No. 3. (1992). *Treaty on European Unity including the Protocols and Final Act with Declarations*, Maastricht, 7 February 1992 [The Treaty is not in force], as presented to Parliament, May 1992. London: HMSO.

Ferguson, Adam. (1767). *An Essay on the History of Civil Society*, ed. by Duncan Forbes. Edinburg University Press, 1966.

Freeman, John R. (1989). *Democracy and Markets*. Ithica and London: Cornell University Press.

Friedland, Roger, and A.F. Robertson. (1990). *Beyond the Marketplace: Rethinking Economy and Society*. New York: Aldine de Gruyter.

Friedrich, Carl J., and Zbigniew K. Brzesinski. (1956). *Totalitarian Dictatorship and Autocracy*. Cambridge, MA: Harvard University Press. (reprint ed., Frederick A. Praeger, 1961*ff.*).

G.H. (1985). "L'institut de l'enterprise propose une 'flexibilité' des départs à la retraite," *sub* "ÉCONOMIE/Social." *Le Monde* (29 Jan.): 41, 43.

Gide, Ch., and Ch. Rist. (1947). *Histoire des Doctrines économiques*, 7e éd. Paris: Recueil Sirey.

Gide, Ch., and Ch. Rist. (1948). *A History of Economic Doctrines*, trans. by R. Richards and E.F. Row. Boston: D.C. Heath and Co.

Gray, Alexander. (1933). *The Development of Economic Doctrine*. London: Longmans, Green and Co.

Gregory, Paul R., and Robert C., Stuart. (1992). *Comparative Economic Systems*, 4th. edn., Boston: Houghton, Mifflin Co.

Hebblethwaite, Peter. (1993). "CELAM: In Wake of Santo Domingo, Political Struggle Between Vatican, Local Church Continues/Final Report: 'Small but Substantial Changes'." *National Catholic Reporter* 22(12) (Jan. 22): 12–13.

Heckscher, Eli F. (1955). *Mercantilism*, rev. ed., trans. by M. Shapiro; ed. by E.F. Soederlund. London: George Allen and Unwin.

Herbertson, Dorothy. (1950). *Frédéric Le Play*, ed. by V. Branford and A. Farquharson. Ledbury, Herefordshire: Le Play House Press.

Holesovsky, Vaclav. (1977). *Economic Systems: Analysis and Comparison*. New York: Mc-Graw Hill Book Co.

Jannet, Claudio. (1893). "French Catholics and the Social Question." *Quarterly. Journal of Economics* (7) (Jan.): 135–161.

John XXIII. (1961a). *Mater et Magistra: de recentioribus rerum socialum processibus ad christiana praecepta compondendis*, 15 Maii 1961, in *Acta Apostolicae Sedis*, LIII: 8 (15 Iulii): 401–464.

John XXIII. (1961). *Mater et Magistra: Christianity and Social Progress*, 15 May 1961, trans. by Wm.J. Gibbons, S.J. New York: Paulist Press.

John Paul I. (1978). "The Virtue of Christian Hope." *L'Osservatore Romano*, English weekly, ed., N. 39 (548), (Sept. 28).

John Paul II. (1981a). *Laborem Exercens: de labore humano*, 14 Sept. 1981, in *Acta Apostolicae Sedis* 73(a) (8 Nov.): 577–647.

John Paul II. (1981b). *Laborem Exercens: On Human Work*, 14 Sept. 1981, in *L'Osservatore Romano*, English weekly ed. (Sept. 21): pp. 1–13.

John Paul II. (1987). *Solicitudo Rei Socialis: On Social Concern*, Rome: St. Peter's Cathedral, 30 December.

John Paul II. (1991a). *Centesimus Annus: On the Hundredth Anniversary of RERUM NOVARUM*, Libreria Editrice Vaticana, 1 May.

John Paul II. (1991b). *Centesimus Annus*, 1 May 1991, in *Acta Apostolicae Sedis* 83(10) (9 Oct.): 793–867.

John Paul II. (1992). *Catéchisme de l'Église Catholique*. Paris: Mame-Librairie Editrice Vaticane; Mame/Plon.

Ketteler, Wm.Em. von. (1864). *Die Arbeiterfrage und das Christenthum*, 3te Aufl. Mainz: Franz Kirchheim.

Ketteler, Wm.Em. von. (1981). *The Social Teachings of Wilhelm Emmanuel von Ketteler*, trans. by Rupert J. Ederer. Washington, DC: University Press of America.

Lebaube, Alain. (1985). "Le Projet de Contrats formation-reclassement." "*économie*: sociale," *Le Monde* (Jan. 26): 21.

Leo XIII. (1891a). *Rerum novarum: De conditione opificum*, 15.05.1891, in *Acta Sanctae Sedis* 23 (1890–91): 641–670.

Leo XIII. (1891b). "Della Questione Operaia." *La Civiltà Cattolica*, ser. 14, vol. X, fasc. 984 (25 maggio): 641–675.

Leo XIII. (1891c). "The Condition of Labor," 15 May 1891, in *Five Great Encyclicals*. New York: Paulist Press, 1939.

Leven, Bozena. (1993). "Change in Living Standards during Poland's Transition from Central Planning to a Market Economy." Paper presented at ASSA Meeting, Anaheim, CA, Jan. 5–7.

Lindblom, Charles E. (1977). *Politics and Markets: The World's Politico-Economic Systems*. New York: Basic Books.

Loucks, Wm.N., and J.W. Hoot. (1948). *Comparative Economic Systems*, 3rd ed. New York: Harper & Bros.

Machiavelli, Niccolò. (1924). *Il Principe*, ed. Michele Scherillo. Milano: Ulrico Hoepli.

Machiavelli, Niccolo. (1985). *The Prince*, trans. by Harvey C. Mansfield, Jr. Chicago and London: University of Chicago Press.

Malina, Bruce J. (1986). *Christian Origins and Cultural Anthropology: Practical Models for Biblical Interpretation*. Atlanta: John Knox Press.

Malina, Bruce J., and Thomas O. Nitsch. (1991a). "The Bishops' Pastoral Letter and the Poverty Problem: Early vs. Contemporary Concerns and Doctrines." Paper presented at Sixth World Congress of Social Economics, Omaha, Aug. 9–11.

Malina, Bruce J., and Thomas O. Nitsch. (1991b). "The Bishops' Pastoral Letter and the Poverty Problem: Early vs. Contemporary Concerns and Doctrines." *Humanomics*, 7(2):40–70.

Marx, Karl. (1883). *Das Kapital*, Iter Bd., 3te Aufl. Hamburg: Otto Meissner.

Marx, Karl. (1954). *Capital*, Vol. I, trans. 3d (1883) German ed. by S. Moore and E. Aveling, ed. F. Engels. Moscow: Progress Publishers.

Marx Karl, and Frederick Engels. (1975). *Collected Works* (*MECW*), Vol. 3. New York: International Publishers.

Misner, Paul. (1991). *Social Catholicism in Europe: From the Onset of Industrialization to the First World War*. New York: Crossroad Publishing Co.

Mulchay, R.E., S.J. (1952), *The Economics of Heinrich Pesch*. New York: Henry Holt.

Mun, Thomas. (1669). *Englands Treasure by Forraign Trade*. London: Robert Home.

National Conference of Catholic Bishops. (1986). *Economic Justice for All: Pastoral Letter on Catholic Social Teaching and the U.S. Economy*. Washington, D.C: United States Catholic Conference.

Newfarmer, R. (1984). "Multinationals and Marketplace Magic in the 1980s." In Ch.K. Wilber (ed.), *The Political Economy of Economic Development*, 3rd ed. New York: Random House.

New York Times. (1992). "Poland: A Success Story," as in the *Omaha World-Herald*, Met. Ed. (Dec. 18): 8.

Nitsch, Thomas O. (1963). "An Economist Views *Mater et Magistra*." *Catholic Business Education Review* 14(2) (Winter): 32–34.

Nitsch, Thomas O. (1964). "Schumpeter and Catholicism: A Comment." *Review Social Economy* 22(2) (Sept.): 104–110.

Nitsch, Thomas O. (1980). "On the Origin, Renaissance and Recrudescence of *Politikē Oikonomia*." *Midsouth Journal of Economics* 4(2):83–97.

Nitsch, Thomas O. (1982). *On the Smithian vs. Unsmithian Nature of Marx's Concept of Alienation*. Omaha: College of Business Administration, Creighton University.

Nitsch, Thomas O. (1983–1984). "Hegel: A Neglected Link in the Smith-Marx Connection." Review of paper presented at 15th annual Atlantic Economic Conference, Paris, March 13–18, 1983, as submitted to the *Atlantic Economic Journal*.

Nitsch, Thomas O. (1985). "Hegel: A Neglected Link in the Smith-Marx Connection." *Atlantic Economic Journal* (*Anthology*), 13(1) (March): 98.

Nitsch, Thomas O. (1986). "Social Economycs: A Typology." Paper presented at 61st annual conference, WEAI, San Francisco, July 1–5.

Nitsch, Thomas O. (1987). "Social Catholicism, Marxism and Solidarism." *Forum for Social Economics* 17(1) (Fall): 1–20.

Nitsch, Thomas O. (1988). "Social Economics: The First 200 Years (Unabridged Manuscript Version)." Creighton University.

Nitsch, Thomas O. (1990a). "Social Economics: The First 200 Years." In Mark A. Lutz (ed.), *Social Economics: Retrospect and Prospect*. Norwell, MA: Kluwer Academic Publishers, pp. 5–90.

Nitsch, Thomas O. (1990b). "*Centesimo Anno*: The Social Encyclical of May 1991," *Forum for Social Economics*, 21:1/2 (Fall 1991/Spring 1992): 1–17; submitted 28 Oct. 1990.

Nitsch, Thomas O. (1992a). "Catholic Social Economy and the Social Question: Founders and First-Positors." More complete version of paper presented at Sixth World Congress of Social Economics, Omaha, Aug. 9–11, 1991; this version, Summer 1992.

Nitsch, Thomas O. (1992b). "Marx on Man's Sociality by Nature: An Inexplicable Omission?" *International Journal of Social Economics* 19: 108–120.

Nitsch, Thomas O. (1993). "*Centesimo Anno—Centesimus Annus*: A Follow-up." Forthcoming in *Humanomics*, 9(4).

Nitsch, Thomas O., and Bruce J. Malina. (1984). "On the Role of a Transcendent in Human Economy." Paper presented at 59th annual conference, Western Economic Association, Las Vegas, June 24–28.

Nitsch, Thomas O., and Bruce J. Malina. (1989). "On the Role of a Transcendent in Human Economy." *Humanomics* 5(1):33–59.

Noblecourt, Michele. (1985). "L'entreprise au coeur du dialogue social, *sub* "ÉCONOMIE" and billed (p. 1) as "SOCIAL: L'Entreprise devient le lieu des negotiations patronat-syndicats." *Le Monde*, Dern. Ed. (3 avril): 27: 3–6.

Noblecourt, Michele. (1988). "Une enquête du ministere des affaires sociales/ L'individualisation totale des salaires a de nouveau progrèsse en 1986," *sub* "ÉCONOMIE/Sociale." *Le Monde*, Dern. Ed. (8 avril): 27.

"Nouvelles measures . . . pour la fonction publique" and "Nouvelle secretaire général pour la Federation de la chimie CFDT [Confederation Française et Democratique du Travail]." (1988). *sub* "ÉCONOMIE/Social." *Le Monde* (8 avril): 28.

Patton, Robert D., and Clinton Warne. (1963). *The Development of the American Economy*. Chicago: Scott, Foresman.

Paul VI, et al. (1965a). *Gaudiam et Spes: constitutio pastoralis de ecclesia in mundo huius temporis*, 7 Dec. 1965, in *Acta Apostolicae Sedis* 63(15) (7 Dec.): 1025–1120.

Paul VI, et al. (1965b). "Pastoral Constitution on the Church in the Modern World (*Gaudiam et Spes*)." In Walter M., Abbott, S.J. (eds.), *The Documents of Vatican II*. New York: America Press, pp. 199–386.

Pekkarinen, Jukka, Matti Pohjola, and Bob Rowthorn (eds.). (1992). *Social Corporatism: A Superior Economic System?* Oxford: Clarendon Press.

Pesch, Heinrich, S.J. (1904*ff.*) *Lehrbuch der Nationaloekonomie*, esp. Vols. I–III, 2nd–4th eds. Freiburg i. Br.: Herder & Co., 1924–0–26; 1st eds.

Peschke, Karl H., S.V.D. (1992). *Social Economy in the Light of Christian Faith*, Ordo Socialis No. 7, 2nd ed. Trier: Paulinas-Verlag.

Petr, Jerry L. (1990). "Economic Reforms in Socialist Economies: An Evolutionary Perspective." *Journal of Economic Issues* 24(1) (March): 1–15.

Pius XI. (1931a). *Quadragesimo anno: De ordine sociali instaurando*, 15.05.1931, in *Acta Apostolicae Sedis* 23(6) (1 Iunii): 177–288.

Pius XI. (1931b). "*Quadragesimo Anno*: Reconstructing the Social Order," 15 May 1931, in *Five Great Encyclicals*. New York: Paulist Press, 1939.

"Pope Warns Against Unregulated Economy." (1992). John Paul II's World Peace Day Message, *National Catholic Reporter*, 29(9) (Dec. 25): 10.

Rodriguez, Alex. (1992). "Una doctrina al gusto de Roma." *El País* (12 Oct.): *sub* "Sociedad," p. 20.

Rollat, Alain. (1987). "Les exigences de la 'conscience sociale'." *Le Monde*, Ed. Internationale, ler–7 (Jan.): 1, 6.

Schneider, Herbert Wallace. (1959). "Corporate State." *Encyclopaedia Britannica*, Vol. VI, pp. 472–474.

Schnitzer, Martin C. (1987). *Comparative Economic Systems*, 4th ed. Cincinnati: South-Western Publishing Co.

Schnytzer, Adi, and Avi Weiss. (1992). "The Failure of Supply Response in Transition: A Market-Based Explanation." *Economic Systems* 16(2) (Oct.): 189–203.

Sheehan, Daniel E. (1991). *Human Development: Abundance and Scarcity*, A Pastoral Letter on the Economy of Northeast Nebraska. Archdiocese of Omaha, NE: January 13.

Sirico, Robert. (1992). "Embracing the Market Economy, In Good Faith." *Wall Street Journal* 74(50) (Dec. 23): A8.

Smith, Adam. (1937). *An Inquiry into the Nature and Causes of the Wealth of Nations* (1776–89), ed. by Edwin Cannan. New York: Modern Library.

"Social: 2/3 des chefs d'entreprises favorables au S.M.I.C." (1985). *sub* "La Vie Économique," *Le Figaro* (25 Mars): 22.

Solo, Robert. (1967). *Economic Organizations and Social Systems*. Indianapolis/New York/Kansas City: Bobbs-Merill.

Villeneuve-Bargemont Alban de. (1834). *Economie Politique Chrétienné, ou Recherches sur la Nature et les Cause du Paupérisme*. Meline, Cans et, Cie, Bruxelles: 111, 1837.

Whitehead, K.D. (1992). "May Catholics 'Dissent' from Papal Social Teachings?" *Fellowship of Catholic Scholars Newsletter*, 16(1) (Dec.): 4–10.

Will, George F. (1992). "At Least One of These, Please." *Newsweek* (Oct. 5): 82.

Williams, Melvin J. (1950). *Catholic Social Thought: Its Approach to Contemporary Problems*. New York: Ronald Press.

Wiser, James. (1986). *Political Theory: A Thematic Inquiry*. Chicago: Nelson-Hall.

5 STATE AND MARKET WHEN COMMAND GOES CAPITALIST

A. Allan Schmid

Countries touting what used to be called command economies have almost disappeared from the face of the earth. The commitment to markets is epitomized by an article in the new Romanian Constitution defining Romania as a market economy and ordering the state to ensure free trade and protect competition (Gray, Hanson, and Ianachkov, 1992). Is it, then, the end of history and arguments about choice of economic system? Are there any choices left? It is the thesis of this chapter that there are options—and that a failure to recognize them is to narrow those who can participate in these choices.

State and Market—Dichotomy or Nexus?

The choices most discussed have to do with how state property is privatized (auctions, vouchers, etc.), monetary policy, how fast to abolish price controls, currency controls, and subsidies, and how much to worry about monopolies. There are two perspectives on these choices. One might be called the *minimalist state* perspective and the other the *state-market nexus* perspective. The minimalist perspective expects that the major role of the state is to (1) put resources into the hands of some private owners as fast as possible (and never upset their plans by future confiscations); (2) facilitate trade among these owners by enforcing their contracts; and (3) enforce competition (although most business agreements can be presumed to be efficiency enhancing). In this minimalist conception there is a clear dichotomy between state and market (Whynes and Bowles, 1981, pp. 12–13). In command economies, the state gave the orders; in the market, the people (consumers) give the orders.

The alternative perspective is not distinguished by the extent of the state (quantitative involvement), but rather involves the unavoidable nexus of state and market (Samuels, 1992). There is no market exchange unless it is clear who the buyer is and who the seller is. But there is much more to it than the ownership of tangible assets in land, apartments, and factories implied above. The state is present anytime there is an opportunity for one person's actions to affect another's, raising the issue of who may proceed without asking others (i.e., is in a position to hear bids to desist by nonowners). The policy issue, then, is not whether the state is involved, but who uses it when interests are incompatible (Schmid, 1989). The incompatibility is not sorted out once and for all with title to exchangeable tangible assets. One question to be explored in this chapter is what is the relationship between who uses the state (has opportunities or rights to sell) and the economic development of the nations of Eastern Europe and the former Soviet republics.

Command and Enablement

What is the difference between detailed central command and the necessarily selective enablement of different interests? The negotiations among a state firm and the central planners and the party involved both tangible and intangible property. Firms strived to control tangible resources such as steel and labor as well as the timely cooperation of other firms providing inputs and further processing outputs. The state firm became "owner" of resources and became obligated to perform via the equivalent of contracts with other firms, all with direction from the state bureaucracy, rather than bids and offers from legally equal firms.

By contrast, in a market economy the decisions to buy and sell are as decentralized as the number of owners who choose to participate in a line of action. But the decision or understanding that all participants have as to who has what opportunities (who is buyer and who is seller) is centralized, collective, and common to the scope of those bound by and playing according to the rules. In that sense, *all economies are centralized.* Even a farmer offering produce at the side of the road has no buyers if they claim the resources used to produce it. This is not to say that multilevel governments are not possible—local, provincial, and national. The state as a collective process by which rights are learned may be formal, such as the nation state, or informal, such as a business corporation, university, or club. The participants may be consciously aware of making a collective decision or spontaneous and unaware of how their individual choices are producing a collective result. All of these systems exact certain costs of entry and exit as they strive to maintain their boundaries. Each may have a particular jurisdiction, and the connecting nodes continually act on and define each other.

Conflict, Economizing, and Coordination

The property rights or institutional foundations of any economy have three interacting elements. One is the sorting out of conflicting interests; the second is the structure of incentives for effort and economizing; and the third is coordination. In the state-market nexus perspective, the state is unavoidably present in every transaction. If there is an opportunity for people to conflict, the state is present. The scope of the state is coterminant with the scope of human interdependence and answers the questions of whose interests count when interests conflict.

Command economies, while counting some successes, have not been successful in eliciting either the full productive efforts of their people or the vigorous pursuit of economizing. Any social system, including the economy, rests on arranging psychological reinforcements consistent with desired activity (and a process for deciding what is desired). Increments of reinforcement must be predictably associated with increments of effort. When people learn that they can improve themselves, they work harder. While command systems do reward those who fill their quotas, the tie of action to reward seems looser than in market systems. Soviet-type economies rely more heavily on nonpecuniary reinforcements, and "profits" are taxed away. The orders of superiors are often personal and capricious (Litwack, 1991). In addition, there are fewer opportunities to try new things when workers and managers are preoccupied with the center's definition of specific performance.

In a command system, it is easy for the center to determine a recipe for producing a given good, but harder to know the opportunity cost of the inputs if used by one firm rather than another because of the loss of information when communicated from the input user to the center and back to input producer (Ericson, 1991). It is the bids of other firms that directly inform the market firm of opportunity costs. Even if the center has some notion of opportunity cost, it has difficulty giving incentives to the firms to economize. In spite of the advantages that market systems have with respect to incentives, Peter Murrell's (1991) survey of the empirical literature shows only small differences in technical and allocative efficiency between market and centrally planned countries. This evidence draws our attention to less dichotomous features of institutional systems. It will be argued below that market information is itself often bounded and rights impacted so that performance is affected by a complex meshing of formal and informal institutions.

The problem for any system to solve involves the incentive to economize and the definition of economizing and hard work. One can economize by saving inputs while holding quantity and quality of output constant. But, for example, if quality is hard for the buyer to measure (information costs), the incentive to economize is the incentive to reduce and hide quality. There is also incentive to push lost opportunities off on others. Use of the environment as a waste sink is a case in point, and observation reveals that both market and command systems can destroy the environment. It is the structure of property rights that determine whose opportunities count and enter into others' calculations of opportunity cost. The hard work of the thief is not to be rewarded, and it is rights that determine who is the thief—for instance, is the user of the environment a thief or a person just using an owned resource? Cost is not just a physical fact of the production function, but a social fact determined by collective choice.

What of coordination? In the command system, the center tries to visualize the recipe for production and order its implementation. Some claim that in the market system no one need be aware of the total recipe of all functions in a marketing chain. Each resource owner need only make an offer and find acceptance for his/her particular function, thus saving on information costs, as Hayek has often explained. This is important as far as it goes. But there is more. Capital must be aggregated; there are problems of assurance and monitoring; there are questions of remedies for breach of contract since not all promises should be executed as first conceived; and there are problems of unavoidably incomplete contracts. If the answers to these questions are not provided by the planner, then each requires a set of rights that makes the market what it is and distinguishes one kind of market from another.

Many activities require the capital of more than one person. There must be some process by which the resources of people who are unknown to each other can be pooled. This is part of the task of company law to be explored below. If the state does not pool resources by command, there must be rules for the private agreements. The interests of the active manager and/or risk bearer, the passive investor, stockholders, bondholders, agents and principals, suppliers, and labor are often at odds, and rights determine who counts.

Coordination and Uncertainty

How are all of these separable and separately owned pieces coordinated? The simplistic answer is that the market does it. But what is the market? It is often suggested that it is simply the individual owners negotiating and making agreements. But complex cooperation does not just happen. Consider just one instance. The cost of a given activity often depends on scale. Producer A could lower costs if larger (or if the industry were larger); Buyer B could go into production only if A were larger and had lower costs than at present. But A makes no investment waiting for several B's to grow and make possible a larger demand for A's product. Each waits for the other. Today's prices don't contain much information on tomorrow's potential prices because of the interlocked production functions. Murrell (1991, p. 62) observes that "potential entrants have to formulate their own general equilibrium model to calculate how expected returns vary with their own and other agents' entry." In this context, Arrow (1987, p. 208) adds that "the superiority of market over centralized planning disappears. Each individual agent is in effect using as much information as would be required for a central planner." Neither market nor plan automatically solves these coordination problems where there is uncertainty and economies of scale. We must search for useful mixtures. The volume of missed opportunities for coordination is difficult to measure since these opportunities leave little evidence behind except the fact that some nations seem to get left out.

The problem of excess capacity is the obverse of missed investment opportunities. Prices today may indicate that a profit is to be made in product X. A firm makes new investments only to discover when the production is on line that a number of other firms made the same decision; therefore, there is excess capacity, and asset losses occur (Richardson, 1960; Shaffer, 1990). The larger forms of this are called real estate cycles, or in agriculture the corn-hog cycle, or just business cycles. Another example of production's missing the mark is when firms stay in place too long.

Investments are sunk only to be made redundant by changing preferences or better technologies.

The welfare state is in part a response to the persistent failure of present market institutions to prevent unbearable losses to immobile assets, both physical and human. The new market economies have the same instincts as the old and wish they could afford the "transfers" that the richer states pay to their citizens left behind. The International Monetary Fund (IMF) and rich donors insist that the new market states be less merciful and resist the practice that the richer states themselves have never resisted as they aid their farmers, coal miners, car and airplane makers. Analytically, the very concept of transfer payment is rights defined. If redundant resource owners knew what they know now, they would have demanded higher returns or assurances before the investments were sunk. If the rights regime had been different, the payments to the redundants would be forfeited escrow for unfilled expectations rather than transfers. The redundant would be suing for breach of contract rather than coming with hat in hand (Beermann and Singer, 1989; Singer, 1988).

The reader might suspect that these examples of under- and overproduction were included to make an argument for central planning again—which the former Socialist nations have been trying to get rid of. But that is not the argument here. Rather, it is to remind us that developmental coordination is not automatic by either command or market.

Property rights relative to coordination can take many forms. In private market economies when someone disappoints another, it could be the basis of a court suit. Commercial law is mostly used to encourage actions consistent with promises (act of commission) rather than to facilitate agreements that otherwise never happen (act of omission). But that is not to say that there are not other institutions used and that they are the same in all market economies. In the German economy the large commercial banks play a role in coordinating investments via credit and stockholding both in the sense of getting a series of interrelated investments to come on line at the same time and to avoid overcapacity. In Japan, the giant interlinked banks and industrial and distribution firms (*Kiertsu*), in cooperation with the government's Ministry of Trade and Industry, have had some success in staking out a position of interlinked investments to develop new products and industries (Thurow, 1992). Could it be that the former socialist countries will adopt a more primitive form of market capitalism that cannot compete with the more modern forms that exist around the world? The German and Japanese systems are not exactly central planning, but they are not exactly a system of isolated individual contracts either. Property rights do play a role in whether private quasi-planning activities occur. The active role of German banks in corporate development would be illegal in the United States.

Property and Plan

As noted above, commercial law is more adapted to preventing breach of contract than failure to contract. Everyone agrees that coordination is built on the expectation that others' promises will be kept. But it is not efficient to force all promises to be physically executed. A better use of the resource may have become evident since the promise was made. The higher return from breach may allow a Pareto-better solution where the promisor can be better off while still giving the promisee the value expected. Although this is clear in principle, a lot of legal resources are incurred in establishing just how much better off the promisee reasonably could have expected to be.

But the bigger problem is that of incomplete contracts. It simply is not possible for the parties to know fully what to contract for. And when it becomes clear later, there is opportunity for one party to gain at the other's expense. Again, concern about this opportunism may thwart some potential cooperation. The central planner would try to make adjustments as events unfolded. The court necessarily plays this role in market economies as one party sues another. Or can it escape by insisting that it just executes the original meaning of the contract? But words don't speak for themselves. As the court searches for meaning, it can ask itself what fair is and how the resolution of the conflict will affect the path of development in the future (assuming it does not choose simply in terms of who paid the judge more). The court, unlike the central planner, does not issue directives for production quotas and the like, but its decisions provide the precedent and example by which firms learn to coordinate their actions. Firms copy successful firms and avoid practices that have resulted in others losing court suits.

Auctions and Complex Coordination

One theme of the previous discussion might be summarized by saying that auctions don't go very far in modern economies. In an auction, goods are already produced and are offered for sale. On the basis of the prices realized, the producers think again and decide to reallocate their resources accordingly in the next period. Price contains all the needed information in this simple world. The motivating power of auction opportunities can be seen in the reforms of Chinese agriculture. When farmers were given the right to work on the land individually, there was a significant increase in output of vegetables and meat. The farmer could produce more by working harder, taking the goods to the nearest population center, and making exchanges on the street. There are few cooperators to be coordinated in this scenario. But the next stage has been slower. To go beyond working harder to working together smarter, life gets more complicated. Fertilizer must be acquired on credit or capital otherwise assembled. The common irrigation system must be maintained. The needs of processors need to be matched to farmer capacities. At some point some new varieties are needed from researchers, and so on. As the interdependencies complicate, the state is no longer simplistic and apart from the market but inextricably part of its fabric. A case analogous to the Chinese experience can be seen in the explosion of retail trading in the former Soviet bloc countries. This activity is simple and similar to an auction, and thus the property rights can be simple. This is in sharp contrast to manufacturing where the uncertainties of coordination have limited new investment.

Development Theory and the State-Market Nexus

Does the system of property rights need implicitly to contain a substantive theory of development? Or can it simply be procedural—a process of exchange? In other words, does law matter? One answer is supplied by Douglass North (1990). His study of economic history leads him to emphasize rights clarity, no government expropriation of rights once set, and institutions that lower transaction cost. In this view the substance of the law is less important than the process. Give the rights to some people (almost any people), don't change them, and make trade as frictionless as possible.

The alternative (perhaps supplementary) view is represented by Alexander Field (1991), also an economic historian. He notes that the location of a right often has income effects and that there are substantial transaction costs no matter how we try to eliminate them. This means that the substance of law matters. Who has to buy from whom matters. And it is unlikely that the direction of bids and acceptances that favors certain sectors at a certain stage and type of economic development will also be suitable for another stage. This clearly was the case when the law facilitated the transition from an agrarian to an industrial economy in the United States (Schmid, 1992). The idea that law matters is also consistent with the theory of Ronald Coase who has made it clear that existence of transaction costs does mean that the location of an exchangeable right affects what a resource is used for (and that it is critical for income distribution).

With this as conceptual background, let's turn to an examination of some of the company and contract law now being revised in the former Soviet bloc countries. Commercial law does not have the popular attention given to factor ownership questions, but most of these countries are revising or creating new rules. Can these laws simply duplicate those in the rich countries? What if all the rich countries don't have the same laws? Does it make any difference which ones are chosen? Have these laws been evolving toward the true and the beautiful and thus only need to be copied for those nations that want to be modern? This conception makes the task largely a technical matter for lawyers. Or are there alternative substantive paths to be chosen requiring political resolution of conflicts? There are as many efficient outcomes as there are property rights distributions. It is quite clear that distributive choices are being made when land is returned to former owners or when factory shares are given to former employees or the general public. It is less clear that distributive choices are made when the commercial code is being discussed. Even less clear is whether it makes any difference for the path of economic development. This chapter is addressed to raising some questions rather than making a case for one rule or the other.

Company Law

Company law refers to the procedures for forming a company—a grouping of people with some shared purposes. It includes corporate forms, rights, and duties of shareholders, including voting rules. Gray and colleagues (1991, p. 9) observe that "the development of most company law reflects the constant shifting of protection for various interests, whether the company, creditors, the investing public, managers, employees, or the national economic interests of the state." When they address the case of Poland they opine that "[t]he coming years should witness the natural evolution of Polish company law as it seeks to protect newly emerging social and financial interests." What is meant by natural evolution? Since these interests are not always compatible, is it nature that decides whose interests count? Is it a matter of just incorporating new interests as they come along or does the law have something to do with selecting what interests emerge?

The provision that is most easily understood is the granting of permission to form a company. Poland follows a pattern of countries molded on civil law rather than common law and thus requires approval by a notary and payment of stamp fees. At the moment there are few notaries, and they receive 3% of equity capital up to 250 million zlotys, plus .01% of equity capital over 250 million. Stamp duties are also significant. These requirements can best be understood simply as taxes and can be evaluated as any tax.

The consequence of corporate forms offered is a bit less obvious. Poland offers two: limited liability company and joint stock company. Both offer limited liability and require transparency, but differ primarily in publicness. The Polish limited liability company is similar to the French S.A.R.L. (*société à responsibility limitée*), the German GmbH (*Gesellschaft mit beschranker Haftung*), and the closely held private corporation in Anglo-American law. The shares are transferable (so the market is embraced), but the company's permission may be required (the market is circumscribed). The concept here is that in a small company the success of the business depends on personal relationships and trust among the capital contributors who are also probably active in management. This relationship could be upset by indiscriminate sale to new unknown stockholders. Most otherwise market-friendly countries of the world allow this limitation to the market. Stockholders in a small firm active in its management may not contribute effort to the firm in proportion to their capital contribution. So the limited liability company allows voting representation to differ from capital share. Control may be more concentrated than ownership of shares. It is judged that the financial condition of the small closely held corporation is inherently more transparent than a large corporation where many shareholders have no first-hand knowledge of the firm. Thus, the closely held firm is not required to have as extensive reporting requirements as larger public corporations.

The Polish joint stock company resembles the French S.A. (*société anonyme*), the German AG (*Aktiengesellschaft*), and the Anglo-American public corporation. The minimum capital requirement is larger than that for the closely held company above. In most industrial countries, when a firm reaches a certain size (49 stockholders in France) it must become a public corporation subject to more stringent financial reporting requirements. The common distinction between public and closely held companies is not followed through in Poland who allows both forms to restrict the sale of stock. Perhaps Poland is anticipating the consequences of unfriendly takeovers of large firms. Some scholars regard the threat of takeovers as a performance-enhancing incentive for managers, while others argue that they induce managerial myopia (Tirole, 1991; Jensen, 1988). Hostile takeovers were common in the United States in the 1980s but infrequent in Germany and Japan. Again, it appears that not all markets are the same.

Even large firms may need stockholder loyalty to weather the financial storms of emerging market economies (exit versus loyalty, in Hirschman's terms—see Hirschman (1970)). There will be differences of opinion among stockholders as to whether the assets are better liquidated or should be held for expected better days. Some countries may want to make it harder for unfriendly takeovers so that the going concern in temporary trouble is preserved, while others may feel that the greater danger is hopeless firms who carry on too long.

Interest-bearing corporate shares are not allowed in Poland and most Western countries. However, they are allowed in Hungary and the former Czechoslovakia. The Polish rule means that those who want the extra security of interest obligations can't be voting stockholders. Recall that German and Japanese banks are large corporate stockholders as well as holders of interest-bearing securities and thus participate more fully in corporate policy. Gray and associates (1991, p. 11) argue that "interest bearing shares might prove useful in countries trying to encourage private ownership of companies by an inexperienced and risk-averse population." This is a case where Hungary and the Czechs have not followed modern Western practice, but have chosen a set of rights that they judge to fit their circumstance better.

Corporate Governance

Articles of association and shareholders agreements are the place where founders indicate something of their decisions on the form of corporate governance. The questions most commonly addressed are rules of voting and quorums at stockholder meetings. But perhaps more important is the internal organization of the company. The literature comparing business organization in the United States and Japan reminds us that coordination of the factors involved in a business can be quite different among countries that are equally committed to markets (Ouchi, 1981; Aoki, 1990). The fact is that much of the coordination is inside firms and nonmarket, though not necessarily hierarchical. There are many choices to be made with respect to organization by products, functions, or regions, a process that has parallels with the organization of the central planning agency. Alfred Chandler's (1977) study of economic history suggests that organization or structure of the firm follows the choice of business strategy. Strategic innovative decisions to develop technology and new markets change the firm's economic environment and require different internal organization than the merely adaptive firm searching for cost-effective ways to deploy its resources for known technologies (Lazonick, 1991; Storper and Walker, 1989).

Much of the choice of firm organization is not related to formal law. But some of it is particularly as it is affected by the administration of antitrust law. Historically, the long-time U.S. prohibition of one corporation's holding stock in another had a lot to do with the organization of multifunction firms (Horwitz, 1992, p. 83). This is an area that deserves further inquiry under current conditions existing in the former Soviet bloc countries.

In the former Soviet bloc countries corporate governance has focused on the participation of labor. Swaan and Lissowska (1992, p. 32) argue that self-management in Poland affected the behavior of management. "In order to avoid any conflict both with the worker's council and with the authorities, managers preferred to refrain from any initiative on the market and to concentrate upon bargaining with the authorities." However, they observe that the enterprise councils in Hungary were an impetus for behavioral change, and they attribute the difference not to formal laws but to legitimization and trust at the national level.

It is interesting that in Yugoslavia where worker participation was most developed, the idea is now virtually abandoned in private firms in Slovenia (Gray and Stiblar, 1992). Worker participation in management was debated but omitted from their new constitution. It is doubly ironic that this is probably rooted in a desire to be like the West, although German law requires worker participation in corporate boards. Again, are the former socialist countries going to revert to a more primitive form of capitalism?

Bankruptcy and Capitalism

Capital markets are secured by interests in real property. Mortgage lending commonly requires that title be given up if the loan is defaulted. It would appear then that the former Socialist countries must learn to accept the jobless, the homeless, and the landless in the name of progress. Mistakes are inevitable, and many will be beyond the fault of the individual participants in the newly emerging market economies. Gray, Hanson, and Ianachkov (1992, p. 14) opine that "[f]oreclosure on the property—and thus the possibility of eviction—will become a necessity if truly private mortgage lending is to emerge. This will clearly take a major change in attitude as well as a rethinking of the legal framework for eviction and foreclosure." Maybe this is the end of history, and capitalist institutions have reached the zenith of accomplishment. Then again, maybe not. As noted above, these failures are part of the seedbed for the welfare state (and in fact were the seedbed for communism). Some institutional creativity is sorely needed if this institutional cycle is not to be repeated.

Contract Law

The inexorable state-market nexus is clear in the choice of what contracts to enforce. The state may not avoid the choice of where to place its sanctions. Are some private agreements unworthy of being enforced? For example, in the United States, a real estate contract discriminating on the basis of race will not be enforced. It may be agreed to between buyer and seller, but other parties feel aggrieved. As in all rights, the issue is who can participate in a transaction. If all agreements are to be supported, the effect will cancel other areas of substantive law that are the vehicle for third party rights. For example, a contract might release a firm from charges of negligence with respect to the safety of its workers or consumers. In the abstract it sounds good that the state should not second guess the agreements of its citizens, but the unavoidable issue is which citizens count. The Hungarian civil code embraces the rule of *laesio enormous*, and the court is required to weigh the substantive fairness of all contracts. American common law was once similar (Horwitz, 1977). Has American law evolved to the apex of truth and beauty worthy of emulation by all, or should each nation ask what it wants to make of itself and if its needs at the beginning of its capitalist experience are different than the already rich nations?

Inequality of bargaining power is one of the problems in contract enforcement. Are these inequalities greater in the former Soviet bloc than in the contemporary industrialized countries? The perceived fairness of the application of state power may be part of the equation adding to legitimation of the state. Even in the richer countries there are debates about contracts of adhesion, and German and United Kingdom laws differ from those in the United States. Many contracts are not really negotiated item by item. Rather, the bigger, more powerful party offers a take-it-or-leave-it contract. Shall the state then enforce these contracts? Daniel Ostas (1992, p. 520) argues that these are vital matters for public policy and that the "Hungarians and Poles must determine for themselves the degree to which the state will support one-sided exchanges." He dramatizes the point by saying that adhesion contracts look a lot like a contract under central planning—namely little choice on one side. He further notes that the language of contracts may be different from everyday customary terms, and if the courts enforce the express legal language with regard to privately drafted penalty clauses, repossession clauses, and warranty disclaimers, the effect may be very one sided.

Contract law technically refers to what agreement prevails if the particular matter is not explicitly described in the contract. So if the parties did not think to address some issue that later turns out to be crucial, the court supplies the provision according to custom, precedent, or code. Consider the case of partially performed contracts. Until 1930, U.S. courts did not enforce these contracts (Horwitz, 1992). Has the United States now found the truth to which others must move or was there some functional reason for this practice at the time or did it represent a political choice between competing interests that changes over time as different groups get control of government? Suppose that a firm has agreed to pay a certain sum of money on a given date but that the other party has only partially delivered the promised good. If the firm is forced to pay and then counter-sue for delivery, it may be bankrupt before the sequence is completed. Many observers of Eastern Europe note that legal resources are scarce, but little attention has been paid to whether this fact has implications for the substance of law. It may be better not to enforce one side of an agreement if the other side cannot also be enforced with speed. It can be imagined that the needs of start-up firms of timid entrepreneurs may be different than large, foreign-financed firms. And the needs may also be different where risks can be spread to third party insurers than when some equitable distribution of the costs of unfillable promises is needed to keep both parties going. Going concerns should be husbanded in fledgling market economies with poorly developed insurance markets among other things.

The trend in the United States is to place less reliance on the courts supplying missing provisions to contracts. On the one hand, firms buy more legal resources and try harder to cover everything in the contract. This may not make as much sense where these resources are very scarce and particularly not available to new firms. If start-up firms cannot have some faith that unforeseen events that were not covered in a contract will not be settled in a fashion to share the costs, it may be part of the picture of new enterprises that never happen.

On the other hand, firms that develop long-standing and continuing exchange partners neither rely on contracts nor resort to the courts for formal adjudication of unforeseen problems. They work them out amicably so that the business relationship continues. To win a big settlement and lose the continuing customer is bad business. This becomes part of the business culture, but it can be expected to be in lessor supply in new market economies. So the details of contract law may be more important there than in mature capitalist countries.

While this chapter has emphasized formal law, custom and business culture are equally important institutionally. There are many problems in coordination that cannot be handled well by any explicit public policy and law (Swaan and Lissowska, 1992). Consider an unsolved coordination problem even in the United States. The warehousing of goods would be much more efficient if pallet size were standard. For pallets to be of standard size has implications for the size of boxes a firm uses to ship its products. Supposedly, this was the kind of problem that central planning was designed to solve. But the record is not good. Great differences exist among industries with respect to their ability to solve these coordination problems involving the development of new technologies. Formal law and government encouragement may help, but informal custom and culture dominate these collective actions. More research is needed to understand if these are just random events or whether their evolution can be enhanced.

Conclusion

Theory and observation suggest that the state-market nexus perspective is the most useful way to describe the historical evolution of capitalist economies and explore the options in the contemporary transitions under way. Informed choice of the legal foundations of a market economy requires a theory of development (answering the question of whose interests contribute the most to where a nation wants to go). Thus it is a matter of political choice, not just a matter of technical economics or law. There are plenty of choices to be made even after privatization is complete. The leading market economies are not all alike, and their further evolution may well be affected by the new market economies if they do not become entombed in a primitive capitalism long abandoned by the leaders.

History is not complete. Major ideologies still divide both academy and politics. Some are convinced that the lesson of the Soviet experience is that all must "abandon the Faustian urge to control, to know in advance, and thus to allow economic outcomes to arise naturally as the unpredictable consequences of market interaction" (Ericson, 1991, p. 26). To label something as natural has provided psychic balm for many for centuries. But what is natural? Is it s/he who can grab an opportunity with little collective help other than that of clan and kin? Does it look like the Mafia? Many former Soviet bloc citizens suspect that all private firms look a lot like the Mafia. Yes, let it happen. Social science knowledge of causality will always be limited. But we can proceed less blindly. Some undesirable things that can happen can be blunted by some conscious, deliberative collective choice, and some other things need a particular type of collective help if they are to happen at all. Our ideological perspective will still play a role in who chooses the legal foundations of the market.

Acknowledgments

I want to thank James Shaffer, Warren Samuels, and David Reisman for stimulating my thinking on this chapter.

References

Aoki, Masahiko. (1990). "Toward an Economic Model of the Japanese Firm." *Journal of Economic Literature* 28(1):1–27.

Arrow, Kenneth J. (1987). "Rationality of Self and Others in an Economic System." In Robin M. Hogarth and Melvin W. Reder (eds.), *Rational Choice: The Contrast Between Economics and Psychology*. Chicago: University of Chicago Press, pp. 201–216.

Beermann, Jack M., and Joseph W. Singer. (1989). "Baseline Questions in Legal Reasoning: The Example of Property in Jobs." *Georgia Law Review* 23(4):911–995.

Chandler, Alfred D., JR. (1977). *The Visable Hand: The Managerial Revolution in American Business*. Cambridge: Harvard University Press.

Gray, Cheryl, and Franjo D. Stiblar. (1992). *The Evolving Legal Framework for Private Sector Activity in Slovenia*, Policy Research Working Papers WPS 893. Washington, DC: The World Bank.

Gray, Cheryl W., Rebecca J. Hanson, and Peter G. Ianachkov. (1992). *Romania's Evolving Legal Framework for Private Sector Development*, Policy Research Working Papers WPS 872. Washington, DC: The World Bank.

Gray, Cheryl W., et al. (1991). *Legal Framework for the Private Sector Development in a Transitional Economy: The Case of Poland*. Policy Research Working Papers WPS 800. Washington, DC: The World Bank.

Ericson, Richard E. (1991). "The Classical Soviet-Type Economy: Nature of the System and Implications for Reform." *Journal of Economic Perspectives* 5 (Fall): 11–28.

Field, Alexander. (1991). "Do Legal Systems Matter?" *Explorations in Economic History* 28: 1–35.

Hirschman, Albert. (1970). *Exit, Voice and Loyalty* (Cambridge, Mass.: Harvard University Press).

Horwitz, Morton J. (1977). *The Transformation of American Law, 1780–1860*. Cambridge: Harvard University Press.

Horwitz, Morton J. (1992). *The Transformation of American Law, 1870–1960.* Oxford: Oxford University Press.

Jensen, M. (1988). "Takeovers: Their Causes and Consequences." *Journal of Economic Perspectives* 2: 21–48.

Lazonick, William. (1991). *Business Organization and the Myth of the Market Economy*. Cambridge: Cambridge University Press.

Litwack, John M. (1991). "Legality and Market Reform in Soviet-Type Economies." *Journal of Economic Perspectives* 5 (Fall): 77–90.

Murrell, Peter. (1991). "Can Neoclassical Economics Underpin the Reform of Centrally Planned Economies?" *Journal of Economic Perspectives* 5 (Fall): 59–76.

North, Douglass. (1990). *Institutions, Institutional Change and Economic Performance*. Cambridge: Cambridge University Press.

Ostas, Daniel. (1992). "Institutional Reform in East-Central Europe: Hungarian and Polish Contract Law." *Journal of Economic Issues* 26(2):513–523.

Ouchi, William G. (1981). *Theory Z: How American Business Can Meet the Japanese Business Challenge*. Reading, MA: Addison-Wesley.

Richardson, G.B. (1960). *Information and Investment.* Oxford: Oxford University Press.

Samuels, Warren J. (1992). "The Legal-Economic Nexus." In Warren Samuels (ed.), *Essays on the Economic Role of Government*, Vol. 1. New York: New York University Press, pp. 162–186.

Schmid, A. Allan. (1989). "Economy and State: An Institutionalist Theory of Process and Learning." In Warren J. Samuels (ed.), *Fundamentals of the Economic Role of Government.* New York: Greenwood Press, pp. 173–178.

Schmid, A. Allan. (1992). "Legal Foundations of the Market; Implications for the Formerly Socialist Countries of Eastern Europe and Africa." *Journal of Economic Issues* 26 (Sept.): 707–732.

Shaffer, James D. (1990). "Selective Perceptions and the Politics of Agricultural Policy Analysis." *Choices* (Third Quarter): 17–21.

Singer, Joseph W. (1988). "The Reliance Interest in Property." *Stanford Law Review* 40(3):611–751.

Storper, Michael, and Richard Walker. (1989). *The Capitalist Imperative: Territory, Technology, and Industrial Growth*. Oxford: Basil Blackwell.

Swaan, Wim, and Maria Lissowska. (1992). "Enterprise Behaviour in Hungary and Poland in the Transition to a Market Economy: Routines as a Barrier to Change." *Research Memorandum Series*, TI-1992/84, Tinbergen Institute, University of Amsterdam.

Thurow, Lester. (1992). *Head to Head*. New York: William Morrow.

Tirole, Jean. (1991). *Ownership and Incentives in a Transition Economy*. Working Paper Series. Washington, DC: Institute for Policy Reform.

Whynes, David K., and Roger Bowles. (1981). *The Economic Theory of the State.* Oxford: Martin Robertson.

6 SCHUMPETER AND CAPITALISM IN AN ERA OF TRANSITION

David Simpson

Introduction

In this chapter I propose to assess the validity of J.A. Schumpeter's prediction of the gradual extinction of capitalism in the advanced countries, to be succeed by a form of socialism. Whereas the conventional wisdom has it that this prophecy, like so many other economic forecasts, has proved to have failed, I shall argue that his predictions and the reasoning behind them, while not correct in every detail, seem to have every chance of being proved correct. This is all the more remarkable when it is remembered that these predictions were made more than 50 years ago. The first edition of *Capitalism, Socialism and Democracy* was published in 1942 in the middle of the Second World War.

The central message of the book was a simple one: that capitalism, as a system of economic and political organization, carried within itself the seeds of its own destruction. Capitalism was doomed to fail, and the symptoms of decline were already visible in the economic and political systems not only of the United Kingdom but also of the United States. The successor state to capitalism would be some form of socialism.

This message did not arouse a great deal of interest at the time. Leading professional economists were still dazzled by the bright intellectual lights of *The General Theory*. Schumpeter found that not only his two-volume 1939 work *Business Cycles*, on which he had lavished so much scholarly effort, was apparently rendered redundant by the *The General Theory*. The same book also overshadowed his *Capitalism, Socialism and Democracy. The General Theory* appeared to offer an operational plan for saving capitalism, and with it democracy, while the Schumpeterian prediction had undertones of historical inevitability which were perhaps uncongenial to the Anglo-American mind.

As Haberler has pointed out (Haberler, 1981), Schumpeter must have gained some satisfaction from Keynes' posthumously published article (Keynes, 1946), in which he recommended that "the classical medicine" be allowed to work, that is, that the recession be allowed to run its course. Had he been alive today, Schumpeter would have been able to take even more satisfaction from the apparent unwillingness of the governments of the advanced countries to adopt Keynesian policies to cope with the current recession, which in the United Kingdom is the longest recession since the Great Depression. Schumpeter would have felt that this fell into the category of "a remedial recession," that is, one that was necessary in order to compensate for previous errors and to provide a basis for future sustainable developments. In the words of the contemporary British prime minister, the pains of a recession are "a price well worth paying" (Singer, 1993).

Now, however, with the general recognition of the inappropriateness of Keynesian remedies for the ills of the mixed economy, or fettered capitalism as Schumpeter would have called it, there has been a revival of scholarly interest in Schumpeter's work (Swedberg, 1991; März, 1991; Allen, 1991). Some of these studies dwell as much on the author's life as his work; no one who wants to complete his or her understanding of the character of Schumpeter should neglect the memoir by his Harvard colleague and fellow countryman, Gottfried Haberler, published only a few months after his death (Haberler, 1950).

The essence of Schumpeter's vision about the breakdown of capitalism that is set out at length in *Capitalism, Socialism and Democracy* can be conveyed in one sentence from page 61 of the book:

> The thesis I shall endeavour to establish is that the actual and prospective performance of the capitalist system is such as to negative the idea of its breaking down under the weight of economic failure, but that its very success undermines the social institutions which protect it, and "inevitably" creates conditions in which it will not be able to live, and which strongly point to socialism as the heir apparent (Schumpeter, 1942).

Fourteen years earlier Schumpeter had put forward the same idea:

> Capitalism, whilst economically stable and even gaining in stability, creates, by rationalising the human mind, a mentality and style of life incompatible with its own fundamental conditions, motives and social institutions, and will be changed, although not by economic necessity and probably even at some sacrifice of economic welfare, into an order of things which it will be merely a matter of taste and terminology to call socialism or not (Schumpeter, 1928).

It is significant that the author places the word "inevitably" in the first passage within quotation marks.

Schumpeter was much too wise to accept the doctrine of historical inevitability. This feature distinguishes his work from that of Marx. Schumpeter was careful to emphasize that his predictions amounted to no more than pointing out historical tendencies that could be arrested or even reversed. In general, he was skeptical of the ability of economists (or anyone else, for that matter) to predict the future:

> An economist can no more foretell the future than can a doctor say when one of his patients will next have a road accident, and what his injuries will then be.

From the first two passages above it is clear that Schumpeter followed Marx not only in believing that capitalism will eventually be replaced by socialism but also that this change would be brought about by factors endogenous to the capitalist system itself. But whereas, in Marx's case, capitalism would disappear in an abrupt and violent collision of economic and political forces, Schumpeter had a very different vision. There would be a steady and gradual decomposition of pure capitalism, "a quenching of capitalist attitudes and institutions." Of course, the concept of pure capitalism is an abstraction. No historical circumstances ever fit that description exactly. Even at one moment in time, there are different patterns of capitalism (Albert, 1991).

According to Schumpeter, the most important factor in the decline of capitalism is the decline in the motivation of the entrepreneur, the hero of the early stage of pure capitalism. The modern business corporation, itself a product of the capitalist process, "socialises the bourgeois mind." The modern corporation executive acquires something of the psychology of a salaried worker employed in a bureaucratic organization.

Meanwhile, the increasing size of firms undermines the concept of property or of freedom of contract. The figure of the working proprietor of a firm, characteristic of early capitalism, has simply disappeared from the contemporary mixed economy. The contract of employment, which once involved a personal link between two individuals, has now become stereotyped, bureaucratic, and impersonal. In Schumpeter's words, "the capitalist process takes the life out of the idea of property."

An increasing size concentration of firms also means that the political attitudes of society are profoundly changed by the elimination of a host of small and medium-sized firms. Schumpeter anticipated that the mixed economy, or "operating the capitalist economy in the labour interest," as he put it, could not be sustained in the long run. It had the disciplines of *neither* the competitive forces prevailing in the traditional capitalist market economy *nor* the sanctions of a Soviet-style planned economy. Competition within a pure capitalist market economy eliminates all activities that no longer have an economically useful function. Such redundant activities are eliminated by decree in a planned economy (if and when they are recognized). But in a mixed economy, it is frequently possible for those who have a vested interest in uneconomic activities to use the democratic political process to protect and thus to perpetuate such activities.

In the absence of incentives or sanctions, the mixed economy would therefore have to rely on self-denial or at least self-restraint on the part of those taking part in the economic process. Individuals would have to act in the interest of the economy as a whole rather than in their own material self-interest. It would therefore appear unlikely that the mixed economy could survive for long as a viable form of economic organization. With an increasing proportion of uneconomic activities, the pressures for change would become irresistible. Thus Schumpeter anticipated that there would be a gradual transition of the mixed economy toward a state of greater government control and regulation which he would call socialism.

Many of those who read *Capitalism, Socialism and Democracy* when it first appeared mistook Schumpeter for a Socialist. Haberler says that this mistake was made even by the editor of the German edition of the book (Haberler, 1981). Other defenders of capitalism criticized the author's attitude as defeatist. In the preface to the second edition of his book, Schumpeter replied: "I deny entirely that this term (defeatism) is applicable to a piece of analysis . . . the report that a certain ship (capitalism) is sinking is not defeatist. Only the spirit in which this report is received can be described as defeatist. The crew can sink down and drink. But it can also rush to the pumps" (Schumpeter, 1950, p. xv).

Elsewhere in the book Schumpeter is discussing industries in the United Kingdom that could be socialized without serious loss of efficiency. At the bottom of the list is agriculture. Schumpeter writes:

> If he (the socialist) insists also on nationalising land—leaving, I suppose, the farmer's status as it is—i.e., transferring to the state all that remains of ground rents and royalties, I have no objection to make as an economist.

To this statement, however, he adds the following footnote:

> This is no place for airing personal preferences. Nevertheless I wish it to be understood that the above statement is made as a matter of professional duty and does not imply that I am in love with that proposal which, were I an Englishman, I should on the contrary opposed to the best of my ability (Schumpeter, 1950, p. 231).

It is not difficult to find the origins of Schumpeter's vision of the individualist economic order and its counterpart, the democratic political system, as being doomed to be succeeded by the interfering collectivist state. According to Samuelson (1981), Carl Menger, the founder of the Austrian school, had become convinced that capitalism was dying. This conclusion, says Samuelson, accounted for the scholarly sterility of the last 25 years of Menger's life.

It is interesting to speculate to what extent Menger's views concerning the demise of capitalism were influenced by his environment. Vienna at the turn of the century was a city of extraordinary social, cultural, and political change. The election of a socialist mayor in 1987, who took into municipal ownership the tramways and electric power and gas companies of the city, and the assassination of the Empress Elizabeth in 1898, seemed to portend growing instability. These changes were mirrored in the cultural and intellectual life of the city. Among the notable creative spirits in the cultural ferment of the period were the psychologist Freud, the painter Kokoschka, the composer Schoenberg, and the dramatist Kraus.

Menger passed on this pessimistic vision to the later members of the Austrian school. Both Schumpeter and Hayek, as well as von Mises, absorbed the implicit belief that capitalism was on the brink of destruction. Each of them reacted to this message in different ways. In 1927 Mises wrote surely the most intellectually devastating assault ever mounted on socialism (*Socialism*, 1951), while Hayek spent most of the later part of his life analyzing the functioning of capitalism, highlighting in particular its beneficial aspects. He also wrote a polemical warning (Hayek, 1944) about the dangers of postwar socialism. This book stressed the socialist roots of Nazism, but it was an unfashionable view and the book was received with an embarrassed silence. Schumpeter was much more detached: *Capitalism, Socialism and Democracy* represents a careful analysis of the reasons for what be believed was the forthcoming decline of the capitalist system.

Superficially, Schumpeter's analysis resembles that of Marx, and he never disguised that part of his thinking that he owed to Marx. However, as we shall see, Schumpeter's analysis of the demise of capitalism was based on reasons entirely different from those of Marx. In Schumpeter's vision, capitalism is destroyed by its success, not its failure. The most important element in its destruction is the spread of rationalism. Capitalism would end not with a bang but a whimper, with the transition to socialism being so gradual that it would be impossible clearly to mark the boundary of the passage from the former state to the latter.

Reasons for the Decline of Capitalism

Pure capitalism can be defined as an economic system characterized by the private ownership of capital, the division of labor, the allocation of resources by the market, and the minimum of government intervention. In such a system, according to Schumpeter, competition takes place principally through the medium of innovation. Innovation is something brought about by competition between entrepreneurs. The driving force of competition that causes entrepreneurs to innovate is not just the prospect of profit, but the threat of loss arising from the actual or potential innovative behavior of rival entrepreneurs. Schumpeter is careful to emphasize that it should not be supposed that innovation takes place by employing means of production which are previously unemployed. While this is possible, it is not the essence of the phenomenon. Innovation means simply putting existing factors to work in different ways.

The fact that innovation requires the bidding away of existing resources from their employment in other firms is one reason why competition through innovation is quite disruptive. Another reason is that specific forms of capital and labor with highly specialized skills rendered redundant by rival innovations elsewhere do not easily migrate to more successful firms and industries, as assumed by neoclassical theory. The value of such capital is more often destroyed, as, for example, after the switch in demand for transport services from railways to cars and airlines. In the case of specific labor skills, competition incurs significant economic costs such as the costs of unemployment and retraining as well as that of job search. Thus the typical path through time of the capitalist economy is not a smooth one, but is marked by periodic upheavals at the level of the firm and, less frequently, the industry, and by irregular fluctuations in the economy as a whole. Schumpeter's metaphor of a "perennial gale of creative destruction" is well chosen and contrasts strongly with the moving equilibrium depicted by steady-state growth theory.

In *Capitalism, Socialism and Democracy*, Schumpeter explains the mechanism according to which, in his view, pure capitalism would gradually give way, through an intermediate stage of controlled or fettered capitalism, to an economic system wholly controlled by government, which could be called socialism. Unlike Marx, Schumpeter made control and not ownership the test of socialism.

Increasing government control would take three main forms, according to Schumpeter: the growing regulation of business activity, increasing levels of taxation, and widening public ownership. Three further features distinguish the process of transition: an increase in concentration of the ownership of property (with a concomitant shift in political attitudes), the withering of the entrepreneurial function, and the growth of an anti-capitalist mentality.

Under pure capitalism, the Schumpeterian entrepreneur has a number of identifying features. He is moved by the desire to found a family fortune; therefore, he is content to take a long view of the required return on investment. He may also be moved by the creative satisfaction that comes from getting things done, and by the desire to prove himself superior to his competitors. He is possessed of an aptitude, entrepreneurship, that is distributed rarely among the population, like a talent for singing. He will typically launch a new firm, controlled by himself, as the vehicle for introducing an innovation. What distinguishes the entrepreneurial function from all others is that the entrepreneur innovates.

However, with the continued evolution of capitalism, the function of innovation and with it the role of the entrepreneur are expected to change. Innovation would become a routine function, carried out by existing companies, not new firms. The individual entrepreneur would gradually become extinct since his function would increasingly be performed by committees operating inside large firms. As the function of the entrepreneur becomes redundant, his or her social status would decline: so, too, would that of the whole bourgeois class. Not only would the function of innovation become routinized in this period of fettered or controlled capitalism; so, too, would the function of invention. These changes would, in Schumpeter's view, follow from the gradual extension of what he called "the range of the calculable" as capitalism progressed.

These were, and are, bold predictions. Have subsequent events shown them to be correct?

In 1981, in approaching the 40th anniversary of the publication of *Capitalism, Socialism and Democracy*, a small number of distinguished scholars conducted a reappraisal of this work (Heertje, 1981). Running through most of the diverse contributions was the implicit assumption that Schumpeter's prediction of the decline of capitalism had been falsified. The survival, indeed the flourishing, of capitalism in the postwar period was a fact so much taken for granted that it seemed unnecessary to spell it out.

Ten years further on, with the complete collapse of socialism in the Soviet Union and in Eastern Europe, and with all forms of socialism apparently in retreat throughout the world, whether in the developing countries or in Scandinavia, such predictions seem even more unrealistic, perhaps even absurd. However, as we shall see, there is still a case to be made in favor of Schumpeter's prediction.

The Decline of Capitalism

Consider four principal dimensions or yardsticks by which the metamorphosis of capitalism into socialism might be measured. They are: (1) the ownership of the means of production; (2) the organization of the economy; (3) the distribution of income; and (4) values and culture.

The Ownership of the Means of Production

From the standpoint of pure or classical Marxism, ownership is the most important, indeed the only, acceptable criterion of progress toward socialism. While various forms of guild socialism, cooperative forms of ownership, and even municipal socialism were not only preached but actively practiced in many of the advanced countries in the nineteenth and twentieth centuries, the orthodox Marxist position that socialism was to be equated with state ownership of all productive assets was never seriously challenged in countries that actually professed themselves to be socialist. The single exception to this rule was Tito's Yugoslavia, a deviation which, while legitimized by references to the textual works of Marx and Lenin, owed its existence in part to the particular historical circumstances in which the communist state in Yugoslavia came into existence, and in part to the personality of Tito himself. In principle, as opposed to practice, the primacy of state ownership as the sole criterion of socialism was, of course, the subject of the interminable debates to which socialist intellectuals in the Western countries were addicted.

Marx believed that ownership of productive capital in an advanced society would pass overnight from private ownership into the hands of the state, acting on behalf of the working class, during a violent political revolution. Schumpeter had an entirely different vision of this transition, in which the question of ownership played a lesser part.

We may note with the advantage of hindsight that Schumpeter was surely right to play down the significance of ownership. When operated at arm's length, as in the case of British Petroleum, some French banks and insurance companies, and some Italian industrial companies, state-owned concerns have not differed significantly in behavior and performance from their privately owned counterparts. In most cases, of course, governments and parliaments in the Western world have been unable to resist the temptation to interfere in the operation of state-owned companies, with consequences that have been all too apparent.

Nevertheless, it must be acknowledged that, using the orthodox Marxist criterion of private versus state ownership, the progress toward socialism that seemed to characterize most, if not all, of the advanced countries in the 35 years after World War II, began to be reversed in the 1980s. Privatization has become a world wide phenomenon, spreading from the advanced to the developing countries in much the same ways as the Socialist message had done in the immediate postwar era. Therefore, if the proportion of productive assets owned by the state is to be the criterion of the extent to which a given country has passed from capitalism to socialism, then there can be no doubt that Marx was wrong. But while Marxists have to accept this measure, Schumpeterians do not. Schumpeter clearly attached little importance to the question of the ownership of productive assets per se. For him, the key issue was that of government control over the private sector of the economy.

The Organization of the Economy

The centrally planned economy is the characteristic form of economic organization associated with classical or Marxist socialism. One can justify this statement, not in terms of textual authority or philosophical argument, but by reference to the actual practices of states that professed themselves to be socialist. Once again, Yugoslavia was the exception.

To the Marxist, therefore, a second yardstick by which an economy could be said to have progressed toward socialism was the extent to which its economic activity was centrally planned.

To Schumpeter, again, a movement to a planned economy, although probable, was of minor importance. Instead, capitalism would gradually be suffocated under a widening and thickening blanket of regulations and taxes, responding to the political demands, via the democratic system, of interest groups, notably the trade unions.

There was plenty of evidence to be found in the first half of this century in support of his thesis, not only in the United States and the United Kingdom but in the other leading industrialized countries as well. Even as late as the mid-1970s in the United Kingdom, it might have been argued that Schumpeter's predictions had a degree of plausibility.

But in retrospect it seems that the tide began to turn in the late 1970s, and that the postwar trend to ever more controlled and taxed market economies began to be reversed with accelerating rapidity in the 1980s. The counter-revolution in favor of the free market, led simultaneously by Mrs. Thatcher in the United Kingdom and President Reagan in the United States, was a program composed primarily of removing state-owned companies to the private sector (in the United Kingdom) and of deregulation of previously regulated markets, notably the airline industry (in the United States), while in both countries a program of lower rates of income tax was enacted. In the case of the United Kingdom, statutory reductions were also made in the lawfully permitted powers of trade unions.

The type of program stated in these two countries has significantly altered the characteristics and behavior of the two economies concerned. It has unleashed previously restrained spirits of enterprise, resulting, at least in the United Kingdom, in discernible improvements in productivity growth. At the same time negative results have emerged such as increased market volatility, leading to large-scale unemployment and a growing inequality in the distribution of income.

Most important, the British and American programs of privatization and deregulation have been widely imitated not only throughout the rest of the industrialized countries but also in the developing countries and, most dramatically of all, in the countries of Eastern Europe and the former Soviet Union. In the latter countries, those living examples of Marxist socialism, the overthrow of the political dictatorship of the Communist party has been accompanied by a program of selling state-owned industry into private hands, and the replacement of the planned economy by the free market as the principal method of allocating national resources.

In these circumstances, how can it be seriously argued that Schumpeter's predictions have any validity?

Leaving aside for one moment the question of the permanence of the Thatcher-Reagan counter-revolution in the advanced countries, it can readily be conceded that the changes in the developing countries are both desirable and unlikely to be reversed. But it is the advanced countries on which Schumpeter was focusing his attention. It may be conceded for the purposes of argument that there has been a tendency within the last decade to abolish many forms of regulation and control in advanced market economies. But what of taxation? Here the case for Schumpeter is strong.

The chronic federal deficit in the United States is common knowledge. It is also well known that the size of the deficit mounted rapidly during the years of the two Reagan administrations. A similar phenomenon can be seen in most of the advanced countries. Governments everywhere are wrestling with actual or potentially chronic budget deficits, arising from an apparently insatiable demand on the part of their populations for the free or subsidised provision of welfare services, notably pensions, but also medical care, educational services, and unemployment, and other forms of social security benefits. At the same time, there is a deep reluctance to pay the taxes necessary to fund such services.

Until World War I, as Drucker points out, no government in history could obtain more than about 5% or 6% of the national income of its people through taxation (Drucker, 1993). But the growing monetization of the economy that came with industrialization and the development of international money markets meant that by World War I even the two poorest participants could tax and borrow in each year more than the total annual income of their respective populations. There no longer seemed to be any limits to the amounts that government could tax, borrow, or spend. And, using taxes and expenditure, the government of the modern state could, above all, redistribute personal incomes.

In his 1918 paper, "The Crisis of the Tax State" (Schumpeter, 1954), Schumpeter was the first economist to point out the implications of these possibilities. In particular, he pointed to the danger of the demand for public expenditure outrunning the willingness or the ability of society to pay for it. This could lead to a crisis:

> If the will of the people demands higher and higher public expenditures, if more and more means are used for purposes for which private individuals have not produced them, if more and more power stands behind this will, and if finally all parts of the people are gripped by entirely new ideas about private property and forms of life—then the tax state will have run its course and society will have to depend on other motive forces for its economies and self interest (Schumpeter, 1954, p. 24).

By "the tax state" Schumpeter meant what he would later call fettered capitalism.

Of the many weaknesses that afflict the mixed economy of the present day, the insatiable demand for government spending is surely the most threatening.

It is a far more serious threat than the chorus of anti-capitalist sentiment which, at the time of writing, is rising once again, having been apparently silenced during the later Thatcher years. Will this chorus of criticism survive the recovery from the recession? My guess is that it will. The quality of modern life in the mixed economy has deteriorated so much that it cannot be repaired with the sticking plaster of another temporary boom in output. Whatever satisfaction that may be derived from increasing quantities of consumer goods cannot compensate for the negative features of increasing inequality, congestion, and pollution that characterize daily life in the cities of the advanced countries. Nevertheless this dissatisfaction is unlikely to be critical.

Much more likely to accelerate the demise of the capitalist system, even in its fettered form, is the probable failure of governments in democratic countries to satisfy the demands of their citizens for health, medical care, and educational services as well as social security benefits. Since the wish-list is open-ended, the demand is, in principle, infinite.

It was precisely this dragon that Mrs. Thatcher and President Reagan set out to slay. They failed. The statistics show that for the seven leading industrialized countries in the world, every one, with the exception of the United Kingdom and Germany, experienced an increase in the ratio of government expenditure to GDP between 1979 and 1989. By 1992, both Germany and the United Kingdom had exceeded their 1979 ratio.

Apart from privatization and deregulation, what was mainly achieved in the 1980s in the United States, United Kingdom, and elsewhere was a reduction in income tax rates (although not the overall tax burden since, especially in the United Kingdom, the burden of indirect taxes rose). But that was the politically popular part.

The consequence of rising government expenditures in the 1980s coupled with reductions in tax rates has inevitably been a rise in government indebtedness. Again, taking the leading seven industrialized countries, from 1981 to 1990, the gross public debt as a percent of nominal GDP or gross national product (GNP) rose in all countries except the United Kingdom.

It is true that many circumstances do not warrant worry about rising government debt: war, recession, and viable public sector investment projects, for example. However, it is surely ominous when the debt-to-national-income ratio rises during a long period, such as the 1980s, without war or recession and with continually rising productivity. Furthermore, as Green (1993) points out, an increase in government indebtedness can set in motion processes that might threaten the stability if not the viability of the system. In other words, the build-up of debt can become sufficiently great so as to become a limiting factor in fiscal policy.

As Drucker has pointed out:

> The governments in all developed countries—and in most developing ones as well—have become such heavy spenders that they cannot increase their expenditures in a recession. But that is, of course, the time when, according to all modern economic theory, they should do so in order to create purchasing power

> and with it revive the economy. In every single developed country governments have reached the limits of their ability to tax and their ability to borrow. They have reached these limits during boom times, when they should, according to modern economic theory, build up sizeable surpluses. The fiscal state has spent itself into impotence (Drucker, 1993, p. 121).

When the real interest rate rises above the economy's growth rate and a primary deficit exists, then the debt ratio must rise. As the debt-to-income ratio rises, so does the risk that the debt will be repudiated.

Green puts forward an alternative view: the real problem of the contemporary mixed economy may not be a secular rise in the debt-to-national-income ratio but instead a "knife-edge" disequilibrium relationship between the demand for public services and the productivity of the economy. In the 1960s and 1970s too much attention, says Green, was paid to the former, at the expense of the latter. In the 1980s, the position was reversed. Certainly, this seems a correct reading of the situation in the United Kingdom, when in the late 1980s the then Chancellor of the Exchequer was using a large budget surplus to reduce the national debt. Only five years later, the size of the projected deficit constrains the present freedom of movement of the Chancellor of the Exchequer, both in the micro and macro aspects of fiscal policy.

However, Green concludes, a secular rise in the debt-to-income ratio also poses an intergenerational problem. In the short term, it simply leads to "scrimping" on essential public services, but in the long term it can lead to civic impoverishment and "growing inequalities between those with the wherewithal to provide substitutes for public services and those without." Perhaps the most important intergenerational transfer is civilization itself. Green quotes Oliver Wendell Holmes when he says that "taxes are what we pay for civilized society."

Politicians who have said that they would increase taxes have simply not been elected. The classic example was Walter Mondale in the 1974 U.S. presidential election. President Bush, seeking election in 1988, promised not to increase any taxes (the famous "read my lips—no more taxes" pledge). President Clinton in the 1992 election made promises not to increase the taxation of the middle classes. Similar promises were made by Chancellor Kohl in the Federal German elections held after reunification in 1990. Prime Minister Major in the British general election of 1992 even pledged to reduce rates of income tax further, although at an unspecified future date.

All these candidates must have known that it was most unlikely that they would be able to keep their promises. The fact that they made them at all reflects the pressure of expectations put on them in the competition for votes that characterizes contemporary capitalist democracy. Yet they were lying, as Schumpeter anticipated. According to Allen (1992), Schumpeter's entries in his private diary included such aphorisms as "Democracy is government by lying."

On the other side of the budget, Mrs. Thatcher and President Reagan were both elected on programs of reducing public expenditure. In this case, knowing the strength of their convictions, it may be accepted that they both did truly believe in this proposition, and both tried as hard as they could to achieve a reduction. Yet two years after Mrs. Thatcher left office, the proportion of public expenditure to GDP in the United Kingdom is higher than it was when she came into office. President Reagan's legacy is an increased federal government deficit as well as increased public expenditure.

Drucker (1993) claims to have detected evidence that democracy in the United States is declining as the result of elected representatives fleecing their constituents to enrich special interest groups. He points to the steady decline in voting participation in the United States, and claims that in all the advanced countries there is a concurrent decline in public interest in the functions of government, and in policy issues. Instead, he says, voters increasingly vote on the basis of "what's in it for me?"

It may be objected that a fatal flaw in democracy as a political system does not mean that capitalism is necessarily condemned. But one does not have to be a Marxist to agree that contemporary forms of Western democracy are inextricably linked to the capitalist system. Indeed, this argument is advanced with as much vigor by proponents of the market economy or of free enterprise as it is by those on the Left.

The Distribution of Income

Despite all the rhetoric about social justice that characterizes the Marxist and non-Marxist tradition in socialism, the concept of equality of income does not seem to have played a major part in Marx's own thought. Indeed, if the distribution of income in the Socialist state is to be made independent of production, and organized instead to serve the principle of "to each according to his need: from each according to his ability," then it is evident that the resulting distribution of income would be unequal, to the extent that needs are unequally distributed throughout any given population. It will, of course, be a different distribution from the unequal distribution according to ability that would be characteristic of pure or unfettered capitalism, and different again from the post-tax distribution characteristic of the fettered capitalism of the contemporary advanced countries.

While some in the non-Marxist socialist tradition not only preached equality of incomes but actually established short-lived experimental communities that practiced absolute equality of income distribution, it is not a principle that was practiced in the socialist countries themselves. Indeed, the widening gap between the living standards of the governing political class, that is, members of the Communist party, and those of the rest of society was one of the factors that finally undermined the system.

What is astonishing in retrospect is the quite open way in which, in a nominally socialist society, discrimination was practiced between the elite and the rest of society. In the USSR and the other communist countries of Eastern Europe, there was privileged access for the ruling group to the enjoyment of large cars, large flats, country houses, and foreign travel. In a society where the quantity and quality of consumer goods available to the general population was notoriously inadequate, exclusive access to certain shops that were well supplied with goods not available elsewhere was reserved to members of the Communist party. Despite the fact that such behavior was devastatingly satirized by George Orwell in *Animal Farm*, and criticized by some unorthodox socialist intellectuals such as Milovan Djilas, the practice continued right up to the collapse of the system.

It may therefore be asked whether distribution of income can legitimately be considered as an appropriate dimension for measuring the supposed capitalist transition. We would argue in the affirmative, since it is clear that for Schumpeter as for most other writers on this subject, pure capitalism was a state in which the distribution of income was determined by earning ability (including, of course, the earning power of owned wealth), entirely untrammelled by taxation or regulation. An essential element of the transition sketched by Schumpeter was the increasing burden of taxation laid upon the upper and middle classes to which the entrepreneurs belonged. Thus, a movement toward greater equality in the distribution of income in a society is an indicator of movement in the direction away from pure capitalism and toward socialism.

While for most of this century, rates of taxation on the upper income groups in the advanced countries have increased, after the Thatcher-Reagan counter-revolution the higher rates of tax at the upper end of the income scale in both the United States and the United Kingdom were reduced. This practice has been imitated in other advanced countries such as Sweden, long renowned for its egalitarian ethos.

As far as reducing very high marginal rates of tax on the rich are concerned, it seems to have been a case of relaxing the stranglehold on the goose's neck so that a continuing supply of golden eggs can be obtained. That the politics of envy is alive and flourishing in the advanced countries is evidenced by the promises of both President Clinton in the United

States and the Labour party in the United Kingdom, in their respective 1992 election campaigns, to increase once again tax rates at the upper end of the income range. Even more remarkable has been the way in which the British monarchy has been compelled by a recent upsurge of public opinion to pay income taxes, something that it had not done for more than 50 years.

In both the United States and the United Kingdom during the 1980s, standard measures showed increases in inequality in the distribution of income. But Drucker (1993) argues that taxation has made little difference to the distribution of income. Citing Pareto, he contends that only two factors determine the distribution of income in a country: productivity growth and culture. About the United States, Drucker claims that as long as productivity was increasing, that is, until the late 1960s or early 1970s, then income distribution became more equal. But once productivity increases began to disappear, a phenomenon that he dates from the beginning of the Vietnam War, inequality began to increase. Differences in taxation between the Nixon-Carter years on the one hand, and the Reagan years on the other, made little difference.

Drucker goes on to claim that income distribution in the United Kingdom has become less equal in the last 30 years, as productivity has stopped growing. However, the rate of growth of productivity in the United Kingdom increased in the 1980s under Mrs. Thatcher.

Values and Culture

It will be recalled that the central part of Marx's vision of the transition from capitalism to socialism was the transfer of political power from the middle class to the working class. Although this has not happened suddenly and violently, as Marx had predicted, it certainly has happened, and nowhere is this revolution more clearly illustrated than in the culture and public values of the societies of the advanced countries.

In the era of pure or classical capitalism, which might be approximated in the case of the United Kingdom and the United States by the period from 1875 to 1910, the culture and values that were publicly espoused and disseminated through the media of the time were essentially those of the middle classes, as Marx never tired of pointing out. While the aristocracy may have had different values (in some respects more akin to those of the working classes), they were prudent enough to keep them to themselves, and in public paid lip service to the values of the middle classes. As Oscar Wilde observed of London's upper class society of that period: "Hypocrisy is the tribute which Vice pays to Virtue."

Whatever the private behavior of individuals may have been, it is not difficult to write down some of the characteristic values that were, at least outwardly, publicly approved in the society of that period.

There was a work ethic of earnest endeavor, associated with, if not parsimony, at least deferred gratification—in some cases, deferred until after death. Self-denial was accompanied by a culture of duty to others, by integrity, and by public responsibility. Speech and written forms of address were modest and formal to the point of pedantry. The same was true of clothing. In the arts, there were aspirations to what was believed to be good taste, even if the performance sometimes fell short. These public values were epitomized in the public architecture, notably the town halls of the great industrial cities of England. Despite higher levels of industrial pollution than exist today, the main public places of these cities were kept clean and orderly. Such values were also reflected in the only national medium of communication of the period, the press. Later, the same values were reflected in Lord Reith's BBC.

These public values were most strongly espoused and propagated by the middle classes. The working classes had somewhat different values, which only found public expression in the music halls and, in the United States, in the burlesque theaters. Any wider expression was frowned upon.

Working-class values of this period tended toward immediate consumption rather than saving. Speech and dress were informal, and personal behavior tended toward generosity rather than parsimony or frugality.

One hundred years ago the counterpart of today's mass media was a small number of newspapers. Radio broadcasting began only in the 1920s, but as recently as the 1950s in the United Kingdom at least it still continued to broadcast middle-class values. In this period, the working classes were forced to listen to Radio Luxembourg or else the BBC's Light Programme. Television broadcasting did not begin in Britain until the late 1930s, but as recently as the 1950s, presenters were still wearing formal evening dress on television in the evenings. Today, because of the pervasiveness of film, video, and television as media of communication as well as the mass circulation tabloid newspapers, public values are much more obtrusive than they were a century ago. It is impossible to escape them, unless one is a hermit.

The values reflected in the mass media of today are the polar opposite of those of the Victorian middle classes. A commercial television station, TV AM, which won its broadcasting franchise in the United Kingdom some five years ago with a declared "mission to inform," was quickly forced to abandon its approach. It had to adopt "a mission to entertain," as the former approach proved insufficiently attractive to advertisers.

In newspapers, the popular tabloids have not evolved to become more like *The Times* of 100 years ago. Quite the reverse; the self-styled "quality" newspapers have lowered their standards to become much more "popular" in taste and appeal, while the popular tabloids compete with each other in a circulation war of ever lowering standards.

In the United States, opinion surveys show that the great majority of people today identify themselves as "middle class," yet it is clear that, as in the United Kingdom, the values they appear to espouse resemble those of the Victorian working class much more closely than those of the middle class of that period.

Just as politicians drawn from the aristocracy and from the working class felt obliged 100 years ago to pay lip service to middle-class values in order to get elected, so today they must pay lip service to working-class or populist values. To get the Republican nomination for president in 1988, George Bush was required to use in public populist phrases that were quite incongruous. In the United Kingdom, the present Conservative prime minister feels obliged to broadcast his belief in "a classless society," a state that is as difficult to imagine as an economy without firms.

Whereas 100 years ago, the prevailing standards in values, culture, fashion, and all forms of public behavior were set by a tiny handful of middle-class or upper-middle-class people, this group has now lost all social as well as political influence. Like the former metropolitan elites in a newly independent colony, the presence of this elite group in society is tolerated, as long as they do not attempt to exert any influence over the new order.

To summarize, then, contemporary values and culture appear to be based on self-indulgence rather than self-denial. Hedonism has replaced the work ethic. Speech and clothing are informal. Public responsibility has been replaced with the principle of "whatever you can get away with." Litter and graffiti, if not encouraged, are at least tolerated in a growing number of Western cities. In private as well as in public life, middle-class values have been overthrown. The class war is indeed over, and, as Marx and Schumpeter predicted, the middle-class values that predominated in the heyday of unfettered capitalism have been comprehensively defeated.

It is not an accident that this should be so. Marx's vision of the circumstances in which the proletariat would overthrow the bourgeoisie would appear to be one in which the accumulation of capital was a completed process. In other words, the stage of quasi-abundance of commodities had been reached, a stationary state where it was implicit that consumer wants could be satisfied by the existing stock of capital. Technical progress as well as further capital accumulation were redundant, and the economic problem could be reduced to one of administration. The whole economy would be like one gigantic public utility, and the economic problem for a socialist society would resemble the organization of the water supply in a country where there was an abundant rainfall.

Although advanced societies may not reach this state of quasi-abundance in the foreseeable future, we are certainly moving toward it, or perhaps approaching it asymptotically. The advanced countries are rich enough to be able to support the large fraction of their population who do not work, including the 10% or so of the labor force who are unemployed at the present time.

In such a society of quasi-abundance—the only circumstances in which it seems that a system of classical or Marxist socialism possibly could work—there is no need for traditional middle-class values. They would become redundant.

Even in our present state of semi-transition, there are some indications that the pace of effort in the more advanced countries is relaxing. In the United Kingdom and the United States, an increasing proportion of each generation of the middle class sees no reason not to work less and play more than its predecessors. In the advanced countries, the number of hours worked on average has shown a steadily downward trend. Williams has calculated that, when the supply of labor is measured by hours offered through a working life, the reduction in the supply in the United Kingdom between 1870 and 1980 is almost 50% (Williams, 1983). Even Germany and Japan are showing signs of being less workaholic than they used to be. It is therefore entirely appropriate that we should be observing changing attitudes toward work, leisure, personal saving, and consumption.

The Socialization of the Labor Market

Although in Schumpeter's view the transition from capitalism to socialism would be gradual, which it was, he also speculated that a watershed or critical milestone would occur with the socialization of the labor market. By this he appears to mean what we nowadays would call a permanent statutory incomes policy.

During the 1960s and 1970s, the United Kingdom and other European countries, and even briefly the United States, experimented with statutory incomes policies, although they were invariably temporary. These experiments failed, not only in terms of their economic objectives but also politically. The unpopularity of Mr. Callaghan's wage increase limit of 5% contributed to his defeat in the 1979 general election. With Mrs. Thatcher coming into power, incomes policies were consigned to the category of the unthinkable.

Even today, with a reassessment of the Thatcher-Reagan policies, no one has suggested the possibility of re-introducing statutory incomes policies. Yet it does seem that the perennial problems of inflation and unemployment are still present in the United Kingdom, if not in the United States, and that the problem of unemployment is getting worse over time. In each succeeding business cycle since the end of World War II, the level of unemployment, both at the peak and the trough of the cycle, has been higher than its predecessor. For those who believe that the price of labor is the most important single determinant of the demand for labor, the observed coincidence of secularly rising unemployment, together with rising real wages for those fortunate enough to be in employment, once again brings the question of incomes policies back on the agenda.

Conclusions

In this chapter we have examined Schumpeter's famous prediction that in the second half of the twentieth century, capitalism would be in a state of transition from the pure form, characteristic of the period 1870–1914, toward a different form of economic organization that might be called socialism. This intermediate or transitional stage Schumpeter referred to in *Capitalism, Socialism and Democracy* as controlled or fettered capitalism. In an earlier work he had referred to it as the "tax state." It is perhaps more familiarly known as the mixed economy.

The question at issue is whether the changes that have been observed in the almost half-century since World War II in the economies of the most advanced countries, that is, the leading industrialized countries of the world, indicate a movement in the direction of socialism, or not. Up to the 1970s, it seemed as if a plausible case could have been made in favor of Schumpeter's thesis. In the 1980s, Mrs. Thatcher and President Reagan introduced a series of measures explicitly directed at rolling back the boundaries of the state and, as they saw it, reversing the drift toward socialism. Notable among these measures were the privatization of state-owned industries, the deregulation of those industries that were privately owned but tightly controlled by the state, and a reduction in rates of income tax, especially at the upper end of the income range. These policies at first appear to be successful in terms of the performance of the British and American economies in that decade and were widely imitated throughout the world. The example of the Thatcher-Reagan counter-revolution was followed not only in other advanced countries but also in the developing countries as well as in the formerly socialist countries of Eastern Europe and the former Soviet Union.

Has this counter-revolution been truly successful, or does it represent no more than a pause for breath in the long march into socialism? It depends what dimensions or criteria are used to measure progress toward socialism. In this chapter, progress according to four different yardsticks was examined.

The first criterion, the extent to which productive assets in a society are publicly owned, is the only worthwhile criterion of progress toward socialism so far as classical or Marxist socialists are concerned. For Schumpeter it is a criterion of lesser importance. On the yardstick of public ownership, the verdict is clear: in the advanced countries since the Second World War public ownership is widely recognized to have failed to deliver a satisfactory performance in economic terms. It also appears to have failed to deliver hoped-for improvements in industrial relations. By contrast, the newly privatized industries appear already to be showing an improved performance. So, on this criterion, there has been no movement in the advanced countries toward socialism; if anything, the reverse has been true.

The second yardstick, the organization of the economy, is the one on which Schumpeter would have preferred his predictions to have been judged. It was the increasing fettering of the pure capitalist economy by an ever-growing range of regulations and taxation which Schumpeter felt would be the principal symptom of the transition to socialism. In this chapter, it has been argued that the growing indebtedness of most of the advanced countries during the 1980s showed that the crisis anticipated by Schumpeter as early as 1918 was approaching. The apparently insatiable demand of the citizens of the advanced countries for publicly provided health and education services and social security benefits seems to be unmatched by their willingness to vote for the tax increases required to pay for these benefits.

The third yardstick is the distribution of income. To the ordinary person, a greater equality of the distribution of after-tax real income is perhaps the simplest and most obvious measure of any transition toward socialism. Problems of measurement mean that a verdict of this point must remain ambiguous. It has long been recognized that one of the weaknesses of the democratic process is that coalitions may use it to alter market outcomes in their favor. In particular, it was feared that the poor majority might gang up on the rich minority. Now, however, it seems that there is a rich majority in most of the advanced countries.

The fourth yardstick, values and culture, is the counterpart of Marx's "social and political superstructure." Here, the outcome is surely unambiguous. Whereas at the turn of the century the public values of the advanced countries were clearly middle class, these values have been everywhere completely overturned. Traditional working-class values now constitute the accepted norm of public behavior in the advanced countries. Seldom can a revolution be so complete without a shot being fired. It is true that the timing and nature of the transition have been different in different countries, as one would expect. As far as the United Kingdom is concerned, middle-class values have held sway as late as the 1950s; from the 1960s onward, however, their demise has been rapid.

For Schumpeter, the entrepreneur was a heroic figure whose function was uniquely valuable in the capitalist system. For this socially useful function, he deserved the respect and esteem of society, and up to about the First World War he did indeed enjoy that respect and esteem in most of the advanced countries. Decline can be detected after the First World War, accompanied by a growth in the influence of an anti-capitalist mentality, also anticipated by Schumpeter.

The entrepreneur, acclaimed by Mrs. Thatcher and President Reagan, enjoyed a brief revival of fortune in the 1980s. Once again, entrepreneurs did seem to be men possessed of superhuman qualities, performing a socially useful function while at the same time amassing personal fortunes. With the collapse of the boom at the end of the 1980s, however, their fortunes and reputations appear to have deflated equally suddenly; some even are languishing in jail.

To sum up, then, if we are to judge any movement from pure capitalism toward socialism by the extent of state ownership—the classic Marxist criterion, then it must be recognized that the popular view of socialism in retreat is upheld. If, however, we judge any possible transition from capitalism to socialism by the indicators that Schumpeter himself would have preferred, those representing government control of the economy rather than government ownership, then a rather different picture emerges. The evidence is not unambiguous, but present trends indicate that the Achilles heel of the mixed economy may be the demand for publicly provided goods, services, and transfer payments unaccompanied by commensurate willingness to pay for them. But this does not necessarily mean that it is evolving toward socialism in most of the conventionally understood senses of that word.

Only since 1989 have people in the West realized just how great a failure conventional socialism in Eastern Europe had been. Few people, with the possible exception of von Mises, had anticipated the full extent of the economic, political, and environmental disaster that the socialist experiment turned out to be. Certainly Schumpeter did not. It is fairly certain, therefore, that within the foreseeable future, few people will want to repeat that particular mistake.

But if the term *socialism* is to be disallowed for the state into which contemporary forms of capitalism may be evolving, what term should then be used?

We want to describe the state in which working class or at least populist values prevail, but where private rather than public ownership of productive assets is the norm, and the allocation of resources takes place primarily through the market rather than through central planning. This might sound like social democracy, but if self-restraint cannot be exercised by society in the matter of publicly provided health, education, pensions, and other welfare benefits, then the democratic system itself may be vulnerable. Schumpeter would not have been surprised. Like Hayek, he warned that what he called socialism would be "likely to present fascist features."

References

Albert, Michel. (1991). *Capitalisme Contre Capitalisme*. Paris: Editions du Seuil.

Allen, Robert L. (1991). *Opening Doors: The Life and Work of Joseph Schumpeter*. New York: Transaction Publications.

Drucker, Peter. (1993). *Post Capitalist Society*. Oxford: Butterworth-Heineman.

Green, Christopher. (1993). "From 'Tax State' to 'Debt State'." *Journal of Evolutionary Economics* 3(1): pp. 23–42.

Haberler, G. (1950). "Joseph Alois Schumpeter, 1883–1950." *Quarterly Journal of Economics* (August): pp. 333–372.

Haberler, G. (1981). "Schumpeter's Capitalism, Socialism and Democracy After 40 Years." In Arnold Heertje (ed.), *Schumpeter's Vision*. New York: Praeger.

Hayek, F.A. (1944). *The Road to Serfdom*. London: Routledge.

Heertje, Arnold. (1981). *Schumpeter's Vision*. New York: Praeger.

Keynes, J.M. (1946). "The Balance of Payments of the United States." *Economic Journal* 56: pp. 172–187.

März, Edward. (1991). *Joseph Schumpeter, Scholar, Teacher and Politician*. New Haven and London: Yale University Press.

von Mises, L. (1951). *Socialism: An Economic and Sociological Analysis*, trans. by J. Kahane. New Haven: Yale University Press.

Samuelson, Paul A. (1981). "Schumpeter's Capitalism, Socialism and Democracy." In Arnold Heertje (ed.), *Schumpeter's Vision*. New York: Praeger.

Schumpeter, J.A. (1928). "The Instability of Capitalism." *Economic Journal* (38): pp. 361–386.

Schumpeter, J.A. (1942). *Capitalism, Socialism and Democracy*. New York: Harper and Row (3rd ed., London: Allen and Unwin).

Schumpeter, J.A. (1954). "The Crisis of the Tax State." In A.T. Peacock, et al. (eds.), *International Economic Papers, 4*. London: Macmillan.

Singer, H.W. (1993). A Review of *Joseph A Schumpeter: His Life and Work* by Richard Swedberg in *Journal of Economic Studies.* vol. 19, No. 4, pp. 61–4.

Swedberg, Richard. (1991). *Schumpeter: A Biography*. Princeton: Princeton University Press.

Williams, Sir Bruce. (1983). *Technology Policy and Employment.* Discussion Paper. London: The Technical Change Centre.

7 CULTURAL EVOLUTION, COLLECTIVE LEARNING, AND CONSTITUTIONAL DESIGN

Viktor Vanberg

Though our civilization is the result of a cumulation of individual knowledge, it is not by the explicit or conscious combination of all this knowledge in any individual brain, but by its embodiment in symbols which we use without understanding them, in habits and institutions, tools and concepts, that man in society is constantly able to profit from a body of knowledge neither he nor any other man completely possesses.

—F.A. Hayek (1952b, pp. 149*ff.*)

Central to F.A. Hayek's theory of cultural evolution is the notion that the rules and institutions upon which human social life is based have been shaped in an evolutionary process of trial and error, a process in which experience with the working properties of such rules is accumulated over generations. This experience, it is asserted, is largely implicit in cultural traditions and customary practices, and far exceeds the knowledge that its present beneficiaries could be said to "possess," in the sense of being able to articulate it. Cultural evolution is portrayed as a *process of growth of knowledge*, not so much as a matter of individual persons becoming more knowledgeable as individuals, but in the sense that the knowledge utilized in the societal nexus grows. Cultural evolution is, in other words, viewed as a process of *social or collective learning*, a process in which the problem-solving capacity in society grows.

The merits and shortcomings of Hayek's evolutionary account of social institutions have been extensively discussed, including by the present author (Vanberg, 1986, 1989, 1993). To add yet another to the long list of already existing contributions on the subject can only be justified by the fact that, on the one hand, the reception of Hayek's argument is still subject to considerable ambiguity while, on the other, the explanatory potential of his overall approach appears to be sufficiently large to merit further attempts at clarification. It is in this spirit that I embark on the present project. My purpose is twofold. It is, first, to outline and discuss the general structure of a *Darwinian* theory of cultural evolution, that is, a theory employing—in the realm of cultural phenomena—the same *explanatory logic* that is characteristic of Darwin's approach to biological evolution. In particular, the purpose is to examine how, within a Darwinian framework, the notion of cultural evolution as a process of *collective learning* can be properly specified. My second purpose is to examine what a defensible theory of cultural evolution can be said to imply for the role of deliberate institutional reform and constitutional design. In the process of carrying out these two tasks, I hope to be able to clarify some of the ambiguity that has surrounded Hayek's arguments on these issues. Let me add that, although much of my argument is about Hayek's thoughts, my interest is not in exegesis but, instead, in a systematic assessment of the scope and limits of an evolutionary approach to social institutions.

Darwinian Evolution

The question of how sociocultural diversity and change can be explained has always been among the fundamental concerns of social theorists. Since Charles Darwin's *The Origin of Species* (1859), *evolutionary* accounts have figured prominently among the theoretical perspectives advanced. Yet, the label "evolutionary" has been claimed for a variety of approaches, which are by no means all compatible with each other, or with the logic of Darwin's argument.

Hayek (1967, pp. 103*ff.*, 111; 1973, pp. 22*ff.*; 1978, pp. 264*ff.*; 1979, pp. 154*ff.*) has often stressed that, counter to common belief, the idea of evolution was "older in the humanities and social sciences than in the natural sciences" (Hayek, 1988, p. 24), that "Darwin's work was preceded by decades, indeed by a century, of research concerning the rise of highly complex spontaneous orders through a process of evolution" (*ibid.*). Hayek refers, in particular, to what he calls the "Mandeville-Hume-Smith-Ferguson tradition" (1978, p. 265*n*), a tradition that created an "atmosphere of evolutionary thought in the study of society" (Hayek, 1978, p. 265) well before Darwin developed his biological concept of evolution (Hayek, 1960, pp. 59*ff.*). As Hayek has also noted, this pre-Darwinian tradition has more in common with the basic logic of Darwin's theory than much of the post-Darwinian evolutionary thought that has become known as "Social Darwinism" (Hayek, 1960, p. 59). What makes much of Social Darwinism "non-Darwinian"[1] is its preoccupation with the historicist notion of "laws of evolution" that are supposed to describe stages or phases through which sociocultural development passes (Hayek, 1973, p. 23; 1988, p. 26). Herbert Spencer's "evolutionary" historicism was, in this regard, definitely not Darwinian.[2] Darwin's theory of natural selection is not about the "*course* of evolution"; it is about the *process* of evolution. It provides an account of how, in principle, this process works. It is not meant to explain its particular outcomes or to predict its future "course."[3]

The social theory of the eighteenth-century Scottish moral philosophers was genuinely *evolutionary* in the Darwinian sense.[4] In the same manner in which, later, Darwin was to explain the seeming purposefulness of the "products of nature" as the systematic outcome of a purposeless, "blind" process, the eighteenth-century evolutionists explained how the appearance of purposefulness in the "products of civilization" can be understood as the outcome of a process that is not guided by foresight. In their view—and contrary to the contemporaneously emerging continental philosophy of history—the process of civilization has no predeterminable course, but is "driven from behind" into an open future by the permanent efforts of individual human beings to improve their lot, to solve the problems they face, and to explore new opportunities.[5] In other words, like Darwin's theory of "natural selection" the Scottish philosophers' evolutionary approach reduced teleology to causation,[6] by showing how seeming purposefulness at the social-structural level can be explained as a largely unintended outcome of a process of trial and error.[7] The driving force behind the cumulative process of civilization is seen in the continuous experimenting of individuals who, in pursuit of their own purposes, constantly adjust to new circumstances and modify—deliberately as well as unintentionally—the ways in which they go about doing things. As, in the course of such intentional and incidental experimenting, individuals happen to find better "tools" or practices for solving recurrent problems, they will tend to retain these superior solutions and others will tend to imitate their successful innovations (Hayek, 1960, pp. 28, 32*ff.*).

The essential claims of Darwinian evolutionary theory are that in the process of reproduction, inheritable variations are constantly generated, that these variations tend to differentially affect the reproductive success of the individual organisms bearing them, and that, as a consequence, the distribution of variation within a population will be gradually shifted in favor of those variations that confer greater reproductive success.[8] Or, as Hayek (1967, p. 32) has put it: "The basic proposition . . . is that a mechanism of reduplication with transmittable variations and competitive selection of those which prove to have a better chance of survival will in the course of time produce a great variety of structures adapted to continuous adjustment to the environment and to each other." The theory shows how *adaptiveness* or *functionality* in nature can emerge without foresight. It provides, in other words, an "invisible hand explanation" (Ullmann-Margalit, 1978) for the emergence of functionality. Furthermore, it is an "individualist" account in that it explains changes at the aggregate or macro-level of a population or species in terms of events at the micro-level, namely, the variation and selective retention of characteristics of individual organisms. And it is individualist in its emphasis on the uniqueness of, and diversity among, individuals in a population, an outlook refered to as *population thinking*.[9] Its focus is on the process in which, due to selective pressure, the distribution of individual characteristics within a population—or, in other words, the composition of the population—changes over time.

Darwinian "adaptiveness" is about an organism's capacity to successfully cope with recurrent problems in its environment. To the extent that such capacity correlates with transmittable properties that vary within a population, and to the extent that the population's problem-environment remains sufficiently stable over time, the distribution of properties will gradually, over successive generations, shift in the direction of increased adaptive fit or increased problem-solving capacity. Such gradual, cumulative shift toward increased adaptiveness can be viewed as a process of *collective learning* in the sense that it is the *population* or species, as a trans-generational collectivity, whose problem-solving capacity increases over time. The core principles of Darwinian evolution—namely, "(a) Mechanisms for introducing variation; (b) Consistent selection processes; and (c) Mechanisms for preserving and/or propagating the selected variations"—can, as D.T. Campbell (1974, p. 42) notes, be generalized to apply to all processes which increase the "adaptive fit" of some system relative to its environment (Campbell, 1983, p. 34). Biological and cultural evolution both rely, as Hayek (1988, p. 26) suggests, "on the same principle of selection: survival or reproductive advantage. Variation, adaptation and competition are essentially the same kind of process, however different their particular mechanisms." They can, in particular, be applied to the study of culture.[10]

Cultural evolution can be regarded as a process of "collective learning" in the sense that it consists in the transmission and accumulation, from generation to generation, of knowledge and experience. It is a process of "selective cumulation of skills, technologies, recipes, beliefs, customs, organizational structures, and the like" (Campbell, 1975, p. 1104), "the transmission in time of our accumulated stock of knowledge" (Hayek, 1960, p. 27). "Knowledge" is meant, in this context, in the broadest sense in which it includes any kind of learned problem-solving capacity, pertaining to whatever human beings confront or perceive as a "problem," from the most basic needs of physical survival to the most abstract and refined issues raised by man's intellectual and spiritual curiosity. Transgenerational transmission of acquired (as opposed to genetically programmed) problem-solving capacity is associated with group-life (Campbell, 1983, pp. 32*ff.*), and traces of it can be found in various species for which group-life is characteristic (Hayek, 1967, p. 66; 1973, pp. 74, 163*ff.*; 1988, p. 17; Bonner, 1980; Vogel and Voland, 1988, pp. 103*ff.*; Mundinger, 1980).[11] It is apparent, however, that the role of *culture* in the human species sufficiently exceeds its role even among the higher primates to make it a distinctively human phenomenon.

The "wisdom" accumulated by "evolutionary learning" is, for obvious reasons, "always wisdom about past worlds, a fittedness to past selective systems" (Campbell, 1975, p. 1106). To the extent that the problem-environment changes, what used to be "adaptive" may be rendered useless or even dysfunctional. And such environmental changes are not confined to events that are external to the respective population. Since to each individual organism the composition of the population to which it belongs is a relevant part of its environment, the very process of variation and selective retention produces environmental change, by shifting the distribution of characteristics within the population.

The "backward looking" nature of evolutionary adaptiveness implies that the *more specific*—relative to the environment—the genetically inherited problem-solving capacity is, the more costly adjustments to changes in the environment will be, costly in the sense that the required adjustments in the population's gene-pool may be achievable only over numerous generations, if at all. The reverse implication is that there should be an advantage to a genetically inherited problem-solving capacity that is *less specific* or more open, that relies more on the *individual's* capacity to learn and to adapt to environmental changes.[12] This fact is the clue to homo sapiens' singular position compared to other animals, and it is the clue to the role of *sociocultural evolution*.[13]

My principal concern in the present context is with the issue of how the notion of "collective learning" can be meaningfully and consistently specified in a Darwinian framework without compromising the "original individualistic emphasis of Darwin's theory" (Axelrod and Hamilton, 1984, p. 89). Or, stated differently, my interest is in the issue of how a Darwinian theory of cultural evolution can be specified that allows for an explanatory account of the "wisdom of culture" (Hayek, 1979, p. 155), in the same sense in which Darwin's theory can be said to provide an explanation for the "wisdom of nature."[14] First, however, I want to examine, at least briefly, the relation between *evolution* and *learning* more generally.

Evolutionary Epistemology: Evolution as Learning

Popper has suggested a "Darwinian theory of the growth of knowledge" (Popper, 1972, p. 261) that, together with contributions by F.A. Hayek, D.T. Campbell (1965, 1974, 1987), and others (Radnitzky and Bartley, 1987), has stimulated a new field of study called *evolutionary epistemology* (Hayek, 1988, p. 10; Popper, 1972, p. 67; Richards, 1981, p. 53). The central claim of this approach is that from natural selection to the growth of scientific knowledge the same basic principle can be found operating, namely that of *trial and error-elimination* or *conjecture and refutation* (Popper, 1972, p. 255).[15] As Popper (1972, pp. 242*ff.*) summarizes the general concept: "All *organisms* are constantly, day and night, *engaged in problem-solving*... Problem-solving always proceeds by the method of trial and error: new reactions, new forms, new organs, new modes of behavior, new hypotheses, are tentatively put forward and controlled by error-elimination."

This general notion of trial-and-error elimination can, Popper argues (1972, p. 288), "be applied not only to the emergence of new scientific problems and, consequently, new scientific theories, but to the emergence of new forms of behavior, and even new forms of living organisms." It describes a general, Darwinian method of "learning" which—though its particular manifestations may be different—is essentially the same at various levels, from "the level of the enzyme and the gene ... up to the articulate and critical language of our theories" (p. 149).[16] Such learning consists, Popper argues, "throughout of corrections and modifications of previous knowledge" (1972, p. 259)[17]: "(A)t every stage of the evolution of life and of the development of an organism we have to assume the existence of some knowledge in the form of dispositions and expectations" (*ibid.*, p. 71). Such expectations "which could be framed as hypotheses" (*ibid.*, p. 258) are, according to Popper, "genetically incorporated" in all sense organs as a capacity to distinguish between typical situations that are of importance to the organism.[18]

Of particular interest in the present context are Popper's concepts of *objective knowledge* and of an *objectivist epistemology*. We can, he suggests, distinguish between subjective and objective knowledge, the first of which requires a "knowing subject" (1972, p. 73), while the second has an existence independent of such a subject. Knowledge in the subjective sense consists, in Popper's definition, "of a state of mind or of consciousness or a disposition to behave or to react" (p. 108). It could, he states, also "be called organismic knowledge, since it consists of the dispositions of organisms" (p. 73).[19] By contrast, knowledge in the objective sense is defined as "knowledge without a knowing subject" (p. 109), as knowledge in the "impersonal sense, in which it may be said to be contained in a book; or stored in a library;" or embodied in tools and other artifacts (p. 286).

Popper sees the distinctiveness of human evolution—as opposed to the evolution of other animals—in its intimate interconnection with the growth of objective knowledge (1972, p. 296), with the evolution of artifacts or "exosomatic organs" like "tools, or weapons, or machines, or houses" (1972, p. 238). The world of objective knowledge originates, he argues, "as a product of human activity" but it "transcends its makers" in the sense that it is, to a large extent, "the unplanned product of human actions" (1972, pp. 159*ff.*), the "unintended by-product of actions which were directed at other aims" (p. 117). And he suggests that a "Darwinian explanation of the instrumental character of undesigned institutions" (1957, p. 65*n*) can help us understand "how language and many other institutions which are useful may arise, and how they may owe their existence and development to their usefulness" (1972, p. 117).[20]

Cultural Evolution as Collective Learning

Popper's understanding of how the world of objective knowledge develops and grows over time is, as both authors recognize (Popper, 1972, pp. 160*n*, 117*n*; Hayek, 1979, p. 157), very similar to Hayek's understanding of the process of cultural evolution. A recurrent theme in Hayek's writings is the notion that "the various institutions and habits, tools and methods of doing things, which . . . constitute our inherited civilization" (1960, p. 62) have passed "the slow test of time" (1967, p. 111) and embody the experience of generations. They are, Hayek argues, the "product of long experimentation in the past" (1978, p. 136), of a "process of trial and error, in the course of which more experience has been accumulated than any living person is aware of" (1976, p. 135).[21] Such accumulated experience is reflected in the "manner in which we have learned to order our day, to dress, to eat, to arrange our homes, to speak and write, and to use the countless tools and implements of civilization" (Hayek, 1960, p. 34).

We can, according to Hayek, equate the growth of civilization with the growth of knowledge "if we interpret knowledge to include all the human adaptations to environment in which past experience has been incorporated" (1960, p. 26). Knowledge in this sense includes, in addition to our explicit knowledge, our "habits and skills, our emotional attitudes, our tools, and our institutions—all . . . adaptations to past experience which have grown up by selective elimination of less suitable conduct" (*ibid.*).[22]

The process of accumulation and transmission of knowledge in this comprehensive sense, the "selective cumulation of skills, technologies, recipes, beliefs, customs, organizational structures, and the like" (Campbell, 1975, p. 1104), can be viewed as a process of *collective* learning not only because the body of knowledge, the growth of which is the learning in question, exists only dispersed in many individual minds. It is collective notably in the sense that the storage of knowledge and experience is largely done not in human minds but in cultural traditions that individuals adopt without being aware of their significance and in products of culture which they learn to use without knowing why they work.

Of crucial importance in this process of "cumulative embodiment of experience in tools and forms of action" (Hayek, 1960, p. 33) is the learning of language. Language is important not just as the medium through which knowledge is communicated from generation to generation, allowing for "a growth of explicit knowledge" (*ibid.*). More important, Hayek argues, is the *implicit learning* (1967, p. 87) that takes place in the process of learning a particular language. The structure of language itself implies certain views or theories about the world (*ibid.*, p. 86). By learning a language, we concurrently learn to adopt these views or theories, "we learn to classify things in a certain manner without acquiring the actual experiences which have led successive generations to evolve this system of classification" (1952a, p. 150), we "acquire a certain picture of the world, a framework of thinking within which we henceforth move without being aware of it" (1967, pp. 86*ff.*), and we can make use of a body of experience that we do not possess but which, without our knowing it, "has become incorporated in the schemata of thought which guide us" (Hayek, 1973, p. 31).[23]

The learning of language, and cultural learning more generally, presupposes, as Hayek (1952a, p. 167) notes, the existence of a sort of accumulated "knowledge" that is embodied, as a "pre-existing" system of classification, in our sensory apparatus.[24] These theories about the world that are built into our sense organs reflect, in a sense, the accumulated experience of the species. It is on the basis of, and constrained by, such hard-wired knowledge that individual and sociocultural learning take place. In other words, one can look at *biological evolution*, *individual learning*, and *cultural evolution* as separate, though interdependent, levels of learning. In biological evolution the learning takes place at the level of the species. It is the distribution of traits within the species that shifts in the direction of increased adaptive fit. In individual learning it is the distribution of behavioral propensities or dispositions within a person's acquired behavioral repertoire which becomes more adapted to relevant aspects of the environment. Such learning is linked to biological evolution in the sense that the *capacity* to learn is a matter of genetic endowment. Yet, *what* is learned is dependent on the particular person's environment. Sociocultural evolution, finally, builds upon the capacity of individuals to learn, yet it is about learning at the social or collective level in the sense that the distribution of practices and problem-solutions within "social populations" or groups shifts in the direction of increased problem-solving capacity.[25] Sociocultural evolution, again, conditions individual learning.[26] As individuals find themselves endowed with an unalterable *genetic heritage* that conditions their *capacity* to learn, they find themselves born into the semi-permanent framework of their *sociocultural heritage* that conditions *what* they learn (Campbell, 1975, p. 1105).[27]

The learning that sociocultural evolution involves is "social" in a double sense. It is social in the sense that individuals can learn not only from their own experience but also from their direct or indirect knowledge of experiences made by other persons.[28] And it is social in the sense that it concerns, as explained above, the problem-solving capacity of social populations or groups. To speak of collective learning in this context is, of course, not meant to imply that there are knowing subjects other than individual human beings.[29] It is meant to point out that the accumulation of knowledge that we describe as cultural evolution is not about individuals *as individuals* becoming more knowledgeable but is, instead, a process that occurs at the level of groups, societies, or cultural communities in which individually possessed fragments of knowledge are meaningfully integrated.[30] Along with the growth of knowledge goes a process of *division of knowledge* that necessarily increases the gap between the knowledge that individuals command individually and separately, and the body of knowledge that they can benefit from through their participation in the social nexus.[31] As Hayek (1960, p. 26) puts it: "The more men know, the smaller the share of all that knowledge becomes that any one mind can absorb. The more civilized we become, the more relatively ignorant must each individual be of the facts on which the working of his civilization depends. The very division of knowledge increases the necessary ignorance of the individual of most of this knowledge."

Evolution and Success: Normative Implications of Hayek's Theory of Cultural Evolution

So far, I have mainly sought to explicate the general nature and the underlying logic of a theory of cultural evolution in general, and its Hayekian version in particular, without explicit discussion of the potential normative implications of such a theory. Yet it is, above all, its perceived normative thrust that has made Hayek's evolutionary approach a subject of controversy, a controversy that centers around the issue of what this approach implies for the role of deliberate institutional-constitutional construction and reform. It is this issue that I want to discuss in the remainder of this chapter.

That Hayek intends his evolutionary argument to have normative content, to have implications for how we *should* deal with the institutional framework within which we find ourselves, is quite obvious throughout his writings on the subject. It is, for instance, clearly implied when he talks about cultural evolution as "a competitive process in which success decides" (1988, p. 73), a process that is "guided not by reason but by success" (1979, p. 166), or a process in which "rules become increasingly better adjusted to generate order" (1988, p. 20). And it is equally apparent when he suggests that evolutionary competition leads to "the survival of the successful" (1960, p. 57) and the "selective elimination of less suitable conduct" (1960, p. 26), "to the prevalance of the more effective institutions" (1979, p. 154), to "successful adaptations of society that are constantly improved" (1960, p. 34), or to "practices which have prevailed because they were successful" (1973, p. 18). Yet, while it seems unquestionable that Hayek presumes the process of cultural evolution to select in favor of rules and practices that are, in some sense, "beneficial" (1988, p. 136) or "desirable," it is far less clear what his precise understanding of the working principles of this evolutionary process is, and precisely *in what sense* he considers the outcomes of this process desirable. In fact, a closer examination of his arguments reveals considerable ambiguity.

There is a quite straightforward interpretation of what Hayek might mean when he describes cultural evolution as a beneficial process, namely that the rules and practices that "succeed" in evolutionary competition are beneficial and desirable *for the persons who adopt them.* Such an individualist interpretation would seem to be most consistent with the underlying classical liberal thrust of Hayek's philosophy, and it appears to be implied, for instance, when he notes that most of the "steps in the evolution of culture were made possible by some individuals . . . (who) simply started some practices advantageous to them which then did prove beneficial to the group in which they prevailed" (Hayek, 1979, p. 161), and when he adds that the way in which such innovations come to prevail in a group is "by gradually spreading acceptance" (*ibid.*, p. 167).[32]

Yet, Hayek's arguments on cultural evolution by no means uniformly support the above notion of a process in which individuals experiment with alternative practices and tend to adopt and imitate those that they find to be more advantageous for their purposes. Parts of Hayek's argument suggest a different interpretation, portraying cultural evolution as a process that does not promote what individuals find desirable, but that, instead, selects in favor of rules and traditions that make *the groups in which they are practiced* "successful." Such interpretation is implied when Hayek depicts cultural evolution as a process that does calculate in terms of group success rather than individual benefit, a process in which practices "have prevailed because they were successful—often not because they conferred any recognizable benefit on the acting individual but because they increased the chances of survival of the group to which he belonged" (Hayek, 1973, p. 18). The same interpretation is suggested when Hayek talks of evolved rules as "the result of a process of winnowing or sifting, directed by the differential advantage gained by groups from practices adopted for some unknown and perhaps purely accidental reasons" (1979, p. 155).

Hayek's claim that cultural evolution selects in favor of rules and traditions that are "group-beneficial," but may run counter to what individuals wish (1960, p. 50), can itself, again, be given two different interpretations, both of which find support in his writings on the subject. In one interpretation, this claim can mean that cultural evolution promotes rules that are not directly beneficial to the individual practicing them, but indirectly beneficial in the sense that it is advantageous to be a member of a group in which they are practiced. In other words, they are rules in which persons can be said to have a *constitutional interest* (Vanberg, 1988, pp. 161*ff.*) in the sense that they would wish them to be practiced in the group(s) in which they take part, even if they cannot benefit individually and separately from following them. Hayek has, apparently, this case in mind when he claims that evolved rules "help to make the members of the society in which they prevail more effective in the pursuit of their aims" (1976, p. 21), or when he notes: "The rules we are discussing are those that are not so much useful to the individuals who observe them, as those that (if they are *generally* observed) make all the members of the group more effective, because they give them opportunities to act within a social *order*" (1978, p. 7).

If the notion of group-beneficial is interpreted in the above sense, that is, in the sense of rules in which individuals have a *constitutional interest*, it is compatible with the previously discussed individualist interpretation in the sense that in both cases cultural evolution is claimed to select in favor of rules that make individuals better off, in the first case because the rules directly benefit the persons practicing them, in the second case because individuals benefit from being part of a group in which they are practiced. Yet, there is a critical difference in the explanatory problems that the two kinds of rules pose. It should be obvious that the straightforward evolutionary account that Hayek provides for rules that directly benefit the persons adopting them, cannot be simply extended to rules in which individuals can be said to have a constitutional interest but which do not generate differential benefits to the persons practicing them. The latter rules pose, in technical terms, a collective goods problem. Hayek did, in fact, recognize the difficulty that the difference between the two kinds of rules creates for his individualist theory of cultural evolution, and he sought to solve this problem by recourse to the notion of group selection, that is, by claiming that "cultural evolution operates largely through group selection" (Hayek, 1988, p. 25), that, separate and apart from individual human choices, a selection process operates at the level of groups per se that favors group-beneficial rules and, thus, solves that public goods problem.[33] I have discussed elsewhere[34] why I find Hayek's appeal to the notion of group selection mistaken, and there is no need to repeat the details of my argument here.[35] In the present context it is sufficient to note that nowhere in his writings does Hayek specify the concept of group selection in a manner that would, indeed, solve the collective goods problem, or, in other words, that could explain how cultural evolution comes to select in favor of group-beneficial rules that individuals "have to be made to obey," because, though all would benefit from general adherence to these rules, "it would be in the interest of each to disregard them" (Hayek, 1973, p. 45).

The second interpretation of the notion of group-beneficial rules is explicitly *non-individualist* in the sense that it is not linked, neither directly nor indirectly, to individual benefits. Though such non-individualist interpretation would seem to contradict Hayek's classical liberal philosophy, it seems implied when, in particular in his last book *The Fatal Conceit* (1988, pp. 120*ff.*), he defines group success in terms of criteria like population size or population growth, criteria that are clearly divorced from what individual persons may find desirable.[36] He describes "beneficial traditions" as those that enable "groups following them to grow" (1988, p. 136), and he notes that evolved "rules were shaped mainly by their suitability for increasing our number" (*ibid.*, p. 134).[37] To be sure, at times Hayek argues as if he sees the "population size" criterion connected with individual benefits, for instance, when he notes "that division of labor is limited by the extent of the market, and that population increase is crucial to the prosperity of a country" (*ibid.*, p. 155), or when he asserts that groups "following competitive market practices would, as they grew in numbers, displace others who followed different customs" (*ibid.*, p. 120).[38] Yet these are arguments not about population size as a success criterion per se, but about the merits of market institutions.[39] And to claim that their productivity allows markets to support larger populations than less productive economic orders is quite different from claiming that success in cultural evolution is measured in terms of population size as such, irrespective of what the persons involved might find desirable. It is, however, the latter claim that Hayek seems to make in much of his discussion on the population size criterion, for instance, when he argues that there is no real point in asking whether we find the results of the evolutionary process "good", or whether we *like* them,[40] since, as he assures us, "(i)n any case, our desires and wishes are largely irrelevant" (*ibid.*, p. 134). And not only the criterion of what we as individuals may find desirable, but *any* notion of desirability seems discarded when Hayek declares, "I do not claim that the results of group selection of traditions are necessarily 'good'—any more than I claim that other things that have long survived in the course of evolution, such as cockroaches, have moral value" (1988, p. 27). If that were, indeed, the conclusion of Hayek's theory of cultural evolution, one could only wonder why we should, in our efforts to organize our social life, care at all about cultural evolution.

There is, as the above discussion was intended to show, an implicit shift in the meaning that Hayek attaches to the claim that cultural evolution selects in favor of successful rules, from an interpretation in terms of direct individual benefits, to one in terms of group efficiency that indirectly benefits individuals, and, finally, to an interpretation that sees group success entirely divorced from individual benefits, or even divorced from any recognizable normative standard. It is helpful in understanding the significance and causes of this shift in interpretation,[41] to consider, at least briefly, two related issues. One of them concerns the normative content of the notion of success in a Darwinian theory of evolution. The other concerns the normative connotations of Hayek's concept of the spontaneous order of the market.

Conditional and Unconditional Evolutionary Arguments

In Darwinian theory the claim that evolution selects in favor of what is successful has no normative content. There is no claim that what evolution promotes is beneficial or desirable in any sense other than that it survives. Success is measured in terms of survival; the two are simply not defined independently. Note that the issue of the conceptual relation between success and survival involves two separable problems. One concerns the *explanatory* or *predictive* content of the notion of the survival of the successful. This notion is, obviously, not more than a tautology if success can only be measured in terms of survival. The notion can be given empirical content, however, if other indicators of success can be identified, attributes that are conceptually independent of survival yet are *conjectured* to promote survival. Such attributes can be identified if, and to the extent that, we can specify the relevant selective constraints that prevail in a particular ecological niche. As an example, we can conjecture that under desert conditions the capacity to economize on water consumption is an attribute relevant for survival, and organisms with such capacity can be predicted to be more successful in coping with the problems of their environment than those lacking such capacity. Or, to use an analogy, in a tennis tournament we can conceptually distinguish between a competitor's abilities and his/her survival, in the sense of advancing into the next round of competition, even though, as a factual matter, the two are closely correlated. (They are not perfectly correlated since such factors as pure luck may play some role.)

The other problem concerns the *normative* content of the notion of the survival of the successful. This notion is without normative content if the merits of the successful are only seen in the fact that it survives. Under such interpretation, it would amount to no more than the claim that what survives has the virtue of surviving. Such claim can, obviously, not be disputed, but it is, for the same reason, totally uninteresting. By contrast, the claim that "the successful survives" is of normative content if two conditions are met, namely, if what is "the successful" can, in the sense discussed before, be identified in terms of attributes other than survival, and if these attributes are claimed to be valuable or desirable for reasons other than their mere survival. Different from its mute counterpart, such a claim would not be true by definition, and it could be disputed. As an example, the claim that cultural evolution selects in favor of successful rules, would be an undisputable but empty claim if it were to mean that selection is in favor of the rules that survive. By contrast, it would be a contentful but also disputable claim, if it were to mean that cultural evolution selects in favor of rules that are successful in the sense of allowing the persons who live with them to be more successful in the pursuit of their aims and interests.

As long as we speak of evolution in general terms, without specifying the constraints that condition the evolutionary process, to say that the successful will survive, does not tell us what success means, other than survival, nor does it tell us whether what survives is desirable in any sense other than that it survives. If we cannot say something substantive about what it is that we expect to be successful, we cannot meaningfully discuss whether what survives is desirable. I suggest that we call such statements *unconditional* evolutionary claims. By contrast, to the extent that the terms of evolutionary competion, that is, the nature of the selection constraints, can be specified, we can distinguish, conceptually, between success and survival. We can conjecture what, given specified competitive constraints, is likely to be successful and is, therefore, likely to survive. And we can meaningfully discuss whether what is predicted to be successful, is—in terms of some standard—desirable. I suggest that we call the latter kind of statements *conditional* evolutionary claims.

The second question to be examined here concerns the normative element in the Hayekian notion of spontaneous market order. When Hayek portrays competitive markets as desirable social arrangements, he makes, in terms of the above distinction, a *conditional*, rather than an *unconditional*, claim. His familiar argument concerning the capacity of spontaneous orders to utilize dispersed knowledge, as well as his argument concerning the role of competition as discovery procedure, are both essential building blocks of his case for markets, but they are not the full story. Both these arguments can be made for all kinds of spontaneous order and for all kinds of competition, not only for competitive markets. But Hayek would not want to ascribe to all conceivable kinds of spontaneous social orders and to all kinds of competition the desirable properties that he attributes to markets. When he talks about markets, he does not mean any kind of spontaneous order, and when talks about market competition he does not mean competitive processes per se, irrespective of their terms. By market competition, he means a specific kind of competition, competition "restrained by appropriate rules of law" (Hayek, 1978, p. 125),[42] rules that are supposed to constrain competitive efforts to strategies that serve consumer interests. Market competition is meant to be competition constrained in a manner that ensures that success can only be had by serving consumer interests better, rather than, for instance, by lobbying government for protective privileges. The normative claims that are made for market competition are conditional claims; they are only made for a competitive order to the extent that it has the specified characteristics of markets.

Unconditional claims about unspecified competitive processes can tell us no more than that success will be with those who succeed. They do not tell us on what success will depend, nor do they tell us whether what succeeds is desirable. By contrast, the afore-mentioned conditional claims about *market competition* do tell us that success will be dependent on the ability to serve consumer interests.[43] To be sure, not all competitive settings that we use to classify as "markets" are perfectly constrained in the sense that better service to consumers is the only way to success. But the relevant point in the present context is that Hayek's normative claims concerning the working properties of markets make sense only if interpreted as conditional claims, as claims that are not meant to apply to each and every kind of spontaneous competitive process, and not to everything that is called "market," but only to competition if, and to the extent that, it is constrained in the sense specified above.

It seems obvious to me that Hayek's arguments on cultural evolution have to be interpreted in the light of the above distinction between conditional and unconditional claims. Both kinds of claims can be found in these arguments, and Hayek's failure to separate them clearly is, in my view, the main source of ambiguity. Yet it is, as I suppose, only in its interpretation as a conditional argument that Hayek's theory of cultural evolution makes good sense. In the remainder of this chapter I want to outline the basic contours of such an interpretation and discuss its implications for the issue of institutional reform and constitutional design.

Hayek's Conditional Evolutionary Argument

An analogy that Hayek often uses in his discussion on cultural evolution is that between *rules* and *tools*. Just as tools provide standard solutions to recurrent problems—like a saw that we use to cut wood—rules can, as Hayek suggests, be looked upon as devices that provide standard solutions to problems that persons encounter in their dealings with each other, like, for instance, the problem of deciding who gives way when two drivers meet at an intersection.[44] For ordinary tools—for instance, a plow—we can easily imagine a process in which continuing trial and error leads to steady improvement from very primitive beginnings to highly developed instruments, a process in which individuals constantly experiment—intentionally and unintentionally—with "plowing-instruments" of differing material and shape, adopting and imitating what they perceive as more suitable, and creating inadvertently new variations as they seek to imitate the successful. And we can understand how, in such a process, "learning without insight" can occur, how the plow-instruments come to incorporate the experience of generations of experimentors, without any of the persons using them being aware of, or being able to articulate, the knowledge that is embodied in the tool. Furthermore, because of the very nature of the process—with individuals being the principal experimentors and selectors—we can expect that it selects in favor of what the individuals involved find more desirable.

The purpose of the "rules as tools" analogy is, of course, to suggest that we can think of the evolution of rules in essentially the same manner, that is, in terms of a process in which individuals, by experimenting with alternative practices and adopting or imitating what they consider advantageous, come to benefit from rules that embody experience and knowledge far beyond what they would be able to articulate. Yet it is apparent that the analogy can only support a *conditional claim*: if, and to the extent that, rules can indeed be experimented with and selected upon like ordinary tools, we have good reasons to assume that they evolve in a similar fashion, in a process that is driven by separate individual choices and responsive to individuals' interests.[45] Many of the rules that we follow in living our lives can be looked at in this fashion. This is obviously true for what one may call "personal" rules. Like diet rules, for instance, such rules serve to solve problems that persons recurrently face in organizing their own personal lives. And it is also true for many "social" rules, that is, rules that help persons solve problems that they encounter in their dealings with each other, as long as "individual experimenting" is possible and as long as the principal benefits as well as the costs of a practice fall on those who adopt it.[46] Hayek (1960, p. 62) apparently has such rules in mind when he talks of "voluntary rules" and notes that they "allow for gradual and experimental change." Yet the analogy is clearly not applicable to all kinds of social rules—for instance, not to what Hayek refers to as "deliberately imposed coercive rules," rules which, as he notes, "can be changed only discontinuously and for all at the same time" (*ibid.*). More generally, it is less applicable the less the rules in question are susceptible to individual experimenting and selecting. Also, the notion of *cumulative storage of experience* in traditions that is so central to Hayek's theory of cultural evolution is most plausible for rules or "behavioral technologies" that individuals can separately experiment with and that generate direct benefits to their users. It is less plausible for rules that can only be tried out in collective experiments, in particular if the collective is a political community as opposed to, for instance, a private organization operating in a market environment.[47]

That there are limits to the rules as tools analogy has not been overlooked by Hayek, and it is obvious that he does not want to confine the claims of his theory of cultural evolution to these limits. Central to his theory of cultural evolution, and to his notion of group selection in particular, is the idea that the process of experimenting with and competition among alternative "ways of doing things" is not only a matter of individually chosen practices but is also about institutional characteristics of groups, that is, about rules that have to prove their usefulness in a competition among groups with different orders, rather than individuals with different practices. As Hayek notes, the "competition on which the process of selection rests must be understood in the widest sense" in which it "involves competition between organized and unorganized groups no less than competition between individuals" (1960, p. 37). Yet what exactly he means when he talks of "competition between organized and unorganized groups" is by no means unambiguously clear.

That some kind of group-level competition occurs, and that much of cultural evolution has been played out "in arenas wherein different orders contended" (Hayek, 1988, p. 20) seems unquestionable. What is at issue is not whether some such competition occurs, but *how*, in what ways, it is carried out, and what can be inferred about the outcomes that result under different terms of competition. Competition among firms in a market, rivalry among different crime gangs, and warfare among nations are all subsumable under the label "competition among groups," and in all settings there will be a "survival of the successful." Yet we would hardly expect that the ingredients to success are the same in these different settings. Group-level competition can be thought of in many different ways. It can, as Hayek notes, be a matter of individual migration between groups, of successful groups attracting outsiders (1979, p. 159). It can be a matter of collective choice, one group deciding to adopt a successful practice observed in another group. It can be a matter of warfare or it may happen "entirely peacefully."[48] Hayek can hardly have meant to claim that all these conceivable modes of competition work out "beneficially." In fact, he has expressed his profound doubts about the merits of some of these processes, in particular of political collective choice processes.[49] And it is obvious that he has a conditional argument in mind when he talks about "coercive interference in the process of cultural evolution" (1988, p. 20), or when, with reference to the example of monetary institutions, he argues that "the selective processes are interfered with here more than anywhere else: selection by evolution is prevented by government monopolies that make competitive experimentation impossible" (*ibid.*, p. 103).[50]

To talk of "interference in the process of cultural evolution" or to argue that the "evolution of rules was far from unhindered"[51] only makes sense, of course, if Hayek has a process with specific characteristics in mind, if his arguments on cultural evolution are meant as conditional arguments that apply to an evolutionary process only if, and to the extent that, it exhibits these characteristics. Hayek's claim cannot be that cultural evolution per se, no matter what its selective constraints are, will produce desirable rules, no more than he can claim that competitive spontaneous orders always work beneficially, no matter what the terms of competition are. Nor can his claim be that there is some "natural" process of cultural evolution that should be left alone to work itself out, "unhindered." There is no cultural evolution "per se"; the process always advances under conditions that reflect human constitutional choices. Cultural evolution is *about* human choices; it cannot even be imagined—like biological evolution, in principle, could—as something "not interfered with" by human choices. We can only choose among alternative frameworks within which we let cultural evolution proceed. If we were to impose no constitutional constraints on the terms of competition, it would not mean that we would leave cultural evolution unhindered. It would mean that we choose to let it proceed under an "anything goes" constitution.

Any reasonable interpretation of Hayek's theory of cultural evolution has to start, in my view, from this premise: that, just like his market argument, his argument on cultural evolution has to be understood as a conditional argument about the workings of a *constitutionally constrained process*, a process that is subject to constraints that serve to insure its beneficial workings.

Yet what exactly is the conditional argument that Hayek's theory of cultural evolution entails, what is the reasonable claim that can be distilled out of his many ambiguous and conflicting comments on the subject? Though Hayek never made an explicit effort to state carefully what the relevant constraints of a beneficially working process of cultural evolution are, they can, in part, be inferred from his writings, at least their general nature, if not time-and-place-dependent specifics. The basic thrust of such a conditional notion of cultural evolution is described by the idea of a process that allows, at all levels at which rules and institutions emerge or are chosen, for alternatives to be tried out, and to be exposed to a kind of competition that makes for responsiveness to the interests of the individual persons who are to live under these rules. This individualistic interpretation is, to be sure, in contrast to some of Hayek's arguments that I have reviewed above. Yet it is, in my view, the only interpretation that is consistent with the general classic liberal spirit of his life work.

Constrained Evolution and Constitutional Design

If Hayek's theory of cultural evolution is interpreted, in the above sense, as a conditional theory, it has apparent implications for the issue of institutional reform and constitutional design. If we can specify the conditions under which a competitive evolutionary process works responsively to individual interests, and if we consider such responsiveness desirable, we can seek to establish such conditions through suitable institutional constraints. Or, more generally, if we can identify the constraining conditions on which the beneficial working of the process of cultural evolution depends, it becomes a constructive task to assure that such conditions prevail.

Interpreted as a conditional argument, a Hayekian theory of cultural evolution is not only compatible with the notion of deliberate constitutional construction, it would be incomplete without such a notion. It has to assign an essential role to institutional-constitutional design in two regards. First, deliberate institutional reforms are, on the one side, an essential part of the experimental *input* into the evolutionary process. Though much of this input may indeed, as Hayek (1960, p. 32) suggests, consist of "undesigned novelties that constantly emerge in the process of adaptation," *designed* novelties certainly play an important part as well. There is no contradiction between the notion of deliberate institutional design and the notion of an undesigned evolutionary process in which institutional experience and knowledge accumulate, just as there is no contradiction between the notion of deliberate organized production and the notion of a spontaneous market process in which such deliberate production experiments compete. What is essential in order that the overall process be of an evolutionary nature is not that the experimental novel inputs are undesigned, but that the inputs are subject to competitive selection.

Indeed, Hayek's real concern is apparently not with the issue of deliberate design per se, but with the scope and the competitive nature of such design. He emphasizes, on the one hand, that "although we must always strive to improve our institutions, we can never aim to remake them as a whole" (1960, p. 63).[52] And he stresses, on the other hand, that his critique of the constructivist mind set is not meant as an argument against deliberate experimentation in institutional matters, but an argument "against all exclusive monopolistic power to experiment in a particular field . . . and against the consequent preclusion of solutions better than the ones to which those in power have committed themselves" (1960, p. 70).[53]

Second, deliberate constitutional design plays an essential role in shaping the constitutional framework on which the desirable working of evolutionary competition depends. Hayek recognizes this fact when he notes that what we can reasonably hope to do is to "create the conditions in which society can gradually evolve improved formations" (1979, p. 14).[54] Yet, though recognizing that we can use our general understanding of the evolutionary "process of cumulative growth . . . to try to create conditions favorable to it" (1960, p. 40), Hayek does not explicitly discuss what it would mean, for the issue of deliberate institutional design, "to create favorable conditions." It is certainly misleading to say, as Hayek (1988, p. 74) does, about the evolutionary process of civilization that "by establishing a framework of general rules and individual freedom it allows itself to continue to evolve." Such a statement cannot be meant literally to say that the evolutionary process *itself* "establishes rules and individual freedom." Presumably it is through the efforts of human beings that these things get established, and the central question is, under what conditions these efforts can be expected to promote individual freedom and to be conducive to cumulative evolutionary learning.

It is also misleading for Hayek to argue that people's attempt "to wrest control of evolution—i.e., of the procedure of trial and error—and to shape it to their present wishes . . . only damages the functioning of the process itself" (1988, p. 74). One can certainly say that the process of "evolution cannot be guided by and often will not produce what . . . [people] demand" (*ibid.*), if this is supposed to mean that an evolutionary process of trial and error necessarily will always lead into an unknown, open future. But such a claim would, with equal certainty, be totally unjustified if it were supposed to mean that we cannot and should not seek to create and to maintain framing conditions that promise to make the evolutionary process work in a fashion that we consider desirable. Of course, we cannot "guide" evolution in the sense of directing it toward a specific predefined goal. But we can, and should, seek to guide the evolutionary process in the sense of establishing a framework that secures its desirable working properties, in the same sense in which we seek to guide the competitive market process by an appropriate framework of rules, even though we cannot guide it in the sense of directing it toward predetermined outcomes.

That such guidance of markets and cultural evolution by suitable constitutional constraints is not only possible, but the principal instrument that we have to improve our "social condition," is an insight that can certainly be found in Hayek's work, yet one that he does not unambiguously develop or consistently maintain. Neither the market nor cultural evolution is "self-contained" in the sense that it would automatically produce, out of itself, the constraining framework that make it operate to the benefit of the persons who live with it. As pointed out above, Hayek unmistakenly recognizes this for the market. Consistency requires that it be also recognized for the process of cultural evolution.

Constitutional Design and Evolutionary Learning

The centerpiece of Hayek's theory of cultural evolution is the argument that in all our efforts in problem solving we can never know in advance what works best. All our problem solutions are tentative conjectures that may be challenged and replaced by alternative, superior solutions. The conclusion that Hayek suggests is that, in order to learn how things can be done better, we should explicitly treat our problem solutions as the conjectures that they are, and place them into an environment in which they can be effectively challenged by potentially superior alternatives.

The market is, from this perspective, an arena in which tentative solutions/conjectures for a broad range of problems—whether concerning the production of bread or the organization of large-scale enterprises—can be tried out and challenged, within a framework of rules that define the terms under which the alternative conjectures compete and are selected upon. These rules are themselves conjectures, tentative solutions to the problem of how, by what institutional framework, markets can be made to work best, that is, to the greatest advantage of the persons involved. Here, too, just as in other problem-solving efforts, we cannot know in advance what works best: for instance, how certain property rights can be most suitably defined, or what kind of patent laws are most advantageous.[55] And here, too, if we want to utilize the potential of evolutionary learning, we need to provide for a framework within which alternative conjectural solutions can be tried out and compete in ways that assure responsiveness to the interests of those who live under the arrangement.

Worked out to its logical conclusion, Hayek's evolutionary approach suggests a thoroughly nondogmatic attitude to all dimensions and all aspects of human problem-solving efforts, including, in particular, the various levels of rules that define the terms of human social life.[56] If we take seriously the insight that at no point can we be sure what, in the realm of rules, may work best, and if we seek, therefore, to expose the rules on which we rely to a competitive environment and allow them to be challenged by potentially superior alternatives, we can look at the institutional-constitutional edifice of social life as a multilayered system of rules, in which the rules at any particular layer are subject to competitive constraints that are defined by rules at another level. As an example, since we cannot know what the best way of producing cars is, we provide for a market framework in which alternatives can be tried out under suitable competitive constraints. Since we cannot know what rules may be most suitable for market competition, we should seek to establish a framework—for example, in a federalist political system—that allows for alternative market rules to be tried out, again under constraints that we expect to make for responsiveness to the interests of the persons involved. And, since we cannot know in advance what the best rules for the political choice processes are by which we decide on rule matters, we should seek to expose these rules as well to suitable competitive constraints.

A terminology suggested by Ludwig Lachmann (1963) seems useful to capture the above notion of a multilayered sytem of rules and institutions. With regard to the order of the market, Lachmann (*ibid.*, p. 67) distinguishes between what he calls *internal* and *external* institutions. External institutions, in his terminology, are those that "constitute" the market; they define the framework within which market activities take place. Internal institutions, by contrast, are those that result from the market process itself; they are generated and shaped by market activities. The external institutions, like the tax code or liability laws, define certain terms under which market competition is carried out, and their appropriate maintenance is, as Lachmann (*ibid.*, p. 76) notes, a political task. The internal institutions, like financial instruments or forms of business organization, are created and modified by market participants as they pursue their interests within the constraints that market competition and the external institutions impose.

As defined by Lachmann, the distinction between external and internal institutions is an absolute distinction between two sets of market-related institutions. Yet it can, of course, be generalized as a relative distinction that applies to any adjacent layer of rules or institutions. For any institutional setting we can distinguish between the rules that define constraints within which other rules/institutions may be chosen or simply emerge. In terms of the generalized evolutionary perspective outlined above, a principal task of external institutions, at any level, can be seen in providing for a suitable competitive arena in which alternative internal rules/institutions can be experimented with. Whether the internal rules/institutions are designed or undesigned experiments is of secondary importance, as long as the external institutions insure a competitive environment in which established practices are always exposed to the potential challenge from superior innovations.

Interpreted in the above sense, Hayek's evolutionary argument is not, as Hayek himself seems sometimes to suggest (1952b, pp. 162*ff.*), an argument against a rational approach to institutional matters. It is an argument that can be rationally discussed and defended at the level of constitutional discourse, that is, in discourse on the issue of how we should procede in choosing the rules under which we live. Being aware of the limits of reason and knowing that, in institutional just as in other matters, we cannot know in advance what works best, we can rationally choose to adopt a framework suitable for competitive evolutionary learning. The anti-constructivist skepticism that informs Hayek's evolutionist outlook should not be understood as an advice to abandon every effort to deliberately shape our institutional environment. It should, instead, be understood as an advice to utilize, in our efforts in institutional construction, the explorative potential of a competitive process of trial and error, a process through which we can hope to achieve at least improvement, if not perfect solutions.

The recommendation to rely, in institutional as in other matters, on competitive evolutionary processes, need not at all appeal to blind faith. It can be argued on rational grounds, and Hayek has articulated many of them. Yet these rational arguments can only be *conditional* arguments, arguments about the working properties of competitive and evolutionary processes that operate within certain constraints. They cannot be arguments about unqualified processes of cultural evolution. A recommendation to rely on such processes could, indeed, appeal to nothing else but blind faith.

Conclusion

Hayek's theory of cultural evolution is widely understood as being relevant for the issue of how, according to what principles, we ought to organize the socioeconomic-political order in which we live. Yet, as I have sought to argue above, his account of cultural evolution can only have such relevance if it is interpreted as a conditional argument, in the same sense in which his account of the working properties of market competition is not an argument about competition per se, but a conditional argument about competition within the confines of "appropriate" rules.

Particularly in some of his later writings, Hayek has presented his theory of cultural evolution as an unconditional theory, as a theory not about how evolutionary forces can be expected to work under certain specified conditions, but about cultural evolution per se, as an all-encompassing, secular process that works itself out irrespective of any human effort to establish a desirable institutional order. Such an unconditional theory of cultural evolution can be of interest for various reasons, but it has little to do with the enterprise that, quite clearly, is at the heart of Hayek's life work, namely to contribute to the study of "the problem of an appropriate social order" (Hayek, 1973, p. 4).

It may well be that "our desires and wishes are largely irrelevant" (Hayek, 1988, p. 134) for what will ultimately, in some distant future, survive in the global process of evolution to which Hayek refers. And it may well be that what will eventually emerge from this global process will be quite different from what we, from today's perspective, would consider a desirable social order. Yet, what does such insight tell us about how we should seek to order our social affairs? Little, if anything at all.

We cannot know what will ultimately survive, if alone because the evolutionary process will be affected by future knowledge that, for principal reasons, we cannot have today. Yet, even if we could know, or if we were to believe we knew, would that be a good reason for us to adopt, here and now, an institutional order that we do not find desirable? For instance, if we were to believe that eventually, in some remote future, only a totalitarian kind of social order would survive, should we, therefore, decide to adopt such an order today? To answer this question in the negative is by no means the same as saying that we need not worry about the workability of our plans for institutional reform. It would obviously be naive if we should try to establish a social order that we consider desirable, without examining whether it can be predicted to be sustainable in the world as we know it. And it would be foolish to commit to an order that is predictably not viable. Yet this is a simple matter of prudence that we can appreciate without counseling the type of evolutionary theory at issue here. Prudent institutional choices can only be made from the set of *viable alternatives*.

Beyond what viability considerations can tell us, it would be futile to speculate about—and adjust our institutional choices to—what might ultimately survive. Whether what we find desirable may ultimately survive or not, within the limits of the viable we have no better criterion for choosing than our preferences.

Acknowledgments

I am grateful to Richard Adelstein and Wolfgang Kerber for their helpful comments on an earlier draft.

Notes

1. Rindos (1985, p. 66), in "Social Darwinism was not Darwinian." It should be noted, though, that the often stereotypical disdain for Social Darwinism does not do justice to, at least, some of the authors who are usually subsumed under this label. That a more qualified assessment is appropriate in particular for the work of W.G. Sumner is argued in H. Kliemt (1985).

2. For a discussion of the differences between Spencerian and Darwinian evolutionism see Rindos (1985, pp. 66*ff.*) who argues that "(t)he evolutionary models of Spencer and Darwin are based upon totally different sets of assumptions" (p. 68).

3. Hayek (1973, p. 24): "The pretended laws of overall evolution supposedly derived from observation have in fact nothing to do with the legitimate theory of evolution which accounts for the process. They derive from the altogether different conceptions of the historicism of Comte, Hegel and Marx."

4. For the post-Darwin era Hayek singles out Carl Menger as the one whose "evolutionary account of the emergence of cultural institutions" (Hayek, 1988, p. 70) was in the pre-Darwinian tradition: "Carl Menger . . . restated the general theory of the formation of law, morals, money, and the market in a manner which, I believe, had never again been attempted since Hume" (Hayek, 1978, p. 265*n*).

5. Lehmann (1960, pp. 99*ff.*) notes about the "evolutionism" of this period: "By evolutionism . . . is here meant an attempt to . . . trace the origin and gradual development of social and political institutions and of civilization generally . . . and to explain them by the operation of forces or 'laws' inherent in the developmental processes themselves. Human nature is such a force in man's attempt to adapt to his environment and to improve his position. Any kind of 'Providential' order is excluded, and there is a playing down, at least, of the rational factor, of leadership roles and of any over-all political planning. . . . (F)ew ideas more deeply penetrated and more widely influenced the social, political and historical thought of the time than this evolutionary idea. . . . It pervades much of the thought of such major thinkers as Hume, Smith and Ferguson."

6. Popper (1972, p. 267): "Darwin's theory of natural selection showed that it is in principle possible to reduce teleology to causation."

7. Hayek (1960, pp. 59*ff.*): "(T)he evolutionists made it clear that civilization was the accumulated hard-earned result of trial and error; that it was the sum of experience, in part handed from generation to generation as explicit knowledge, but to a larger extent embodied in tools and institutions which have proved themselves superior."

8. In the summary of Chapter 4 of his *The Origin of Species*, Darwin has stated this notion in the following terms: "If under changing conditions of life organic beings present individual differences in almost every part of their structure, and . . . if there be . . . a severe struggle for life . . . , it would be a most extraordinary fact if no variations had ever occurred useful to each being's own welfare. . . . But if variations useful to any organic being ever do occur, assuredly individuals thus characterised will have the best chance of being preserved in the struggle for life; and from the strong principle of inheritance, these will tend to produce offspring similarly characterised. This principle of preservation, or the survival of the fittest, I have called Natural Selection."

9. Mayr (1982, pp. 46*ff.*): "This uniqueness of biological individuals means that we must approach groups of biological entities in a very different spirit from the way we deal with groups of identical inorganic entities. This is the basic meaning of population thinking. . . . (H)e who does not understand the uniqueness of individuals is unable to understand the working

of natural selection." See also Mayr's (1976, p. 28) contrast between the outlook "of the population thinker and of the typologist."

10. Witt (1987, p. 116) suggests that biological evolution and cultural evolution can both be viewed as processes through which *information* is transmitted, information embodied in the gene pool of a population in one case, information transmitted as *cultural heritage* in the other. Boyd and Richerson (1985) similarly base their "dual inheritance theory" of cultural evolution on the notion that genetic and cultural inheritance are two channels along which two kinds of information are transmitted.

11. In the absence of cultural transmission, experience acquired by individual learning is lost with the death of the learning organism. Learning would, in a sense, have to start from zero in every new generation.

12. Campbell (1965, p. 41): "Thus instinct-formation involves a trial-and-error of the life and death of whole mutant animals. A learning process may end up providing a very comparable behavioral repertoire, but does so by trial-and-error responses within the lifetime of a single animal, and using memory rather than genetic structure as the storage process."

13. Rindos (1985, p. 72) refers to culture "as a peculiar manifestation of genetic plasticity."

14. Menger (1985, p. 232) has talked about "(t)he *'intuitive wisdom'* in organically developed social institutions" as posing an explanatory challenge to the social theorist, not "unlike the 'suitability' which in natural organisms strikes the admiring attention of the expert natural scientist." On Menger, see note 4.

15. Popper (1972, p. 112): "(T)here is a close analogy between the growth of knowledge and biological growth; that is, the evolution of plants and animals."

16. Popper (1972, p. 261): "From the amoeba to Einstein, the growth of knowledge is always the same: we try to solve our problems, and to obtain, by a process of elimination, something approaching adequacy in our tentative solutions."

17. Popper (1972, p. 71): "All acquired knowledge, all learning, consists of the modification (possibly the rejection) of some form of knowledge, or disposition, which was there previously, and in the last instance of inborn dispositions." For a similar argument on the primacy of conjectural knowledge or the "primacy of the abstract" see Hayek (1967, pp. 23*ff.*; 1978, pp. 41*ff.*). With regard to such implicit knowledge Hayek talks about the "theorizing" that is "done already by our senses" (1967, p. 24), and he notes that his views in these matters are related to "Karl Popper's argument against 'inductivism'—i.e., the argument that we cannot logically derive generalizations from particular experience, but that the capacity to generalize comes first and the hypotheses are then tested and confirmed or refuted according to their effectiveness as guides to actions" (Hayek, 1978, p. 43).

18. Popper (1972, p. 72): "*(T)here is no sense organ in which anticipatory theories are not genetically incorporated.* The eye of a cat reacts in distinct ways to a number of typical situations . . . : these correspond to the biologically most important situations between which it has to distinguish. Thus the disposition to distinguish between these situations is built into the sense organ, and with it the *theory that these, and only these, are the relevant situations for whose distinction the eye is to be used.*" For a very similar view of the "theory-impregnated" (*ibid.*) nature of our sense organs, see Hayek's reflections on "the intuitive capacity of our senses for pattern recognition" (1967, p. 23).

19. Popper (1972, p. 71): "Knowledge in its various subjective forms is dispositional and expectational. It consists of dispositions of organisms."

20. As an analogy for such unintended, evolutionary growth of institutions Popper (1972, p. 117) mentions the example of animals who "unintentionally" create a path in the jungle, by following—because of its greater ease—an existing track paved by others, and by doing so contribute to making the lane even more convenient for those who come later.

21. Hayek (1960, p. 62): "(T)he evolutionary view is based on the insight that the result of the experimentation of many generations may embody more experience than any one man possesses." Hayek (1967, p. 88): "(T)hose rules which have evolved in the process of growth of society embody the experience of many more trials and errors than any individual mind could acquire." For similar statements, see Hayek (1967, p. 92; 1973, pp. 11, 119; 1976, p. 135).

22. Hayek (1978, p. 10): "This sort of 'knowledge of the world' that is passed on from generation to generation will thus consist in a great measure not of knowledge of cause and effect, but of rules of conduct adapted to the environment. ... Like scientific theories, they are preserved by proving themselves useful, but, in contrast to scientific theories, by a proof which no one needs to know. ... This is the true content of the much derided idea of the 'wisdom of our ancestors' embodied in inherited institutions ..."

23. On the embodiment of knowledge in language see also Hayek (1956/57, pp. 517*ff.*).

24. About such "pre-sensory experience" Hayek (1952a, p. 167) notes: "A certain part of what we know at any moment about the external world is therefore not learnt by sensory experience, but is rather implicit in the means through which we can obtain experience. ... All that we can perceive is thus determined by the order of sensory qualities which provide the 'categories' in terms of which sense experience can alone take place." Hayek's thinking in these matters has been influenced by Lorenz's (1983, orig. 1941) biological interpretation of Kant's categories a priori.

25. Mundinger (1980, pp. 190*ff.*) suggests as a "population definition of culture": "(C)ulture is a set of populations that are replicated generation after generation by learning—on overt population of functionally related, shared, imitable, patterns of behavior (and any material products produced), ... and simultaneously, a covert population of acquired neural codes for those behaviors. ... By populations I do not mean populations of organisms, but rather two non-organism populations: a population of ideas (neural codes), and an associated population of motor patterns (behavioral models)."

26. On the interaction between the processes of individual learning and sociocultural evolution see Langton (1979, 1982).

27. Boyd and Richerson (1985, p. 34) comment on this issue: "The essential feature of culture is social learning, the nongenetic transfer of patterns of skill, thought, and feeling from individual to individual in a population or society. ... (S)ocial learning can create ... socially transmitted traditions that are not directly attributable to genetic factors and immediate environmental contingencies. To understand the evolutionary process of ... cultural transmission one must understand the forces that affect the frequency of different culturally transmitted variants in a population."

28. Campbell (1965, p. 44): "(O)ne of the most obvious economies of social life is the economy of cognition, i.e., of processes whereby the trial-and-error explorations of one member serves to save others the trouble of entering the same blind alleys."

29. As Hayek (1960, pp. 24*ff.*) notes: "Knowledge exists only as the knowledge of individuals. It is not much better than a metaphor to speak of the knowledge of society, as a whole. The sum of the knowledge of all the individuals exists nowhere as an integrated whole."

30. As Hayek (1952b, p. 161) argues: "(T)he only 'reason' which can in any sense be regarded as superior to individual reason does not exist apart from the interindividual process in which, by means of impersonal media, the knowledge of successive generations and of millions of people living simultaneously is combined and mutually adjusted, and that this process is the only form in which the totality of human knowledge ever exists."

31. Hayek (1960, pp. 25, 30): "(C)ivilization enables us constantly to profit from knowledge

which we individually do not possess. . . . It is through the mutually adjusted efforts of many people that more knowledge is utilized than any one individual possesses or than it is possible to synthesize intellectually."

32. Such an individualist interpretation of cultural evolution is also suggested when Hayek (1960, p. 63) notes that it is the "flexibility of voluntary rules which . . . makes gradual evolution and spontaneous growth possible, which allows further experience to lead to modifications and improvements. Such evolution is possible only with rules which . . . can be broken by individuals who feel that they have strong enough reasons to brave the censure of their fellows."

33. Hayek (1988, p. 136) claims for "the evolution of moral orders through group selection" that "groups that behave in these ways simply survive and increase." Such wording is, of course, misleading, since groups per se do "behave" according to moral rules; individuals in groups do. What needs to be explained is, therefore, how individuals in a group come to follow rules that make the group successful. If there is a collective goods problem involved, the simple argument that the respective rules are group-beneficial is per se not sufficient for an explanation.

34. Vanberg (1986). For a differing view see Hodgson (1991).

35. The principal argument against the group selection thesis is that, because of the collective goods problem, the group-beneficial consequences of an individual's behavior are per se not sufficient to explain the exhibiting of such behavior if it is costly to the respective individual. Though individuals who exhibit group-beneficial, yet self-sacrificial, behavior will share, as group members, in the group-benefits that they produce, other group members who do not share in the costs of the group-beneficial behavior will have an even greater net-advantage. As long as no additional factors come into play, factors that correct the distribution of payoffs between the group-benefectors and the free-riders to the advantage of the former, selection works against group-beneficial behavior. This is true for genetically transmitted behavioral programs, as well as for learned behavioral programs. In genetic evolution, the free-riders would—other things being equal—have better prospects to reproduce. (An exception are "social insects," like ants, that reproduce as groups and among which, therefore, interindividual genetic competition is absent.) And this is also true for the transmission of learned rules, on which cultural evolution is based. If no compensating factors are at work, free-riding will generate higher payoffs, and will, therefore, find stronger reinforcement than group-beneficial behavior. In human groups the instruments of deliberate social organization and rule-enforcement can be, and often are, used to provide such compensating factors.

36. The various interpretations of what group beneficial may mean that I try to distinguish here are, by no means, always separated in Hayek's arguments. They often appear intermixed as, for instance, when he notes about the evolutionary process: "(T)hough it clearly produces also much that we . . . do not like . . . , it does bring for ever-increasing numbers what they have been mainly striving for. . . . Man has been civilized very much against his wishes. It was the price he had to pay for being able to raise a larger number of children" (1979, p. 168).

37. In Hayek's *The Fatal Conceit*, heavily edited by W. Bartley—one can even find the extremely strange claim that "*(i)t is not the present number of lives that evolution will tend to maximise but the prospective stream of future lives*" (1988, p. 132; emphasis in original).

38. See also Hayek's (1988, p. 23) argument about rules that evolved, "not because men recognised by reason that they were better but because they made possible the growth of an extended order . . . in which more effective collaboration enabled its members, however blindly, to maintain more people and to displace other groups." See also *ibid.*, p. 120.

39. Hayek (1988, pp. 20*ff.*): "While it [an understanding of cultural evolution] cannot

prove the superiority of market institutions, a historical and evolutionary survey of the emergence of capitalism . . . helps to explain how such productive . . . traditions happened to emerge."

40. Hayek (1988, p. 133): "Yet, as with every organism, the main 'purpose' to which man's physical make-up as well as his traditions are adapted is to produce other human beings. . . . There is no real point in asking whether those of his actions which do so contribute are really 'good', particularly if thus it is intended to inquire whether *we like* the results."

41. The confusion that this shift tends to cause is reinforced by statements like the following from *The Fatal Conceit*: "It would however be wrong to conclude, strictly from such evolutionary premises, that whatever rules have evolved are always or necessarily conducive to the survival and increase of the populations following them. We need to show, with the help of economic analysis . . . how rules that emerge spontaneously tend to promote human survival. Recognizing that rules generally tend to be selected, via competition, on the basis of their human survival-value certainly does not protect those rules from critical scrutiny. This is so, if for no other reason, because there has so often been coercive interference in the process of cultural evolution" (Hayek, 1988, p. 20). In evaluating this argument, or others, from *The Fatal Conceit*, one should keep in mind, though, that this last major publication of Hayek was, as I mentioned before, heavily edited by W. Bartley.

42. Hayek (1988, p. 19) points to an elementary requirement when he notes: "Competition is a procedure of discovery, a procedure involved in all evolution. . . . To operate beneficially, competition requires that those involved observe rules rather than resort to physical force. Rules alone can unite an extended order." See also Hayek (1967, p. 12; 1948, pp. 101*ff.*; 1978, p. 135).

43. And they tell us that what succeeds in market competition can be considered desirable, at least, if we agree with A. Smith's (1979, p. 660) argument that "(c)onsumption is the sole end and purpose of all production," a maxim which, he thought, "is so perfectly self-evident, that it would be absurd to attempt to prove it."

44. Hayek (1960, p. 27): "(W)e command many tools—in the widest sense of that word—which the human race has evolved and which enable us to deal with our environment. These are the results of the experience of successive generations which are handed down. And, once a more efficient tool is available, it will be used without our knowing why it is better, or even what the alternatives are.

These "tools" which man has evolved and which constitute such an important part of his adaptation to his environment include much more than material implements. They consist in a large measure of forms of conduct that he habitually follows without knowing why; they consist of what we call "traditions" and "institutions". . . . Man is generally ignorant . . . of why he uses implements of one shape rather than of another. . . . He does not usually know to what extent the success of his efforts is determined by his conforming to habits of which he is not even aware." See also Hayek (1956/57, p. 519; 1973, p. 113; 1976, p. 21; 1979, p. 163).

45. Whether the image of a process in which individuals are the principal experimentors and selectors is, in fact, appropriate for all kinds of "tools" in the ordinary sense is an issue that can be left aside in the present context. Of relevance here is the issue of whether such an image is appropriate for all kinds of rules.

46. On the distinction between personal and social rules, see Vanberg (1988, pp. 158*ff.*).

47. On this issue see Vanberg (1992, pp. 114*ff.*). Phillips (1945, pp. 255*ff.*) refers to one aspect that is relevant here, when he talks about the role of individual experimenting: "In some fields, however, this cannot be done. . . . An illustration of this is government. . . . The essential difference is that an individual can perform an experiment in physics, whereas it

requires a whole nation to perform an experiment in government." On the difference between technological and social-institutional evolution, see also Campbell (1975, pp. 1105*ff.*).

48. Hayek (1988, p. 131): "Although the displacement of one group by another, and of one set of practices by another, has often been bloody, it does not need always to be so. . . . Many of these processes may then have happened entirely peacefully, although the greater military strength of commercially organised people will often have accelerated the process."

49. See, for instance, Hayek (1960, p. 110): "We have no ground for crediting majority decisions with that higher, superindividual wisdom which, in a certain sense, the products of spontaneous social growth may possess." See also Hayek (1960, p. 111; 1979, pp. 76, 167; 1988, pp. 19, 730).

50. Hayek (1988, p. 103) adds the complaint that "so little private experimentation and selection among alternative means has ever been permitted." See also Hayek (1979, p. 163): "The basic tools of civilization—language, morals, law and money—are all the result of spontaneous growth and not of design, and of the last two organized power has got hold and thoroughly corrupted them."

51. Hayek (1988, p. 20): "The evolution of rules was far from unhindered, since the powers enforcing the rules generally resisted rather than assisted changes conflicting with traditional views about what was right or just."

52. For similar statements see Hayek (1967, p. 92; 1973, p. 65; 1978, p. 19; 1979, p. 167).

53. Hayek (1960, p. 37): "The relevant distinction is . . . between conditions, on the one hand, in which alternative ways based on different views or practices may be tried and conditions, on the other, in which one agency has the exclusive right and the power to prevent others from trying."

54. This role for "constitutional design" appears also to be recognized when Hayek (1952b, pp. 160*ff.*) contrasts two "fundamentally different" attitudes towards institutional reform: "(O)n the one hand the essential humility of individualism, which endeavors to understand as well as possible the principles by which the efforts of individual men have in fact been combined to produce our civilization, and which from this understanding hopes to derive the power to *create conditions favorable to further growth*; and, on the other hand, the hubris of collectivism, which aims at conscious directions of all forces of society" (emphasis added.)

55. Hayek (1988, p. 35): "The institutions of property, as they exist at present, are hardly perfect; indeed, we can hardly say in what such perfection might consist. Cultural and moral evolution do require further steps if the institution of several property is in fact to be as beneficial as it can be."

56. Hayek (1960, p. 23): "If we are to advance, we must leave room for a continuous revision of our present conceptions and ideals which will be necessitated by further experience."

References

Axelrod, Robert, and W.D. Hamilton. (1984). "The Evolution of Cooperation in Biological Systems." In R. Axelrod (ed.), *The Evolution of Cooperation*. New York: Basic Books, pp. 88–105.

Bonner, John T. (1980). *The Evolution of Culture in Animals*. Princeton: Princeton University Press.

Boyd, Robert, and Peter J. Richerson. (1985). *Culture and the Evolutionary Process*. Chicago and London: The University of Chicago Press.

Campbell, Donald T. (1965). "Variation and Selective Retention in Socio-Cultural Evolution." In H.R. Barringer, G.I. Blanksten, and R.W. Mack (eds.), *Social Change in Developing Areas*. Cambridge, MA: Schenkman, pp. 19–49.

Campbell, Donald T. (1974). "Evolutionary Epistemology." In P.A. Schilpp (ed.), *The Philosophy of Karl Popper*, La Salle, IL: Open Court, pp. 413–463.

Campbell, Donald T. (1975) "On the Conflicts Between Biological and Social Evolution and Between Psychology and Moral Tradition." *American Psychologist* 30: 1103–1126.

Campbell, Donald T. (1983). "The Two Distinct Routes beyond Kin Selection to Ultrasociality: Implications for the Humanities and Social Sciences." In D. Bridgeman (ed.), *The Nature of Prosocial Development: Interdisciplinary Theories and Strategies*. New York: Academic Press, pp. 11–41.

Campbell, Donald T. (1987). "Evolutionary Epistemology." In G. Radnitzky and W.W. Bartley (eds.), *Evolutionary Epistemology, Rationality, and the Sociology of Knowledge*. La Salle, IL: Open Court, pp. 47–89.

Hayek, Friedrich A. (1948). *Individualism and Economic Order*. Chicago: The University of Chicago Press.

Hayek, Friedrich A. (1952a). *The Sensory Order—An Inquiry into the Foundations of Theoretical Psychology*. Chicago: The University of Chicago Press.

Hayek, Friedrich A. (1952b). *The Counter-Revolution of Science*. Glencoe: The Free Press.

Hayek, Friedrich A. (1956–1957). "Ueber den 'Sinn' sozialer Institutionen." *Schweizer Monatshefte* 36: 512–524.

Hayek, Friedrich A. (1960). *The Constitution of Liberty*. Chicago: The University of Chicago Press.

Hayek, Friedrich A. (1967). *Studies in Philosophy, Politics and Economics*. Chicago: The University of Chicago Press.

Hayek, Friedrich A. (1973). *Law, Legislation and Liberty*, Vol. 1. London and Henley: Routledge & Kegan Paul.

Hayek, Friedrich A. (1976). *Law, Legislation and Liberty*, Vol. 2. London and Henley: Routledge & Kegan Paul.

Hayek, Friedrich A. (1978). *New Studies in Philosophy, Politics, Economics and the History of Ideas*. Chicago: The University of Chicago Press.

Hayek, Friedrich A. (1979). *Law, Legislation and Liberty*, Vol. 3. London and Henley: Routledge & Kegan Paul.

Hayek, Friedrich A. (1988). *The Fatal Conceit*. Chicago: The University of Chicago Press.

Hodgson, Geoffrey M. (1991). "Hayek's Theory of Cultural Evolution—An Evaluation in the Light of Vanberg's Critique." *Economics and Philosophy* 7: 67–82.

Kliemt, Hartmut (1985). *Moralische Institutiouen-Empiristische Theorienihrer Evolution*. Freiburg/München: Karl Alber.

Langton, John. (1979). "Darwinism and the Behavioral Theory of Sociocultural Evolution: An Analysis." *American Journal of Sociology* 85: 288–309.

Langton, John. (1982). "The Behavioral Theory of Evolution and the Weber Thesis." *Sociology* 16: 341–360.

Lehmann, William C. (1960). *John Millar of Glasgow 1735–1801. His Life and Thought and his Contributions to Sociological Analysis*. Cambridge: Cambridge University Press.

Lorenz, Konrad. (1983). (orig. 1941). "Kants Lehre vom Apriorischen im Lichte gegenwärtiger Biologie." In K. Lorenz, and F.M. Wuketis (eds.), *Die Evolution des Denkens*. München/Zürich.

Mayr, Ernst. (1976). *Evolution and the Diversity of Life*. Cambridge, MA: Harvard University Press.

Mayr, Ernst. (1982). *The Growth of Biological Thought*. Cambridge: Harvard University Press.

Menger, Carl. (1985). *Investigations into the Method of the Social Sciences with Special Reference to Economics*. New York and London: New York University Press.

Mundinger, Paul C. (1980). "Animal Cultures and a General Theory of Cultural Evolution." *Ethology and Sociobiology* 1: 183–223.

Phillips, H.B. (1945). "On the Nature of Progress." *American Scientist* 33: 255*ff*.

Popper, Karl R. (1957). *The Poverty of Historicism*. Boston: The Beacon Press.

Popper, Karl R. (1972). *Objective Knowledge—An Evolutionary Approach*. Oxford: Oxford at the Clarendon Press.

Radnitzky, Gerard, and W.W. Bartley (eds.). (1987). *Evolutionary Epistemology, Rationality, and the Sociology of Knowledge*. La Salle, IL: Open Court.

Richards, Robert J. (1981). "Natural Selection and Other Models in the Histeriography of Science." In M.B. Brewer and B.E. Collins (eds.), *Scientific Inquiry and the Social Sciences*. San Francisco: Jossey-Bass Publishers, pp. 37–76.

Rindos, David. (1985) "Darwinian Selection, Symbolic Variation, and the Evolution of Culture." In *Current Anthropology*, Vol. 26, pp. 65–88 (includes comments by R.L. Carneiro, E. Cooper, P. Drechsel, R.C. Dunnell, R.F. Ellen, C.J.M.R. Gullick, R.A. Hackenberg, J. Hartung, J.H. Kunkel, G.S. Nickerson, P.J. Richerson and R. Boyd [77–83], and a reply by D. Rindos [84–87]).

Smith, Adam. (1979). *An Inquiry into the Nature and Causes of the Wealth of Nations*. Oxford: Clarendon Press.

Ullmann-Margalit, Edna. (1978). "Invisible-Hand Explanations." *Synthese* 39: 263–291.

Vanberg, Viktor. (1986). "Spontaneous Market Order and Social Rules." *Economics and Philosophy* 2: 75–100.

Vanberg, Viktor. (1988). "Rules and Choice in Economics and Sociology." *Jahrbuch für Neue Politische Ökonomie* 7: 146–167.

Vanberg, Viktor. (1989). "Hayek as Constitutional Political Economist." *Wirtschaftspolitische Blätter* 36: 170–182.

Vanberg, Viktor. (1992). "Innovation, Cultural Evolution and Economic Growth." In U. Witt (ed.), *Explaining Process and Change—Approaches to Evolutionary Economics*. Ann Arbor: The University of Michigan Press, pp. 105–121.

Vanberg, Viktor. (1993). "F.A. Hayek." In G. Hodgson, M. Tool, and W. Samuels (eds.), *Handbook on Institutional and Evolutionary Economics*. Aldershot: Edgar Elgar.

Vogel, Christian, and Eckart Voland. (1988). "Evolution und Kultur." In K. Immelmann, et al. (eds.) *Psychobiologie—Grundlagen des Verhaltens*. Stuttgart: Gustav Fischer Verlag, pp. 101–130.

Witt, Ulrich. (1987). *Individualistische Grundlagen der evolutorischen Oukonomik*. Tübingen: J.C.B. Mohr (Paul Siebeck).

8 HEALTH AND CHOICE: THE CONTRIBUTION OF JAMES BUCHANAN

David Reisman

A.L. Macfie, looking to the future, anticipated a renewed need for the unique combination of the analytical and the philosophical, the social and the psychological, that is the lasting gift of the Scottish giants: "If there is a future for sociological economics and politics—and if there is not we shall have to make it—then there is an opportunity for the resurgence of the Scottish tradition and the Scottish genius" (Macfie, 1955, p. 17). Buchanan on health and choice provides convincing proof that the opportunity has indeed made the man and that the Scottish method lives on in the political economy of an influential contemporary who has had the courage to take the wider view.

This chapter is concerned with the contribution of James Buchanan to the collective choice of the optimal health care policy. Divided into two sections, it first examines Buchanan's views on the inconsistencies of the National Health and then considers his analysis of the American private-sector alternative. The conclusion is reached that Buchanan's box of tools is in truth an extension of Enlightenment attitudes and that Adam Smith lives on in the public choice posture of agnosticism and negotiation, consensus and compromise without which "we would surely fight" (Buchanan, 1985, p. 3).

The two sections of this chapter demonstrate that the Mecca of the consistent Virginian is properly to be sought in the methodological individualism of Adam Smith. Logically so, since it is the essence of Buchanan's public choice that good procedures are always and everywhere to be ranked above specific endstates: "As Adam Smith recognized so clearly, . . . there is no agreed upon objective for the participants in an economic nexus, each one of whom seeks only to pursue his or her own privately defined aims (which may or may not reflect narrowly defined economic interest). Absent such agreement, there is simply no external standard by which alternative structures can be evaluated" (Buchanan, 1989a, p. 25). The point of departure is revealed preference. Buchanan, being as skeptical of Samuelson's Social Welfare Function as Smith was of Rousseau's General Will, neither could have had any other: "Agreement is all" (Reisman, 1990, p. 117).

The National Health

Buchanan's first major contribution to the debate about health care and health policy was his Institute of Economic Affairs paper of 1965 on *The Inconsistencies of the National Health Service*. Pro-market thinking in Britain in the eighteenth year of the NHS (and the first year of American Medicare) then centered around user charges, occasionally around means testing, very occasionally around re-privatization. What pro-market thinkers actually found in Buchanan in the first year of Harold Wilson's new Labour government is very likely to have been what they expected to find. There can be no doubt that there is much in Buchanan's paper that is broadly consonant with the views that were then being expressed by John Jewkes, Dennis Lees, Lionel Robbins, Arthur Seldon, and Jack Wiseman. Yet it cannot be denied that there is much as well that would have been more at home in the Italian public finance tradition of Puviani and Einaudi than it was then in the British political culture of vintage Butskellism. The insights that seemed familiar were cited and absorbed. The insights that seemed far-out were neglected and ignored. The result of selective reading in a complacent era was as predictable as it was partial: Buchanan was taken to have written a *plaidoyer* for competitive pricing and commercial top-ups when the true novelty of his analysis lay in the *critique* of a unidisciplinary orthodoxy more at home with the idealized abstractions of welfare economics than ever it was with the far more relevant "problems of collective decision-making" (Buchanan, 1965a, p. 8). Pro-market thinkers praised Buchanan for praising the market. Anti-market thinkers attacked Buchanan for failing the poor. Three years after the publication of *The Calculus of*

Consent, one would have expected a greater appreciation of the distinction that Buchanan was trying to draw between good rules on the one hand, picking winners on the other, when he came in 1965 to examine the *Inconsistencies of the National Health Service.*

Demand was greater than supply in the social health sector, Buchanan said, and the consequence had been a deterioration in the standard of care: "The failures are exhibited by breakdowns in the quality of the services themselves due to the disparity between the facilities supplied and the demands made upon them" (Buchanan, 1965a, p. 9). Failures are essential to the diagnosis of *Inconsistencies*: no consistent democrat would feel that the Service had a case to answer if long waiting times were merely the socially preferred rationing mechanism, if limited availability were only another name for economic scarcity in a world of nonfinite resources, if doctors' complaints were simply the bargaining ploy of rent seekers doomed forever to seek rents. Buchanan's examples of crowding and congestion are not in themselves robust enough to bear out his contention that the system was overloaded virtually to the breakdown point. Besides that, indicators of success exist which go some way toward counterbalancing the illustrations of failure: thus the tendency of a socialized system to rely heavily on preventive medicine in preference to costly cure will ceteris paribus damp down the long-term demand for care, while the redistribution of a fixed budget in favor of the geographically underdoctored and the occupationally underprivileged might be consensually regarded not as breakdown but as felicity by a generous nation prepared to put up with longer waits in exchange. Failures are essential to the diagnosis of *Inconsistencies*, but whether Buchanan actually proves that there has in fact been a breakdown is another matter. Being fair to Buchanan, of course, one would have to concede that no generally accepted statistic on systemic breakdown has as yet been constructed. Objective data on morbidity and mortality are less than ideal from the perspective of the methodological individualist who accepts the logical possibility that unanimity of consensus might rank other goals above health status at the margin. Subjective data are vastly preferable but also seldom available: the deficiency is especially acute in cases of socialized provision or insured payment where negotiated prices cannot be relied on to supply a proxy for intensity of need. One should not, therefore, be too hard on Buchanan for measuring breakdown on the basis of complaints. Perhaps the patients should be more patient about waits, perhaps the doctors should be less greedy about payment—but perhaps qualitative indicators such as complaints are, after all, good grounds for the supposition that the Service is falling victim to its own *Inconsistencies.*

The cause of the mismatch between demand and supply in the Health Service was not, in Buchanan's view, administrative slack or bureaucratic inefficiency—a public choice concern with which he was all too prepared to identify himself in the Preface (published in the same year as the *Inconsistencies*) to Gordon Tullock's *The Politics of Bureaucracy*. The cause was not the result of technical shortcomings, Buchanan said, but rather something as fundamental as the very "structure of the institutions" (Buchanan, 1965a, p. 4). Rational choice in a socialized system must compel the maximizing consumer to expand his/her demand up to the point where marginal utility equals price equals zero. Rational choice in a socialized system must also compel the maximizing voter to restrict the supply of taxation that s/he imposes on him/herself. Rational choice impels the typical consumer to demand more and more: even if fully aware of overconsumption relative to non-zero opportunity cost, still it would be irrational for one among many to forego benefits when the resources saved will not make a measureable difference to total quantities. Rational choice also impels the typical voter to supply less and less: however strongly she is committed to health and care, still s/he will want it to be the others who pay the piper while she him/herself plays the free rider on the tune. As consumer, the typical individual wants to consume more; as voter the typical individual wants to taxpay less; and thus the incompatibility between the private and the public choice of one and the same individual turns out to be the fundamental reason why, in Buchanan's view, the representative calculator will rationally press both for an expansion in services and for a reduction in the taxation that supports the services.

The representative calculator's lot is evidently not a happy one. Even less happy, however, is the lot of the representative politician in a Downs-type economic theory of democracy: whether s/he expands or whether s/he reduces, still s/he would appear to be trapped in an Arrow-type impossibility bind from which no voter-pleaser can expect to emerge successful. And all of this due not to a lack of wisdom on the part of the leadership but simply because of a conflict of roles in a specific institutional environment. Adam Smith, writing of the East India officials, had said that it was the perverse incentives and not the rational individuals that he had most wished to censure for the shortcomings of the corporation. James Buchanan, writing of the National Health Service, has provided no less institutional an account of the intrinsic excess of demand over supply which he regards as the beacon that lights the way to failures on a good day, breakdowns on a bad one.

As ingenious as Buchanan's explanation quite obviously is, nonetheless there are reasons for thinking that the Jekyll and Hyde model of schizophrenia by consent somewhat overstates the gravity of the threat.

On the demand side, it must never be forgotten that medical attention even at a zero user-charge always imposes the nonnegligible costs of time and travel, to say nothing of the nonpecuniary burdens of pain and danger. Care in itself only yields utility, Buchanan has conceded, to "the 'little old ladies'—of both sexes—who literally enjoy trips to the clinic" (Buchanan, 1990a, p. 6); while no one but an extreme hypochondriac would put in for an unnecessary appendectomy merely because it was free. Also, the loyalty of the doctor to the Service as well as to the patient is likely to mean that urgent demands will automatically be ratified (a broken bone will be set, a difficult pregnancy smoothed) but that discretionary treatments (cosmetic surgery, perpetual psychoanalysis) will remain vulnerable to the societal gatekeeper's strict refusal. Such a sensitivity of resource allocation to consensual criteria is one of the most attractive features of the socialized option to the pure constitutionalist. Even, however, where morally unacceptable (perhaps because it refuses treatment for nonmedian complaints), still it undeniably performs the useful function of imposing a limit on demand-led utilization. Since the line must be drawn somewhere, one is compelled to reflect that there are worse decision-making mechanisms that might be employed than the reliance on professional ethic and societal priorities in preference to the overconsumption that is the undesired outcome of uninformed patients' unbridled sovereignty. Had Buchanan acknowledged the crucial role of the doctor as gatekeeper, he would have pleased both the constitutional political economists (provided only that the filters employed by the practitioners be broadly acceptable to ex ante unanimity of consent) and the National Health supporters (provided only that the consensus remember the invisible, the inarticulate, and even the unsavory). Had he done so, of course, his imputation of *Inconsistencies* would have been significantly weakened and he would have had to choose a different title for his paper. Worse things can happen.

On the side of supply as well as on that of demand, there too forces would seem to be operative such as suggest that Buchanan's theory of *Inconsistencies* may somewhat have overstated the gravity of the problem. Buchanan's concern would seem to be the reluctance of taxpayers to pay for the public goods which they as citizens are keen to consume. At one level the fear is as well founded as the saloon-bar commonplace that the meal is the utility, the bill the *dolerosa*. At another level, however, the fear is as meaningless as the *reductio ad absurdum* that the rational citizen in a democracy will consistently press not for low taxes but rather for no taxes at all. Talking realism, the payment of tax is not optional but compulsory: it was in the very year of the *Inconsistencies* that Mancur Olson (who had built on Baumol, who had built on Hume) had demonstrated the value, in *The Logic of Collective Action*, of coercive coordination, consensually imposed, as a means of bringing order to an *n*-persons' Prisoner's Dilemma. Talking legitimacy, the bundle of benefits is selected according to agreed-upon procedures: the voter in the democracy who participates in the game (who, in the limit, actually supports the services) has in that sense no greater a moral right to opt out of the costs than has the diner who plays the free rider immediately after the sweet. Buchanan is in the circumstances placing himself in a difficult position when he predicts that rational supply will fall short of rational demand: assuming that the consumer is aware both of the bundle and of the price, the most that can be said is that we are here in the realm of the *might* but not of the *must*.

Package deals are, of course, unsatisfying compromises; and an entirely separate explanation of the underfunding of the Health Service might have been the British practice of funding health out of general and not hypothecated taxation. General taxation can be applied to the provision of health care. Equally, however, it can be employed to provide education and defense. It might thus have been the case that the underfunding relative to demand which Buchanan identified in the NHS was not the result of the rational health calculus which he infers so much as the outcome of a differently focused calculus on the part of passionate minorities such as childless couples and militant pacifists. Hypothecated taxation, visible and nonfungible, might have been capable, in the Britain of the 1960s, of reducing voter alienation and augmenting tax revenues—very much as Buchanan had suggested in a celebrated defense of earmarking published in 1963. There he had shown, using a two-service illustration, that compartmentalization and unbundling could lead to an increase and not a decrease in the supply of public finance: "Not only will the favored service be allotted a larger share of each budget dollar, but also total spending on both services increases" (Buchanan, 1963b, p. 118). Earmarking, Buchanan said in 1963, was efficient, precisely because "the reference system becomes that of the individual citizen" (Buchanan, 1963b, p. 108). Segregation, Buchanan said in 1963, was sensitive, precisely because it was "one means of insuring more rational individual choice" (Buchanan, 1963b, p. 108). Both in terms of aggregate revenues and of individual participation, in short, the British supporters of a service-specific National Health tax would have had good grounds to look to the Buchanan of 1965 to take a lead. They would have looked in vain: whatever the explanation of the excess of demand over supply, Buchanan in 1965 apparently saw the fiscal *regime* as forming no part of the story.

Buchanan in 1965 diagnosed an excess of demand over supply that he believed to be the result of marked *Inconsistencies* between the demand side and the supply side of a single choice calculus. He also explored reforms that he saw as potential techniques for transcending the arbitrary duality that was the cause of the perpetuated imbalance.

On the side of demand, Buchanan drew attention to the elimination of shortages and surpluses through markets: "Prices would be set by competitive forces and the services finally made available would be determined not through a collective-political decision but by the private decisions of many suppliers responding to expressed demands" (Buchanan, 1965a, p. 17). Taxes being nonzero, the advantage of nonzero prices would be at least to bring demand and supply within the same framework of discourse. Such a restructuring of institutions would reduce the congestion that inevitably arises when consumption is allowed to proceed to the point at which marginal utility becomes equal to zero. It would bring the opportunity cost to the community of the health care inputs in some measure into the individual's own calculus. It would allow positive statements to be made about the optimality of care: clearly, "zero user prices are not demonstrably optimal in themselves" (Buchanan, 1965a, p. 22), and nor are revealed preferences about quantities demanded in an Eden-like environment where the consumer pays no cost in exchange for his/her benefit.

Pricing of care was frequently opposed in Britain in the 1960s with the argument that a flat-rate charge is always a disproportionate burden on a lower income. Buchanan's position is different. It is also characteristic of his attitude to entitlements.

Looking backward, Buchanan shows no interest in the historical origins of the status quo endowments. We start from here, not from there, Buchanan is fond of stressing; and "rectificatory redistribution, if effectuated, must, as a process, involve violation of the contractarian or agreement criteria for fairness" (Buchanan, 1988, p. 206). Property rights are so important in themselves, Buchanan says, that they can only be defined as constitutional matters, not to be settled save behind a veil of ignorance, not to be altered without unanimity of consent such as effectively rules out what socialists would describe as the retributory correction of a past injustice. What exists is where we are *now*, Buchanan would argue; and confiscation by consent, the veil drawn aside but unanimity retained, is less than likely to occur in a world of rational *homines economici*.

Yet redistribution might still occur, Buchanan would maintain; and the reason is that, bygones being forever bygone with respect to the wins and the losses of the historical past, all individuals are truly situated behind a veil of uncertainty when they contemplate the future. Looking forward if not looking backward, in other words, claims can be rethought on an impartial basis and allocations reconsidered in the certain unknowledge that the crippled beggar paying the crippling user charge might turn out one day to be oneself. Rawls would be confident enough about anxiety actually to predict a deliberate policy of skewing economic command in favor of the least advantaged. Buchanan, wavering nervously between agnosticism and indeterminacy, would be prepared to say only that *oughtness* is whatever good procedure throws up as best: "*Any* set of arrangements of implementing fiscal transfers, in-period, meets the constitutional stage Wicksellian test, provided only that it commands general agreement" (Buchanan, 1987, p. 312). Buchanan's tolerant individualism will not be as reassuring as Rawls's Difference Principle to the members of the lower-income groups in some doubt as to how to react to the proposal for prices. What must be stressed is that there is no reason to suppose that the allocative decision (to introduce user charges) will not be accompanied, in Buchanan's case, by a separate, redistributive decision (to top-up purchasing power with cash transfers or health vouchers). There is, of course, no reason to think that it will be; but that is somehow not Buchanan's point. Buchanan's point is that an optimal decision on user charges should not be delayed merely because of the impact of that decision on the distribution of income. The distribution of income, he would say, is important enough to warrant treatment other than at the back door—and nonzero prices are potentially of some value in solving the demand-side problems that had led to the *Inconsistencies*.

As with demand, so with supply, where Buchanan searched for institutional reforms likely to bring the two blades of the scissors into a more viable relationship one with the other. With the underlying problem being an excess of supply over demand, it might have been expected that he would propose not only deterrent charges on the demand side but also an expansion in the supply of resources that was actually being devoted to health. Perhaps this was his proposal and perhaps it was not. With hindsight, and in the light of his later reservations concerning the escalation of costs, his position in 1965 can best be described as perceptively ambiguous. Thus, in the case of the private sector, his proposal was for the unrestricted growth of parallel provision. The state had never come clean about limited entitlements in Britain, Buchanan implied: rather than admitting that the NHS simply did not have the money to live up to the unrealistic expectations it had engendered, it had relied on nonprice rationing through waits and criteria such as had led inevitably to frustration and disappointment. Abandoning open-ended commitments that could not be honored, Buchanan suggested, the state should pre-specify the per capita entitlement to care (in physical units or, employing shadow prices, in economic values) and then rely on "a market or market-like set of institutions to emerge which supplements the publicly-funded, publicly-supplied facilities" (Buchanan, 1965a, p. 18). Such top-up protection would cater both for minority wants (say, for a private room) and abnormal needs (say, for an expensive drug not available in the state scheme). It would also have the attractive philosophical property that it would encourage individuals to put their money where their mouth is with respect to the supply of resources devoted to care. Yet Buchanan never says precisely how the growth in the top-up sector is best to be stimulated. His underlying premise being failure and breakdown, it is by no means clear that the prespecification of state entitlements (even if in the form of "relatively absolute absolutes," constitutionally protected against the competitive bidding of practical politics) will be sufficient to promote the desired expansion in supply: the perception of failure and breakdown in the Health Service had demonstrably not led to a significant expansion in private protection in the years leading up to 1965, and few things can be less conducive to health status than are failure and breakdown. Tax relief would have been a possibility, but it is one that Buchanan has elsewhere rejected as burdensome (since selective exemptions prevent across-the-board reductions) and inequitable (since tax deductions are regressive, worth more at higher marginal rates): "What is needed for efficiency is a pattern of effective price reductions varying with incomes" (Buchanan, 1970a, p. 300), Buchanan has said, and clearly, the price discrimination built into tax relief is the inverse of the desired effect. All of which then raises doubts as to whether Buchanan has in practice isolated the trigger mechanism by means of which the incremental growth in private sector supply is effectively to be brought about.

With respect to public sector supply, Buchanan's position is no less difficult. The economic approach to politics would seem to point to democratic overexpansion of collectivised provision—but the facts speak eloquently in support of containment and control: "Since 1948, total outlay on medical-health care has increased less in Great Britain than in the United States, where it is supplied largely in the market" (Buchanan, 1965a, p. 8). The *homo economicus* orientation would seem to point to self-interested conduct on the part of cynical politicians keen only to please their voters—but the evidence is better compatible with a hypothesis of moralistic self-denial and normative *non*-individualism: "Responsible *collective*, i.e., governmental, decision-makers have not expanded investment in supplying health services to the levels of expressed *individual* demands" (Buchanan, 1965a, p. 9). The market mechanism is often credited with superior economic efficiency—but where spillover benefits are involved (the case of coordinated immunization) or where economies of large scale arise (the case of capital-intensive medicine), there the collectivized option may well prove the more cost-effective one: "If there were no municipal fire departments, it is likely that total outlay for fire protection would exceed the costs of maintaining the fire departments" (Buchanan, 1963a, p. 205). The positive economist is often said rationally to value the precise prediction—but where the payoff from the budget simply cannot be established with any accuracy, there it would be wrong to pretend that one is indeed in a position to say whether it was the land of Shakespeare or the land of Lincoln that had spent more prudently in the area of health: "We can infer nothing at all concerning the 'correctness' or 'incorrectness' of the collective decisions that have been made as regards aggregate levels of provision. The observed facts are consistent with either non-optimal or optimal levels of investment since 1948" (Buchanan, 1965a, p. 22). Undersupply might accompany *Inconsistencies*—and National Health expenditures ought in such circumstances to be expanded. Alternatively, optimal quantities might accompany *Inconsistencies*—and the premium in such a case would be on the leaner pig, not the fuller trough. Overdevelopment, finally, might accompany *Inconsistencies*—and then the task would be to weed out inputs that were no longer dancing to any recognisable tune. Buchanan's conclusions are evidently not as single-valued as the formula for liquid nitrogen. Nor, however, is the complex social kaleidoscope to which they relate.

The American Experience

At the University of Virginia in the mid-1960s Buchanan secured a research grant from the National Center for Health Services Research and Development. His collaborators were two promising doctoral candidates, then unknown except for the names of Mark V. Pauly and Cotton M. Lindsay that were subsequently to be associated with such distinguished work in the field of health economics.

Mark Pauly secured his Ph.D. in 1967: his thesis (entitled "Efficiency in Public Provision of Medical Care") was later to become his standard reference on *Medical Care at Public Expense*, to say nothing of "The Economics of Moral Hazard" that appeared in the *American Economic Review* in June 1968. Cotton Lindsay obtained his doctorate a year after Pauly, submitting a dissertation on "Supply Response to Public Financing of Medical Care in the United States" and then departing on a NATO postdoctoral fellowship for the year's study at the London School of Economics that was to culminate in "Medical Care and the Economics of

Sharing," published in *Economica* in November 1969. Lindsay (by then at University of California at Los Angeles) was clearly more than conversant with British conditions when he prepared, together with his former supervisor, the report for the British Medical Association on "The Organisation and Financing of Medical Care in the United States" that appeared in 1970 in the BMA's compendium on *Health Services Financing*. Buchanan (by then at the Virginia Polytechnic Institute) was himself no stranger to the National Health: Fulbright Visiting Professor at Cambridge from 1961–1962, Visiting Professor at the London School of Economics in Spring 1967, the author of the *Inconsistencies*, a frequent visitor to Britain, he like Lindsay was well placed to make cross-cultural comparisons of rules and institutions.

The contribution to *Health Services Financing* was written at a time when the United States was the world leader in care per capita: the United States in 1970 was devoting 6% of its national product to medical care, and this had risen from 4% in 1929 (when, of course, the Gross National Product was itself lower). The resourcing was impressive, Buchanan and Lindsay said, but the record for all that was disappointing. Medically, the age-specific mortality rates were unsatisfactory and deteriorating. Socially, the large numbers of doctors trained in subsidised medical schools were, in Lyndon Johnson's Great Society, demonstrably not supplying an adequate service for the poor, the elderly, and the isolated. Economically, opportunity costs were being neglected, medical prices were inflating at twice the general rate, and scarce potential was flagrantly being wasted despite the fact that it could so easily mean the difference between life and death. All was apparently not well in the United States at the time when Buchanan and Lindsay published their paper.

Being methodological individualists and not militant ideologues, the general conclusion of Buchanan and Lindsay was that there was a good case to be made in favor of balance: "Essentially," they said, "we remain pragmatists" (Buchanan, 1970b, p. 584). Buchanan and Lindsay were able to see some scope both for the collective and for the private. It may accordingly prove helpful to examine their analysis with respect to each of the two sectors in isolation.

Collective Action

The starting point for collective action is the rational choice of the individual citizens that togetherness is indeed preferable to separability. Their choice will refer exclusively to their own nation, quintessentially unique as each historically delimited aggregate must necessarily be. Their very ability to reach agreement without prohibitive transaction costs and side payments will in itself be proof that they as a nation possess the requisite homogeneity of consensus to be capable of action as a unit. Some collectivities will be too divided even to contemplate the possibility of such action: "The problems become almost unmanageable when it is admitted that different segments of society may have different attitudes toward the appropriate goal of collective action" (Buchanan, 1970b, p. 567*n*). Divided collectivities will forever be condemned by the democratic standards of methodological individualism to private purchase, however deficient. United collectivities will at least possess the option of choosing to socialize and to nationalize. This is not to say that they will inevitably opt for collective action, only to say that a consensual society like Sweden will enjoy a genuine choice between the shared and the individualized that will effectively be denied a conflictual society like India, dependent willy nilly on economic exchange because of a general inability to agree on a viable alternative.

Buchanan and Lindsay chose to treat the United States as a single decision-making unit. In that way they de facto precommitted themselves more to the India than to the Sweden model. Fiscal federalism and the theory of clubs would have done much to alter the balance. Devolution of power (not excluding the exit option and the right to secede) had been a longstanding concern of the farm boy from the Deep South who, warning the British in 1990 against "regulatory 'Brusselsization'" without respect for local diversity, informing them in addition that "Lincoln's decision to fight to preserve union can be viewed as a breaking of the implicit contract that had established the federal structure" (Buchanan, 1990b, pp. 6, 18), was only harking back to the case for "a truly decentralized political structure in the power sense" that he had first made so eloquently no less than four decades earlier: "As the need for an ever-expanding scope of public services increases, with especial emphasis on the social services," he had cautioned the readers of the *American Economic Review* in 1950, "the *laissez-faire* result will be the ultimate centralization of effective political power" (Buchanan, 1950, p. 189). Alarmed by this concentration, he had therefore put forward proposals intended to stem the encroachment of the carpet-bagging monolith. Buchanan was in the circumstances more than favorably disposed to Charles M. Thiebout's *Journal of Political Economy* paper on "A Pure Theory of Local Government Expenditures" that, in 1956, developed a theory of locally supplied public goods selected through the personal mobility of rational migrators. Ultimately he was to judge the Thiebout model of voting with the feet somewhat of a "pseudo-paradigm," incomplete, "indeterminate," and "nihilistic," unable to incorporate the feedback effects on the competing localities of the ever-changing revenue base, weak on the locational rents that arise in the private sector and that make the real choice one of simultaneous maximization subject to a *dual* constraint: "The criterion for optimality is that individuals should locate themselves in space in such a fashion that each person's contribution to total value, private and public, is the same in all locations" (Buchanan, 1972a, pp. 249, 260). Although he undoubtedly had reservations, Buchanan also found much that was much to his taste in Thiebout's idea of individuals with similar demand functions who band together to share non-excludable public goods on a local basis: thus he has expressed the view with respect to differentiation and autonomy, that it must be "the primary purpose of federalism" to "create competition between jurisdictions" (Buchanan, 1980, p. 183). His work on the theory of clubs may in that sense be read not simply as an account of the swimming club but as an interpretation of the fiscal club as well. Larger than the individual but smaller than the nation, the noncentral "consumption ownership-membership arrangement" (Buchanan, 1965b, p. 207) represents a self-selected pool, a voluntarily espoused circumscription that is committed by its charter to the revealed preferences of the local electorate. With local policies being more finely tuned than national, one would have expected methodological individualists like Buchanan and Lindsay to have factored their interpretation of American health policy down to the smallest economic level of analysis. Perhaps because American health policy tends in practice significantly to be formulated at the center, they chose in the event to forego the normative in favor of the positive and to treat the United States as a single decision-making unit. Yet the United States is a large and a complex country; and to that extent the commitment of Buchanan and Lindsay to the analysis of the *what is* may have had the unintended effect of building an India into the account when possibly the nation, broken down into component clubs, might more fruitfully have been described as a series of Swedens.

India or Sweden, what may at least be said about America is that there is some perception in that country of interlinked destinies in the specific area of health: "Some individuals are willing to pay something to see that others consume more medical care than they privately would choose to consume if left to their own devices" (Buchanan, 1970b, p. 563). Some individuals are apparently convinced that private provision unsupplemented leads inescapably to underallocation—and that collective action, necessary and welcome, is best orchestrated through state compulsion and not through voluntary charity: "Each individual may keep his own contribution arbitrarily small if he expects others to provide the balance. A more desirable state of affairs may be attained if all persons collectively agree upon the amount each is to 'contribute'. This provides an 'economic' rationalization of what governments do through the taxation/expenditure process. Via the political process, each person 'agrees' to contribute a certain amount through taxes paid" (Buchanan, 1970b, pp. 563–564). The free rider is the reason for coerced coordination; individuals' agreement alone can legitimate the collective intervention; and the generalization from "some" to "all" indicates that, whatever may be said about the Indians or the Swedes, the Americans at least would seem to have had an openness to public programs that the "natural proclivities" of the rational vote-seeker may have encouraged him/her to exaggerate but for the origination of which the practical politician can him/herself in no significant way be held responsible.

Only political economy (through the calculus of consent) and not welfare economics (the prisoner of objectification and abstraction) can measure the spillovers and interdependencies that cause "all persons" to opt for intervention in the area of health. The perceptions identified, it is helpful if they can be explained; and this Buchanan and Lindsay seek to do in terms of two clusters of externalities.

The first case—the more selfish case—may best be typified by immunization against communicable disease. The higher the percentage of the population protected, the smaller the chance that any one person will catch the disease; but the greater, too, the costs of negotiating agreement and bribing backsliders. Thence the argument that the rational individual, anxious to economize on the curative treatments that are the burdensome tax levied by contagious neighbors, will press the state to take over the task of preventive coordination that, left to the private sector, would have proved to be a prohibitive expense. Economies of scale only reinforce the result, earlier derived by Buchanan in collaboration with Tullock, that collective action in certain circumstances can easily prove the better buy: "Collectivization produces both a greater degree of immunization and a lower cost per person than that which would be present under independent or market adjustment" (Buchanan, 1965c, p. 117). Which is not, of course, to predict that collective action will in actual fact prove the commodity that the consumers choose. Perhaps they will be discouraged by the allocative and disincentive effects that are the excess burden of the tax: "It is possible . . . that the external costs imposed by tax collection would eliminate altogether any net advantages of collectivization" (Buchanan, 1965c, p. 127). Perhaps they will be ignorant of the costs and benefits associated with immunization because of a rational choice made to economize on information and search: "The problem is the familiar one of choosing one's doctor. To choose one's doctor rationally may, in the limiting case, require the acquisition of sufficient information as to make the seeking of the doctor's advice totally unnecessary" (Buchanan, 1989c, p. 141). Perhaps, indeed, the consumers will choose by intuition and prejudice and not employ rationality at all. The most that can be said by way of prediction is that the consumer of policies could do worse than to buy collective action in instances of externalities such as that typified by immunization against communicable disease.

The second case—the more altruistic case—involves the Good Samaritanism that some have called Christian charity and others have associated with the Kantian's commitment to other–regarding conduct, ideally reciprocated. Such a separation of the *quid* from the *quo* is a familiar occurrence in the real world, where starving children in developing countries are seldom asked to pay a user charge in exchange for their famine relief. In the real world, Buchanan has frequently indicated, "we do observe individuals giving up 'goods' to others, including the set of 'others' where the individual units remain unidentified to the donor and wholly outside meaningfully drawn boundaries of personal relationship" (Buchanan, 1972b, p. 19). Stranger gifts of this kind are fully compatible with Buchanan's methodological individualism, which is absolutely consistent in its refusal to conflate perceived self-interest with hedonistic selfishness. Unwilling to "place economic interest in a dominating position" or to impute "evil or malicious motives," Buchanan's consumer-orientated calculus has consistently proceeded on the basis that only revealed preferences, impartially observed, can provide any guidance at all as to the extent to which *persona economica* is also mean and greedy. Nothing can be known in advance of listening and learning save perhaps this, that there is simply no need a priori to "assign net wealth or net income a dominating motivational influence on behavior in order to produce a fully operational economic theory of choice behavior in market or political interaction" (Buchanan, 1987, pp. 306, 307). People's goals are people's goals, but still, Buchanan has repeatedly emphasized, it would be less than likely if the textbook economist's rational pursuit of private gain actually described the whole of human life: "Care must be taken to distinguish between the self-interest assumption, as the basis for a 'logic of choice', and the self-interest assumption as the basis of a predictive, explanatory theory of human action" (Buchanan, 1962a, p. 175*n*). Nowhere is this call for cautious eclecticism more apposite, it would appear, than in the case of medical care, where Buchanan and Lindsay established that people *do* care about others—and "are willing to express this through political process" (Buchanan, 1970b, p. 583). Privatizers will tear their hair and socialists will dance in the street, but the position of the methodologist individualist will remain absolutely clear: the other-orientated consumer apparently ranks some collective action above radical laissez-faire, and it would be intolerant and undemocratic to refuse to satisfy the reasonable demand.

Altruistic externalities established, Buchanan and Lindsay seek to account for popular attitudes with respect to the humanitarian spillover. Their task is more difficult than it was in the case of contagion and epidemic, their explanation a mix of the absolute and the relative. The absolute dimension is picked up by the popular sensitivity to the "*quality* of suffering": "Individuals may be compassionate and seek, simply, to reduce 'suffering' in others" (Buchanan, 1970b, pp. 563, 564). The relative dimension, the more complex with respect to consensus, relates not to isolated illness but rather to the "*distribution* of suffering": "Special attention to shares of medical care may be warranted if this sense of 'fairness' is active. Those concerned to see all enjoy an equal chance to live may be legitimately concerned to see that all are provided with an equal opportunity to obtain medical care" (Buchanan, 1970b, pp. 564, 567). The different dimensions in turn spotlight the disparities between the different populations. The Americans, fundamentally independent in attitude, have adopted a mode of collective action that relies upon medical subsidisation targeted on the absolutely deprived. The British, more concerned with comparative standards and equality of access, have opted instead for common institutions and zero prices. Both countries have developed networks of transfer and delivery that rely on the state to fill the gap where the "typical individual values—hence is willing to pay for—something for which no institution of the private sector can readily arrange. Private unilateral action cannot be counted upon to satisfy these wishes" (Buchanan, 1970b, p. 565). Both countries have departed from spontaneous processes and done so, gains from trade being reaped and no party being made worse off by the rearrangement, in a manner which is clearly "Pareto-relevant" (Buchanan, 1962b, p. 101). Yet neither country has in the event opted for precisely the same institutional response to a market failure in the specific area of health that each has perceived, but also perceived in a slightly different manner.

The neoclassical economist will presumable seek to rank the alternative approaches to collective action in terms of objective criteria such as those of equilibrium and endstate. The constitutional political economist will not. As long as good decision-making rules are employed, he will say, what is chosen by the Americans can only be regarded as that which is efficient for the Americans, what is chosen by the British can only be described as that which is efficient for the British. Methodologically speaking, the individualist can have no other benchmark other than the outcome of "free and periodic elections, open franchise, open entry for parties, candidates, and interests, majority or plurality voting rules" (Buchanan, 1986, p. 55) and the myriad of supplementary mechanisms by means of which the consulting democracy strives sensitively to choose. In the words of Agnar Sandmo: "Buchanan strongly emphasizes that politics is not a process of fact finding or identification of truth but rather of conflict resolution between individuals. This view has strong implications for the way in which economists conceive of their own role in society. Rather than attempting to find 'optimal' solutions to economic problems they should concentrate on finding good decision rules, which all individuals and interest groups will find it in their own long-run interest to adopt for the solution of still unidentified conflicts over resource allocation" (Sandmo, 1990, p. 52). The social engineer, the omniscient robot, and the benevolent despot go out. The cohesive community, the negotiated compromise, and the spontaneous procedure come in. Buchanan "repeatedly emphasises the view that economics is the study of exchange and not the science of choice and optimization" (Sandmo, 1990, p. 55)—and agreement is all.

Private Action

Buchanan and Lindsay have significantly less to contribute concerning the market for health than they do with respect to the state. The main reason is their conviction that medical care is a commodity with unique properties. Medical care can mean the difference between life and death—and no one would want survival itself to be rationed by price to the highest-income bidder. Information about symptoms, treatments, and qualifications is asymmetrically distributed—and the consumer "often ignorant of the quality of the product he is purchasing" (Buchanan, 1970b, p. 547). Anxiety and the option demand lead rationally to precautionary oversupply—and many individuals who never visit the local hospital "would probably be willing to pay something to have a hospital available" (Buchanan, 1970b, p. 574). Future needs are uncertain and unpredictable—and the risk-averse able to hedge their bets through insurance pooling such as makes moral hazard an intrinsic part of the health care story. Buchanan and Lindsay will no doubt be accused by extreme free marketeers of exaggerating the dissimilarities between the market for care on one hand, the market for pins on the other. Oversympathetic though they may well be to the rhetoric and romance of a glamorous area of social activity seldom asked to prove that it is indeed value for money, still Buchanan and Lindsay, in inferring the uniqueness of care, are likely only to be echoing the views of the vast majority of their readers. Such a state of affairs is unlikely be entirely unacceptable to radical subjectivists such as are the members of the Virginia school.

Yet radical subjectivists tend to be more than comfortable with decentralized decision-making mechanisms. Buchanan and Lindsay like other epistemological libertarians tend to have an innate sympathy with the economic exchange. Their conviction that competitive markets are by and large good procedures with fair rules is well illustrated by the following, which refers specifically to success-indicators in hospital capitalization: "Replacing economic signals (though they be in error) with administrative fiat is akin to throwing away the only timepiece in town because it runs five minutes fast. Thus it would seem that basing hospital investment on market signals is likely to lead to more efficient allocation than basing it on no signals at all or on the desires and wishes of a small committee representing a small minority of the community served" (Buchanan, 1970b, p. 561). Perhaps it would, but we start from here; and the American hospital industry, then as now, was dominated by the nonprofit voluntaries that, under little pressure from management or trustees to economize, had in effect cut themselves off from market discipline in order to pursue the blinkered objectives of the medical professionals. Making a market where no market exists is never an easy task; and certainly it cannot be made any easier by the unique characteristics of a commodity that Buchanan and Lindsay believe to be unlike any other. Many would no doubt sympathize with Buchanan and Lindsay when they complain that the voluntaries, properly subject neither to plan nor to rivalry, "combine the worst of both words" (Buchanan, 1970b, p. 585) and ought to be phased out. More difficult, however, is to say how the cat is best to be belled. The hospital service is differentiated and localized. The outside surgeons who contract in are in favor of uneconomic excess capacity lest waits deprive them of fees. The community as a whole is widely believed to be morally opposed to profits put before patients. The process of marketization (which in the case of the voluntaries does not presuppose de-nationalization) is likely in the circumstances to prove so complicated an undertaking as to cause the opponents of hospitals' overcapitalization ultimately to retreat from competition and return to controls. It is by no means easy to say precisely how the hospitals are to be made more cost-conscious through pricing, and Buchanan and Lindsay do not fully spell out what ought to be done. In identifying the allocatively inefficient practices of an overregulated, overprofessionalised industry, however, at least they draw attention to the problem of deadweight wastefulness such as they clearly believe could be reduced in a laudably Pareto-like manner through the restructuring of the rules in favor of a more competitive game.

Patients, too, Buchanan and Lindsay indicate, ought to become part of the new and cost-conscious order. Thence re-emerges the nonzero user charge that had earlier figured so prominently in the context of the *Inconsistencies*. The proposal to reject the "everything free" orientation of the National Health and to rely on the deterrence of pricing—described as "the normal process usually counted upon to check consumption" (Buchanan, 1970b, p. 570)—strongly resembles in 1970 the suggestion made in 1965. Yet there is a significant difference between the British paper and the American one. The British paper, apparently treating token contributions as if they equalled marginal or average costs, gave the rather misleading impression that an author who regards medical care as unique somehow wanted the market for care to resemble the supplying and demanding of apples and pears. The American paper, on the other hand, had the advantage that, acknowledging the ongoing reality of prepayment and insurance, it recognized that charges in the case of care are never likely to go beyond the deductible threshold or the co-insurance proportion to become the textbook price. The American paper, in short, made clear what the British paper had obscured, that cost-sharing will be a disincentive to "whimsical" consumption but to little else—and that the sovereign nail-biter is unlikely to regard with any warmth any attempt to make co-insurance rates so high as to frustrate the purpose for which the insurance was purchased in the first place. Clearly, "one must . . . choose between having uncertainty on the one hand or moral hazard on the other" (Buchanan, 1970b, p. 571). Textbook economists will presumably opt for deterrence but ordinary people demonstrably want protection. Faced with this conflict of loyalties, Buchanan and Lindsay as methodological individuals have no choice but to side with the nervous and the anxious against the rationing and the allocative. They are fully aware of the overconsumption that will be induced by their moderation: an individual expected to pay 20% of the cost might be prepared to spend \$10 on an extra day in the hospital but not \$50, and to that extent the use of \$50 of society's scarce resources to satisfy a want that the consumer him/herself values at \$10 self-evidently involves a social welfare loss. They are fully aware of the problem. By the same token, being democrats, they see that there is no obvious solution. If Ulysses and his crew unanimously reveal a strong preference for cast-iron insurance (public sector or private sector), there is not a great deal the friend of liberty can do to protect them from themselves.

Buchanan and Lindsay, writing about hospitals and patients, are better at identifying problems than at finding solutions: their approach would seem better suited to the analysis of collective than it is to private action. Much the same must be said about their views on doctors, where they nonetheless make interesting proposals for a greater diversity of schools and standards in an attempt to extend the range of consumers' choices: "Those who desire (for income or other reasons) to purchase the services of less highly qualified physicians (at lower fees) are going to be dissatisfied if relatively high standards are set, with price consequently high as well" (Buchanan, 1970b, p. 578). Freer entry could increase the numbers of practitioners—but greater variety could increase the burden of becoming informed. More doctors could mean lower fees—but greater availability could boost the utilization of medical services. Both in terms of search costs and in terms of treatment costs, in other words, the liberalization of supply could provoke an unwelcome upward displacement in the share of care that is not really anticipated by Buchanan and Lindsay, whose approach to care inflation is couched more nearly in terms of limited than of excessive supply: "More and more dollars are bidding against each other for a very limited amount of medical resources" (Buchanan, 1970b, p. 557). The search costs could be kept down, of course, through the occupational licensure of a professional body, while limitation of supply could be reconciled with limitation of demand by means of state manpower policies applied to medical schools in tandem with National Health budgets, stringently capped. The adoption of the British status quo would almost certainly have some success in keeping down the cost of care. Cost containment was not in any case a major concern of James Buchanan when, with Cotton Lindsay, he sent in his report to the British Medical Association.

But things were to change. In 1970 the share of the American national product that was committed to the medical service industry stood at 6%. By 1990 it had doubled and seemed poised to double again before the end of the century. Buchanan by 1990 had reached the conclusion that health care was threatening to crowd out other claims on scarce resources—and that a public bad called out for a collective constraint.

Buchanan did not say that he wanted the ceilings and the priorities to become the responsibility of a British-type National Health Service. What he did say is that the maxima and the criteria, however enforced, should emerge bottom-up from consensus and not be imposed top-down by leadership. Laissez-faire, Buchanan concluded in 1990, did not "offer, for me, a satisfying resolution" (Buchanan, 1990a, p. 17); Leviathan would only stem the escalation at the cost of democracy; and thus the need for the "politics-as-complex-exchange derivation" (Buchanan, 1989b, p. 39) such as alone could make the limitation of freedom an intervention that would popularly be regarded as morally legitimate. Political market or economic market, in short, it is catallactic process, negotiated contract, and revealed preference that alone can tell right from wrong in the ethically charged environment of Buchanan's political economy.

Buchanan's political economy is a "forum for dialogue" (Buchanan, 1990a, p. 5) and an intellectual framework for collective choice. It is also a civilized humanistic contribution in its own right. So much of unidisciplinary economics being narrowly technocratic and often aridly abstract, it is eminently refreshing to encounter a free spirit who, situating himself in the grand tradition of intellectual discourse, is not afraid to postulate links between values and exchanges, cooperation and budgets, spontaneity and property, conflict and constitution. As John Gray has so accurately pointed out, "Buchanan's thought is political economy in the classical sense—the sense in which it was practiced by the Scottish School, and in which it encompasses social philosophy as well as positive or explanatory economic theory. For, as with Smith, Ricardo or indeed Marx, Buchanan's thought composes a system of ideas and comprehends a distinctive perspective of man, government and society" (Gray, 1990, p. 149). Buchanan on health and choice well illustrates the strength of Gray's intuition that in Buchanan the Scots will rise again.

Acknowledgments

The author would like to thank V.J. Vanberg and J.M. Buchanan for their support. This chapter is based on a paper written while the author was a Visiting Fellow at the Center for Study of Public Choice, George Mason University.

References

Buchanan, James. (1950). "Federalism and Fiscal Equity." *American Economic Review*, Vol. 60. In his *Fiscal Theory & Political Economy*. Chapel Hill: University of North Carolina Press, 1960.

Buchanan, James. (1962a). "Politics, Policy and the Pigovian Margins." *Economica* Vol. 29. Reprinted in J.M. Buchanan and R.D. Tollison (eds.), *Theory of Public Choice*. Ann Arbor: University of Michigan Press, 1972.

Buchanan, James. (with W.C. Stubblebine). (1962b). "Externality." *Economica*, Vol. 29. Reprinted in R.D. Tollison and V.J. Vanberg (eds.), *Economics: Between Predictive Science and Moral Philosophy*. College Station: Texas A & M University Press, 1987.

Buchanan, James. (with M. Kafoglis). (1963a). "A Note on Public Goods Supply." *American Economic Review*, Vol. 53. Reprinted in R.D. Tollison and V.J. Vanberg (eds.), *Explorations into Constitutional Economics*. College Station: Texas A & M University Press, 1989.

Buchanan, James. (1963b). "The Economics of Earmarked Taxes." *Journal of Political Economy*, Vol. 71. Reprinted in J.M. Buchanan and R.D. Tollison (eds.), *Theory of Public Choice*. Ann Arbor: University of Michigan Press, 1972.

Buchanan, James. (1965a). *The Inconsistencies of the National Health Service*. London: Institute of Economic Affairs.

Buchanan, James. (1965b). "An Economic Theory of Clubs." *Economica*, Vol. 32. Reprinted in R.D. Tollison and V.J. Vanberg (eds.), *Economics: Between Predictive Science and Moral Philosophy*. College Station: Texas A & M University Press, 1987.

Buchanan, James. (with G. Tullock). (1965c). "Public and Private Interaction under Reciprocal Externality." In J. Margolis (ed.), *The Public Economy of Urban Communities*. Washington, DC.: Resources for the Future. Reprinted in R.D. Tollison and V.J. Vanberg (eds.), *Economics: Between Predictive Science and Moral Philosophy*. College Station: Texas A & M University Press, 1987.

Buchanan, James. (with M.V. Pauly). (1970a). "On the Incidence of Tax Deductibility." *National Tax Journal*, Vol. 23. Reprinted in J.M. Buchanan and R.D. Tollison (eds.), *Theory of Public Choice*. Ann Arbor: University of Michigan Press, 1972.

Buchanan, James. (with C.M. Lindsay). (1970b). "The Organisation and Financing of Medical Care in the United States." In British Medical Association, *Health Services Financing*. London: British Medical Association.

Buchanan, James. (with C.J. Goetz). (1972a). "Efficiency Limits of Fiscal Mobility." *Journal of Public Economics*, Vol. 1. Reprinted in R.D. Tollison and V.J. Vanberg (eds.), Explorations into Constitutional Economics. College Station: Texas A & M University Press, 1989.

Buchanan, James. (1972b). "Toward Analysis of Closed Behavioral Systems." Reprinted in J.M. Buchanan and R.D. Tollison (eds.), *Theory of Public Choice*. Ann Arbor: University of Michigan Press. 1972.

Buchanan, James. (with H.G. Brennan). (1980). *The Power to Tax*. Cambridge: Cambridge University Press.

Buchanan, James. (with H.G. Brennan). (1985). *The Reason of Rules*. Cambridge: Cambridge University Press.

Buchanan, James. (1986). "The Man and the State." Presidential Address to the Mt Pelerin Society. In R.D. Tollison and V.J. Vanberg (eds.), *Explorations into Constitutional Economics*. College Station: Texas A & M University Press, 1989.

Buchanan, James. (1987). "The Constitution of Economic Policy." *American Economic Review*, Vol. 77. Reprinted in R.D. Tollison and V.J. Vanberg (eds.), *Economics: Between Predictive Science and Moral Philosophy*. College Station: Texas A & M University Press, 1987.

Buchanan, James. (1988). "Contractarian Political Economy and Constitutional Interpretation." *American Economic Review (Papers and Proceedings)*, Vol. 78.

Reprinted in J.M. Buchanan (ed.), *The Economics and the Ethics of Constitutional Order*. Ann Arbor: University of Michigan Press, 1991.

Buchanan, James. (1989a). "On the Structure of an Economy: A Reemphasis of Some Classical Foundations." *Business Economics*, Vol. 24. Reprinted in J.M. Buchanan (ed.), *The Economics and the Ethics of Constitutional Order*. Ann Arbor: University of Michigan Press, 1991.

Buchanan, James. (1989b). "The Economy as a Constitutional Order." In W. Sichel (ed.), *The State of Economic Science: Views of Six Nobel Laureates*. Kalamazoo: Upjohn Institute. Reprinted in J.M. Buchanan (ed.), *The Economics and the Ethics of Constitutional Order*. Ann Arbor: University of Michigan Press, 1991.

Buchanan, James. (with V.J. Vanberg). (1989c). "Leadership and Deference in Constitutional Construction." *Public Choice*, Vol. 61. Reprinted in J.M. Buchanan (ed.), *The Economics and the Ethics of Constitutional Order*. Ann Arbor: University of Michigan Press, 1991.

Buchanan, James. (1990a). *Technological Determinism Despite the Reality of Scarcity*. Little Rock: University of Arkansas for Medical Sciences.

Buchanan, James. (1990b). "Europe's Constitutional Opportunity." In J.M. Buchanan et al., *Europe's Constitutional Future*. London: Institute of Economic Affairs.

Buchanan, James. (1992). *Better than Plowing*. Chicago: University of Chicago Press.

Gray, J. (1990). "Buchanan on Liberty." *Constitutional Political Economy* 1: pp. 149–168.

Macfie, A.L. (1955). "The Scottish Tradition in Economic Thought." *Scottish Journal of Political Economy*, Vol. 3, 1955. Reprinted in D. Mair (ed.), *The Scottish Contribution to Modern Economic Thought*. Aberdeen: Aberdeen University Press, 1990.

Reisman, D. (1990). *The Political Economy of James Buchanan*. London: Macmillan.

Sandmo, A. (1990). "Buchanan on Political Economy." *Journal of Economic Literature* 28: pp. 50–65.

Index